the MOTORCYCLE SAMURAI

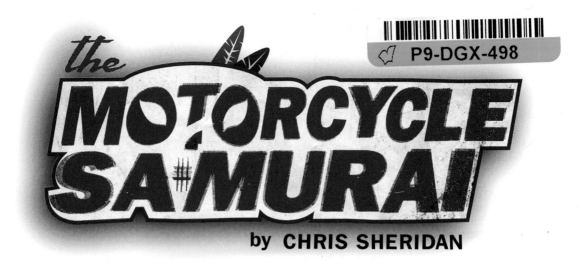

by CHRIS SHERIDAN

VOLUME ONE:
A FIERY DEMISE

TOP SHELF PRODUCTIONS

For Mom and Dad,
with gratitude and love.

The idea that became the story within the pages of this book would not have become a reality without the support, effort, and love of so many.

My wife, Kirsten, for the tireless joy, support, and for always reminding me how fun work and life should be.

Chris Ross for taking the ride, even though the path was not always clear or smooth. Chris Staros & Brett Warnock for taking a chance and making this crazy tale a book. Leigh Walton for helping me to learn my lines.

Jeff Lemire for being so supportive. Geof Darrow for being so mean.

Mark Waid and the Thrillbent team for being champs.

Mike, Margo, Henry, George, & Willa. Kate, Dave, Oliver, & Omar. Kyle, Rich, Michelle, Dehlia & Ellis. Thanks Pops for showing me how easy it was. Elena, Adele, and Remy. Meggie, Lauren, and all my family.

John Roberts, Chip Mosher, and the team at comiXology for finding a platform to tell the tale.

Russell Willis and the team at Sequential for helping showcase the chaos.

Alex de Campi, Gail Simone, Van Jensen, Dusty Higgins, Rob Harrell, and Nate Powell for their dearest support.

Senior Smith and Mister Rathbun, King Kong, Amy H., Leigh BD, Glenn and Joey T. Barry B. and Doug, with Brian Churilla, Vinnie, Josh, Josh, Brian, Cullen and Bill. Shannon for all the Coffee. Dave Stewart, Guy Davis, Jim Gibbons, and Fabian Jr. Thanks Bruce Lee, Elvis P., Steve McQueen, John Ford, John Wayne, The Man With No Name, Sergio Leone, and Quentin, Kurt V., Douglas A., and Raymond C.

The Motorcycle Samurai Book One: A Fiery Demise © & ™ 2015 Powderkeg Press, LLC.

Published by Top Shelf Productions, PO Box 1282, Marietta, GA 30061-1282, USA.

Editor-in-Chief: Chris Staros.

Design by Chris Sheridan and Chris Ross.
Publicity and Marketing by Leigh Walton (leigh@topshelfcomix.com).
Edited by Chris Ross with Leigh Walton.

ISBN 978-1-60309-359-0

Previously published digitally. Printed in Korea.

18   17   16   15   5   4   3   2   1

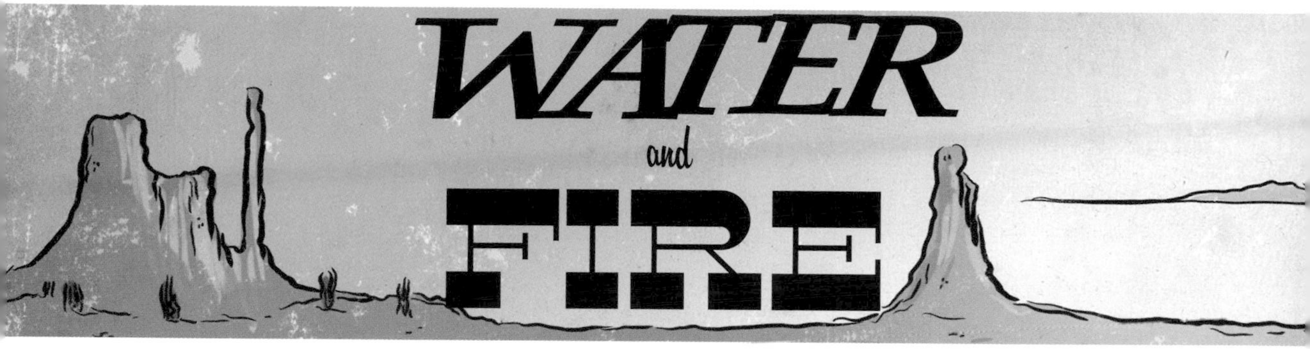
WATER
and
FIRE

PROLOGUE

MOTORCYCLE SAMURAI

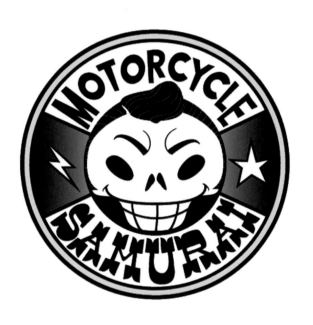

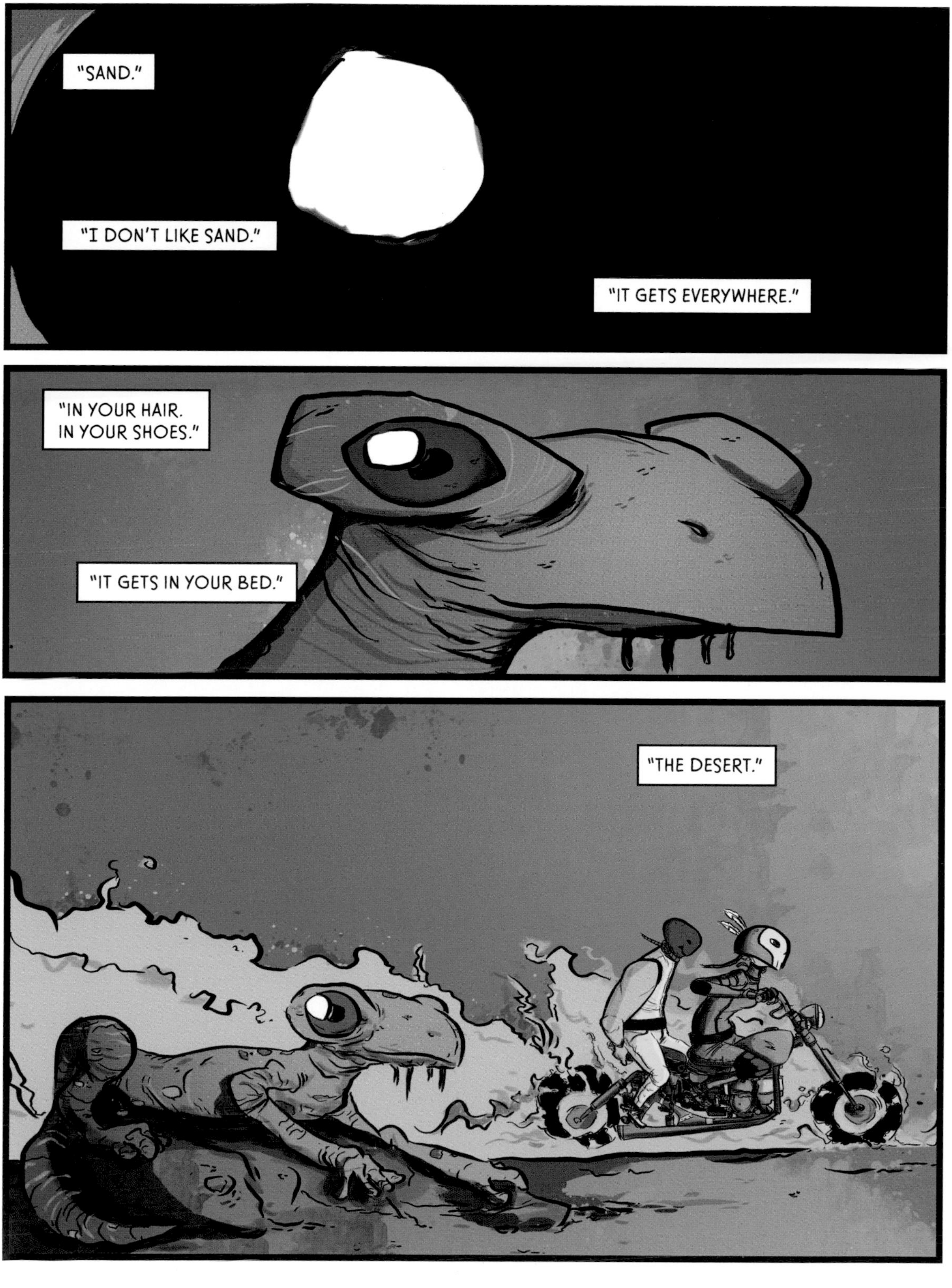
"SAND."
"I DON'T LIKE SAND."
"IT GETS EVERYWHERE."
"IN YOUR HAIR. IN YOUR SHOES."
"IT GETS IN YOUR BED."
"THE DESERT."

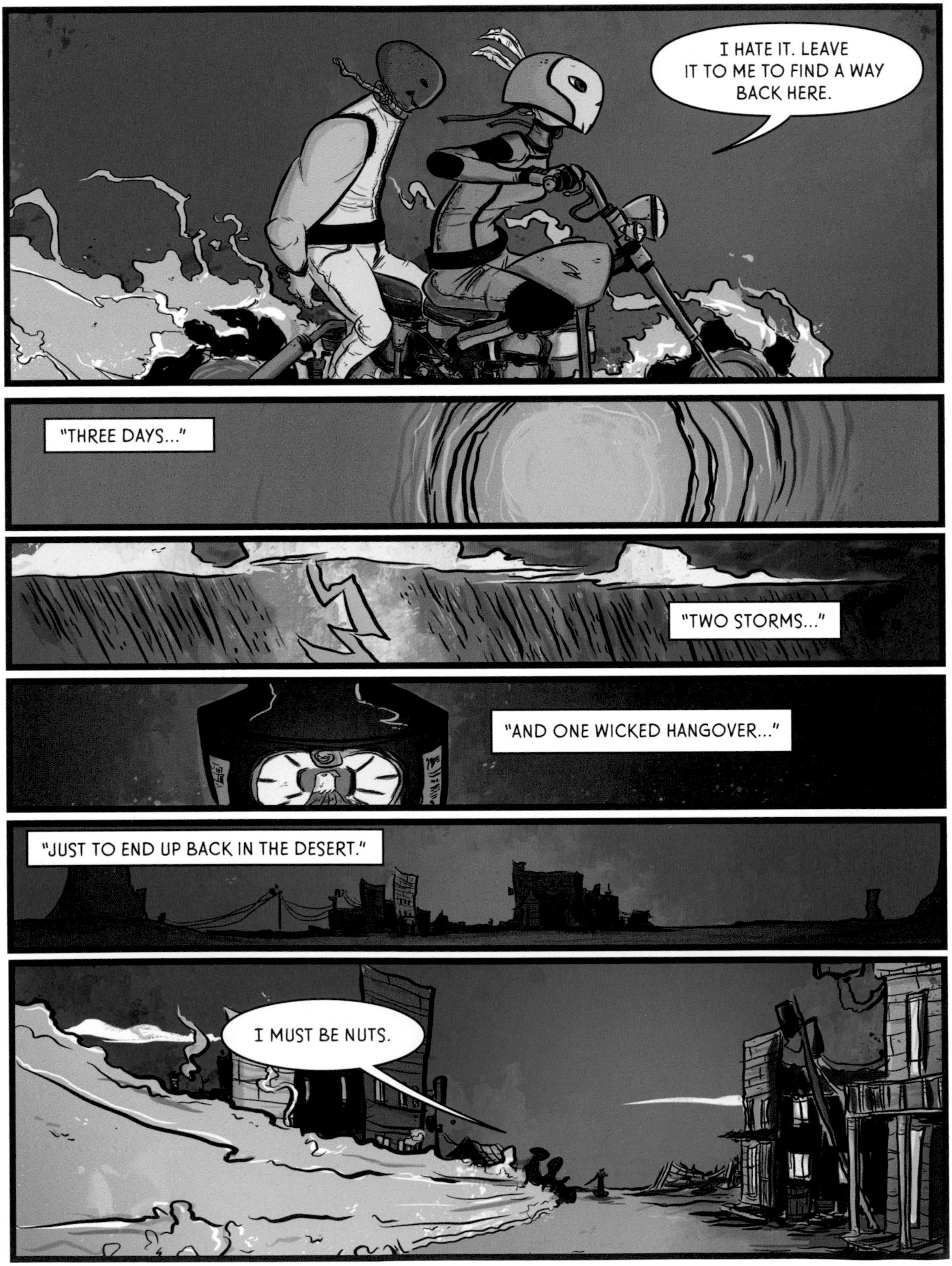

I HATE IT. LEAVE IT TO ME TO FIND A WAY BACK HERE.
"THREE DAYS..."
"TWO STORMS..."
"AND ONE WICKED HANGOVER..."
"JUST TO END UP BACK IN THE DESERT."
I MUST BE NUTS.

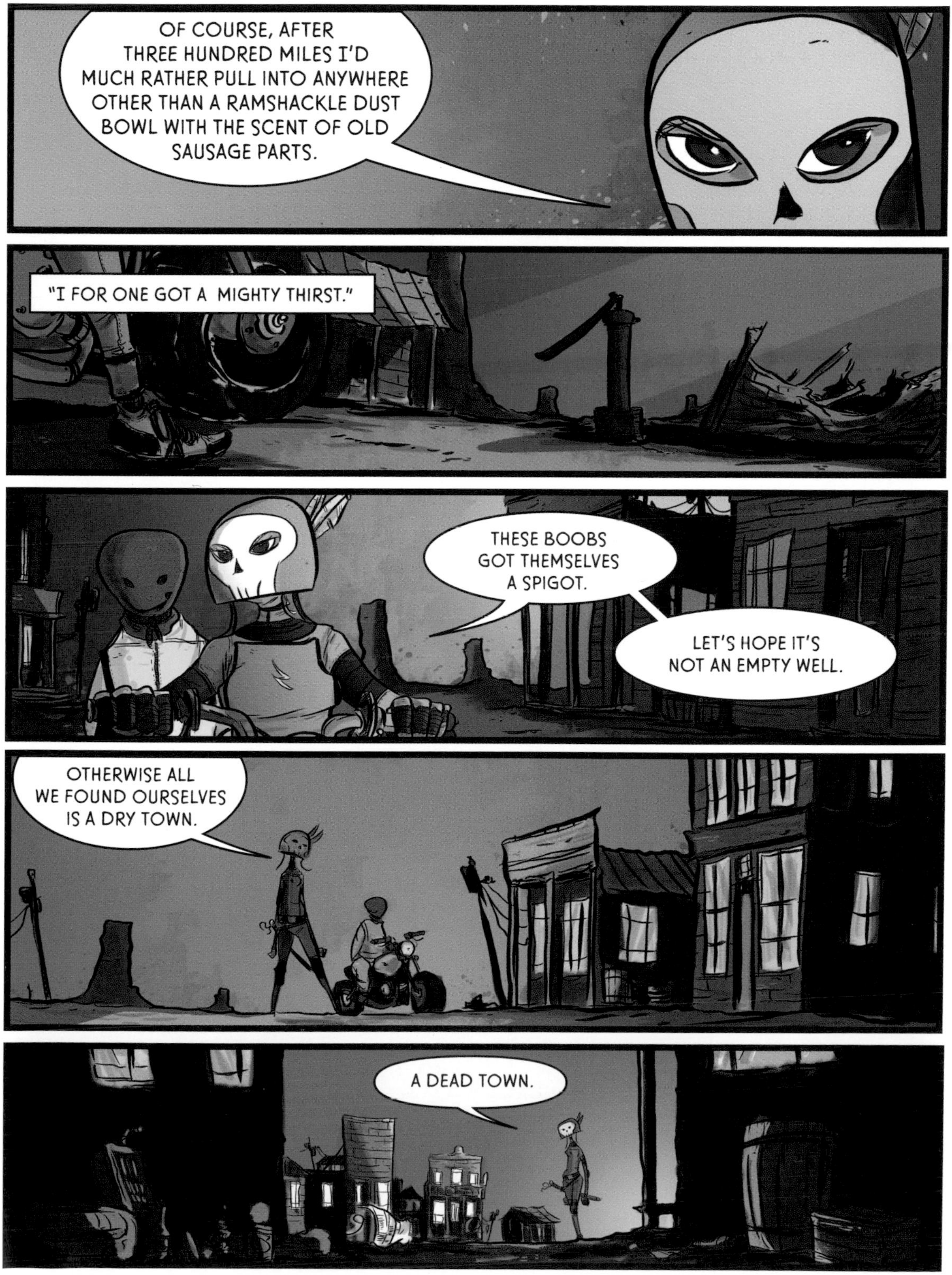
OF COURSE, AFTER THREE HUNDRED MILES I'D MUCH RATHER PULL INTO ANYWHERE OTHER THAN A RAMSHACKLE DUST BOWL WITH THE SCENT OF OLD SAUSAGE PARTS.
"I FOR ONE GOT A MIGHTY THIRST."
THESE BOOBS GOT THEMSELVES A SPIGOT.
LET'S HOPE IT'S NOT AN EMPTY WELL.
OTHERWISE ALL WE FOUND OURSELVES IS A DRY TOWN.
A DEAD TOWN.

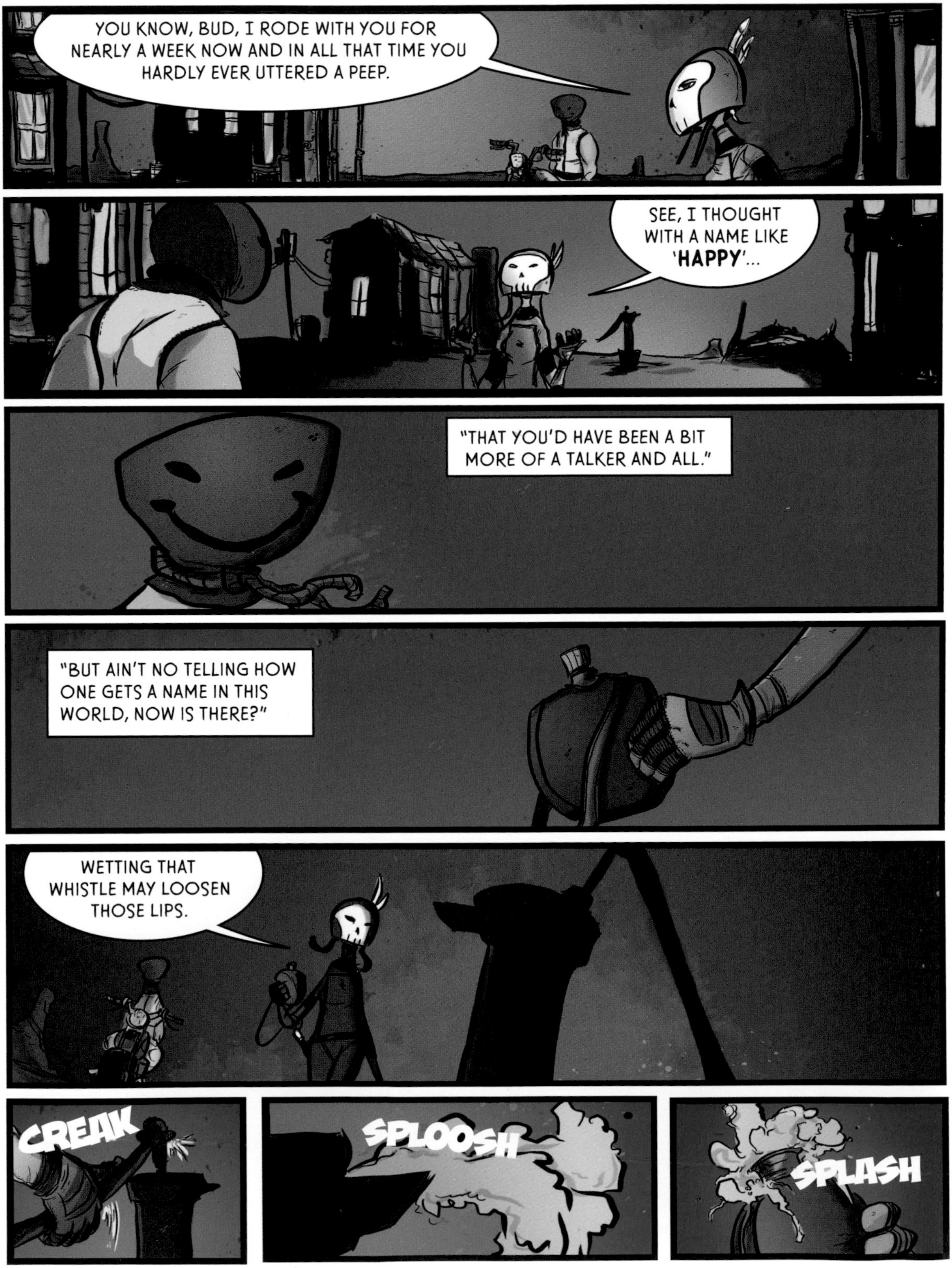
YOU KNOW, BUD, I RODE WITH YOU FOR NEARLY A WEEK NOW AND IN ALL THAT TIME YOU HARDLY EVER UTTERED A PEEP.
SEE, I THOUGHT WITH A NAME LIKE '**HAPPY**'...
"THAT YOU'D HAVE BEEN A BIT MORE OF A TALKER AND ALL."
"BUT AIN'T NO TELLING HOW ONE GETS A NAME IN THIS WORLD, NOW IS THERE?"
WETTING THAT WHISTLE MAY LOOSEN THOSE LIPS.
CREAK
SPLOOSH
SPLASH

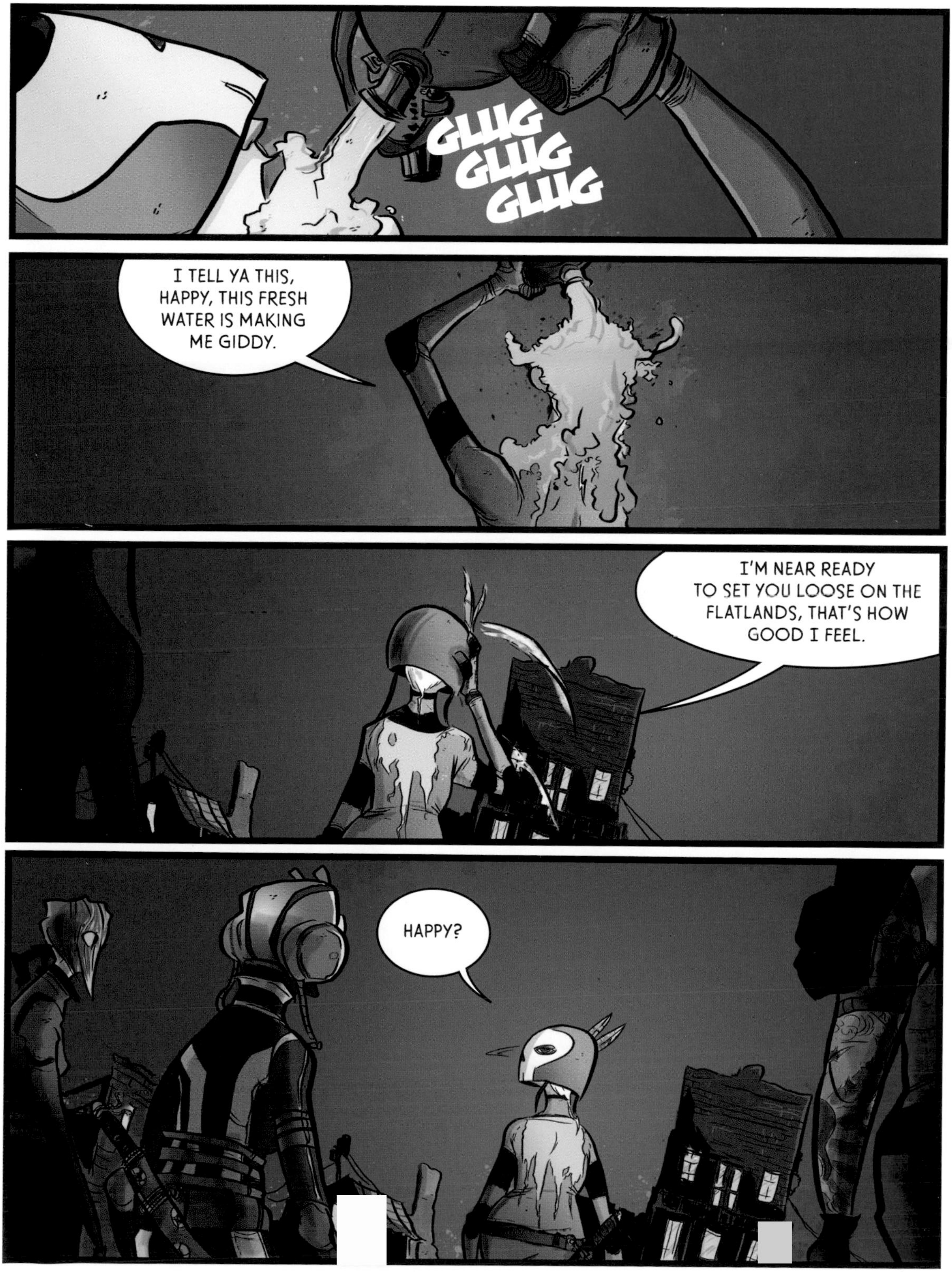
GLUG GLUG GLUG
I TELL YA THIS, HAPPY, THIS FRESH WATER IS MAKING ME GIDDY.
I'M NEAR READY TO SET YOU LOOSE ON THE FLATLANDS, THAT'S HOW GOOD I FEEL.
HAPPY?

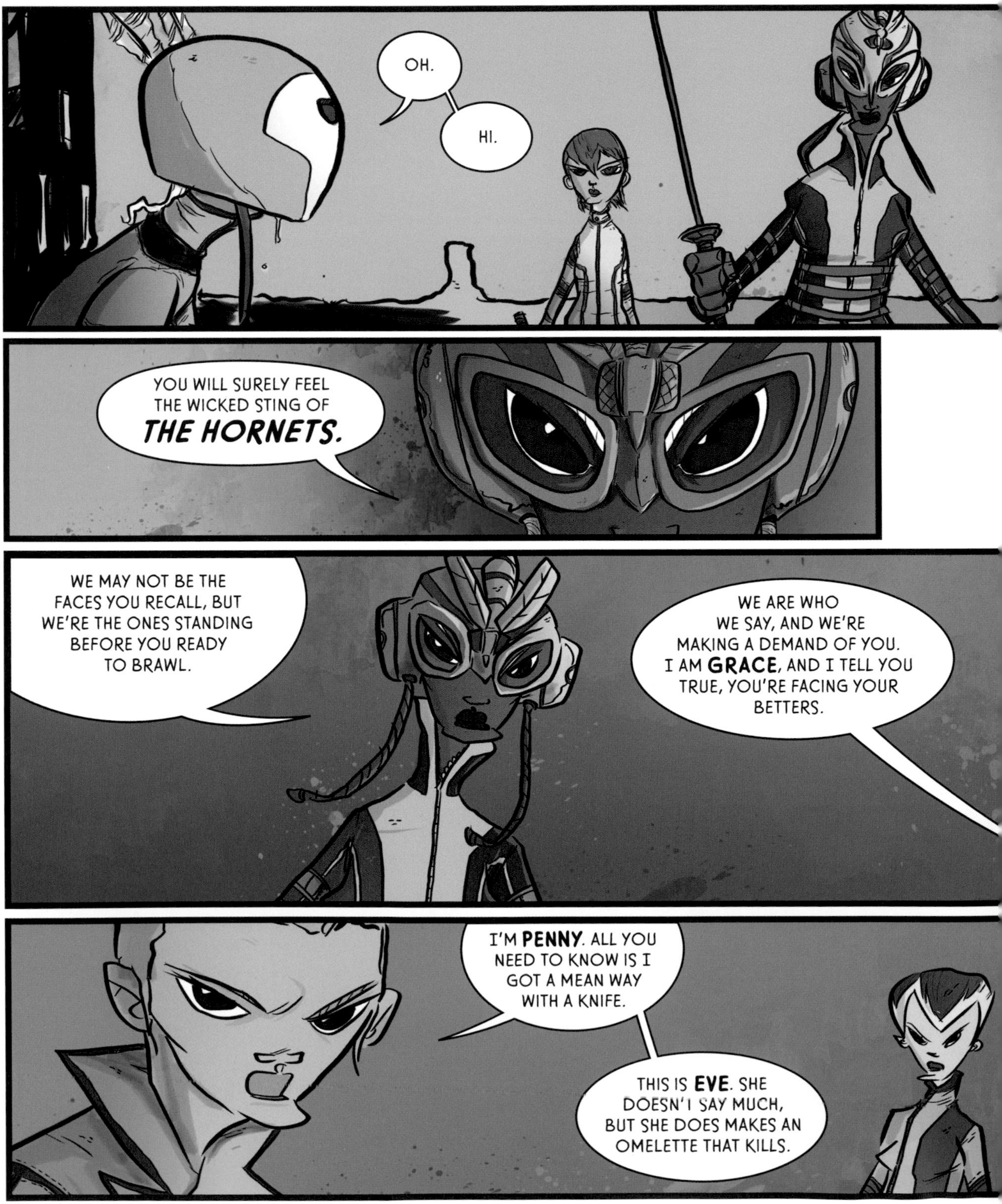
OH.
HI.
YOU WILL SURELY FEEL THE WICKED STING OF *THE HORNETS.*
WE MAY NOT BE THE FACES YOU RECALL, BUT WE'RE THE ONES STANDING BEFORE YOU READY TO BRAWL.
WE ARE WHO WE SAY, AND WE'RE MAKING A DEMAND OF YOU. I AM **GRACE**, AND I TELL YOU TRUE, YOU'RE FACING YOUR BETTERS.
I'M **PENNY**. ALL YOU NEED TO KNOW IS I GOT A MEAN WAY WITH A KNIFE.
THIS IS **EVE**. SHE DOESN'T SAY MUCH, BUT SHE DOES MAKES AN OMELETTE THAT KILLS.

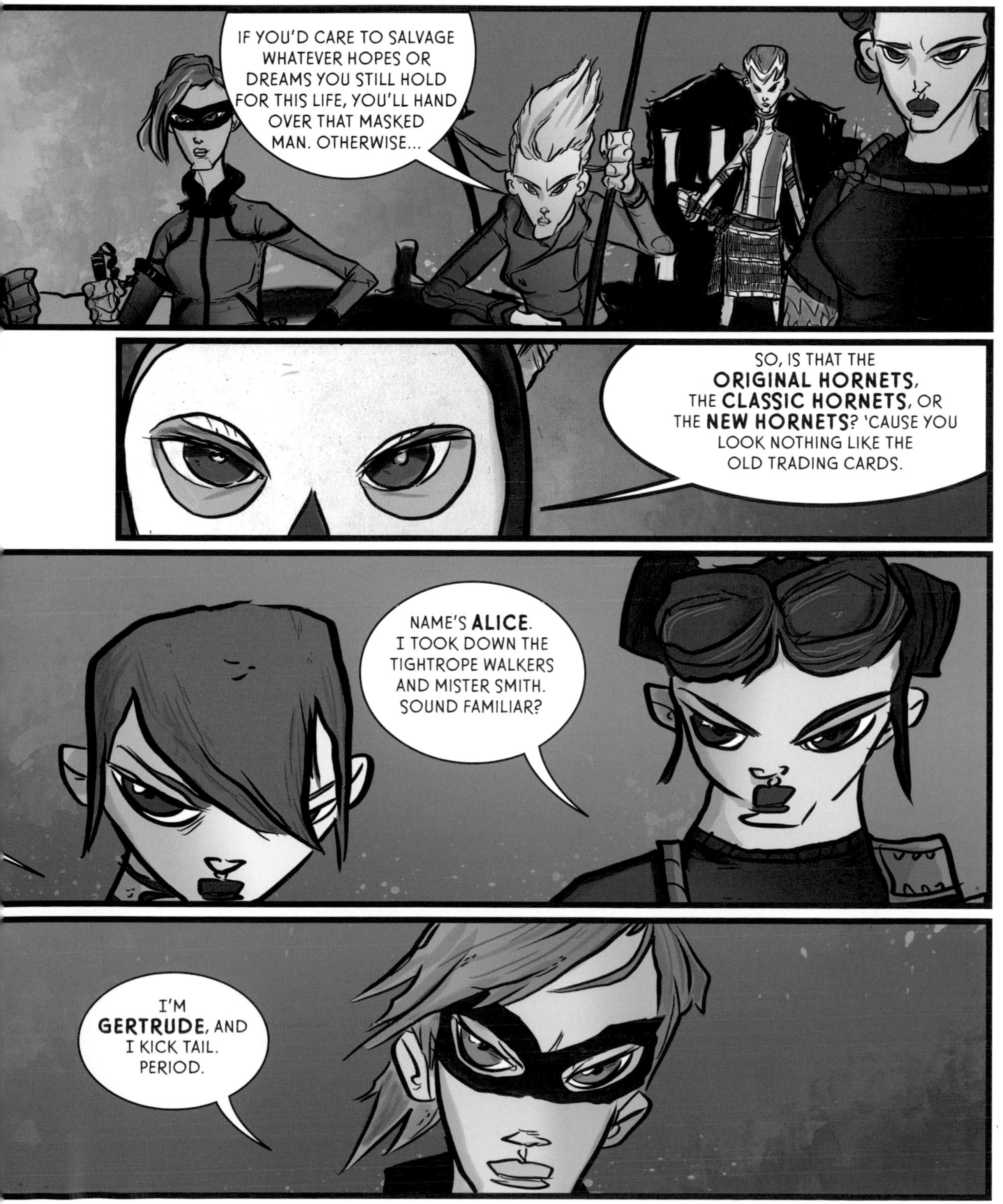
IF YOU'D CARE TO SALVAGE WHATEVER HOPES OR DREAMS YOU STILL HOLD FOR THIS LIFE, YOU'LL HAND OVER THAT MASKED MAN. OTHERWISE...
SO, IS THAT THE ORIGINAL HORNETS, THE CLASSIC HORNETS, OR THE NEW HORNETS? 'CAUSE YOU LOOK NOTHING LIKE THE OLD TRADING CARDS.
NAME'S ALICE. I TOOK DOWN THE TIGHTROPE WALKERS AND MISTER SMITH. SOUND FAMILIAR?
I'M GERTRUDE, AND I KICK TAIL. PERIOD.

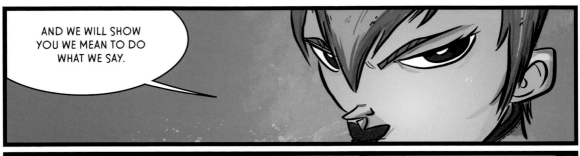

AND WE WILL SHOW YOU WE MEAN TO DO WHAT WE SAY.

"WE WANT THE MAN IN THE MASK. BECAUSE HE IS WORTH SOMETHING TO SOMEONE OF IMPORTANCE."

WELL, WHILE I LIKE YOUR SPIRIT OF COMPROMISE, I AM THE **WHITE BOLT,** FAMED FOR MY HATRED OF BLOODY SAND. THAT AND DISAPPOINTING FOLKS THAT COME MAKING DEMANDS.

BESIDES, I OFFER YOU MY MYSTIC BLADE. IT'S WORTH FAR MORE THAN THE MAN BACK THERE IN THE BURLAP SACK...

NO DEAL. MAKE READY FOR STRUGGLE, BLOOD AND PAIN, YOU LITTLE TWIT. FOR YOU FACE *THE HORNETS*.

I DIDN'T FIGURE YOU TO BE THAT SMART, BUT NOW IT'S JUST A LOT OF MOVEMENT AND UNSATISFYING GRUNTING.

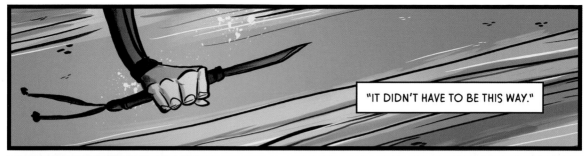

"IT DIDN'T HAVE TO BE THIS WAY."

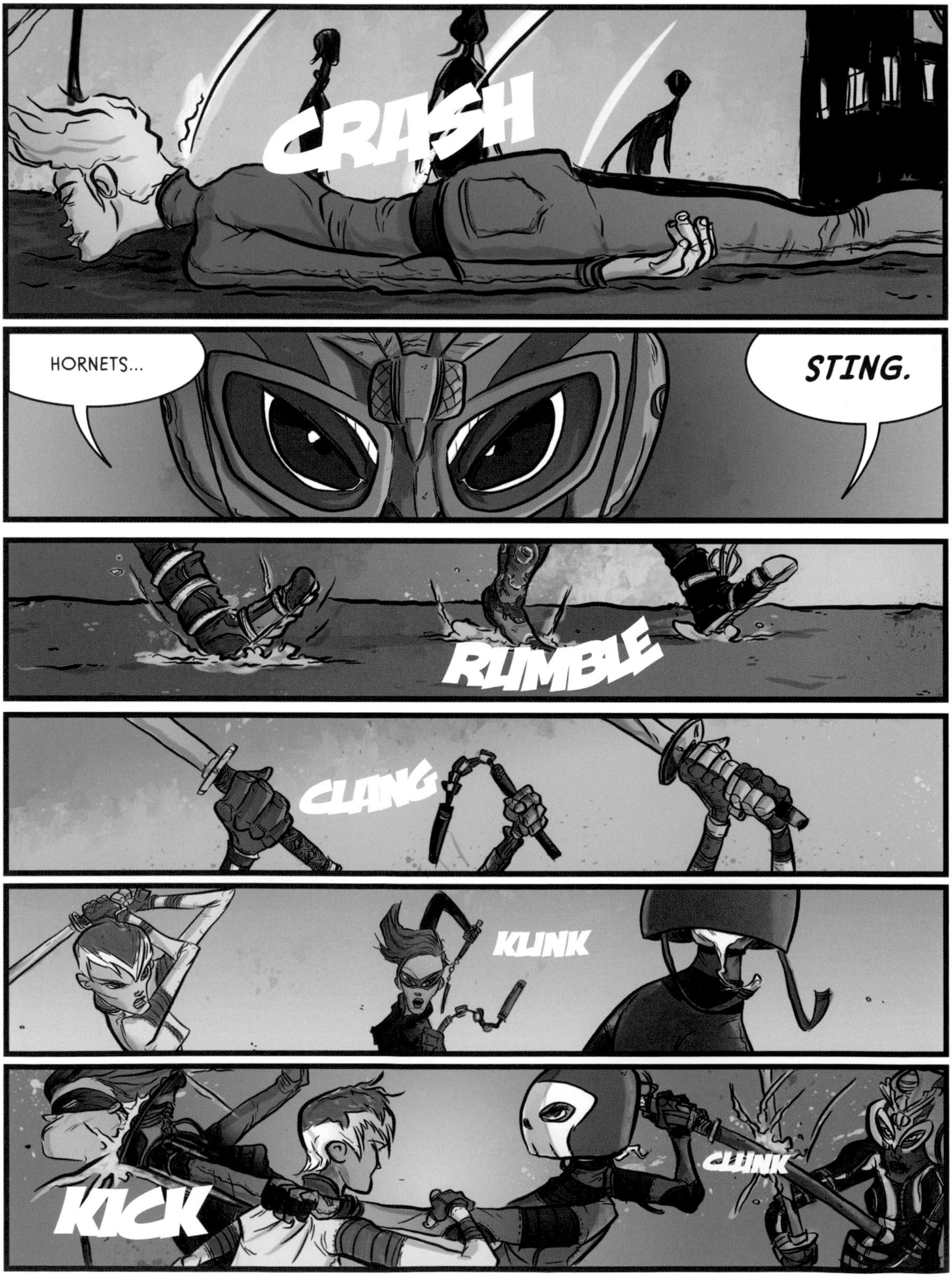
CRASH
HORNETS...
STING.
RUMBLE
CLANG
KLINK
KICK
CLINK

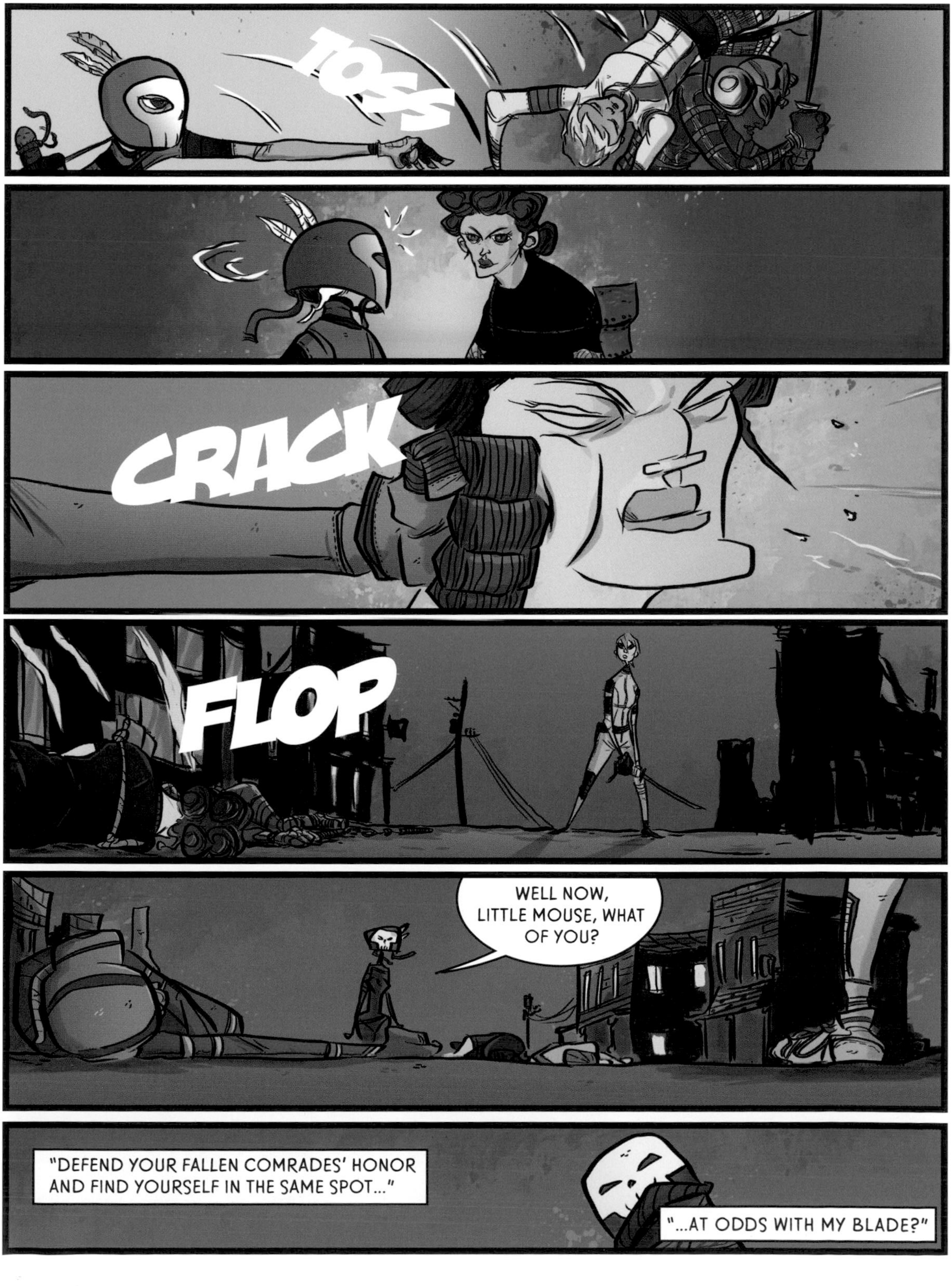
TOSS
CRACK
FLOP
WELL NOW, LITTLE MOUSE, WHAT OF YOU?
"DEFEND YOUR FALLEN COMRADES' HONOR AND FIND YOURSELF IN THE SAME SPOT..."
"...AT ODDS WITH MY BLADE?"

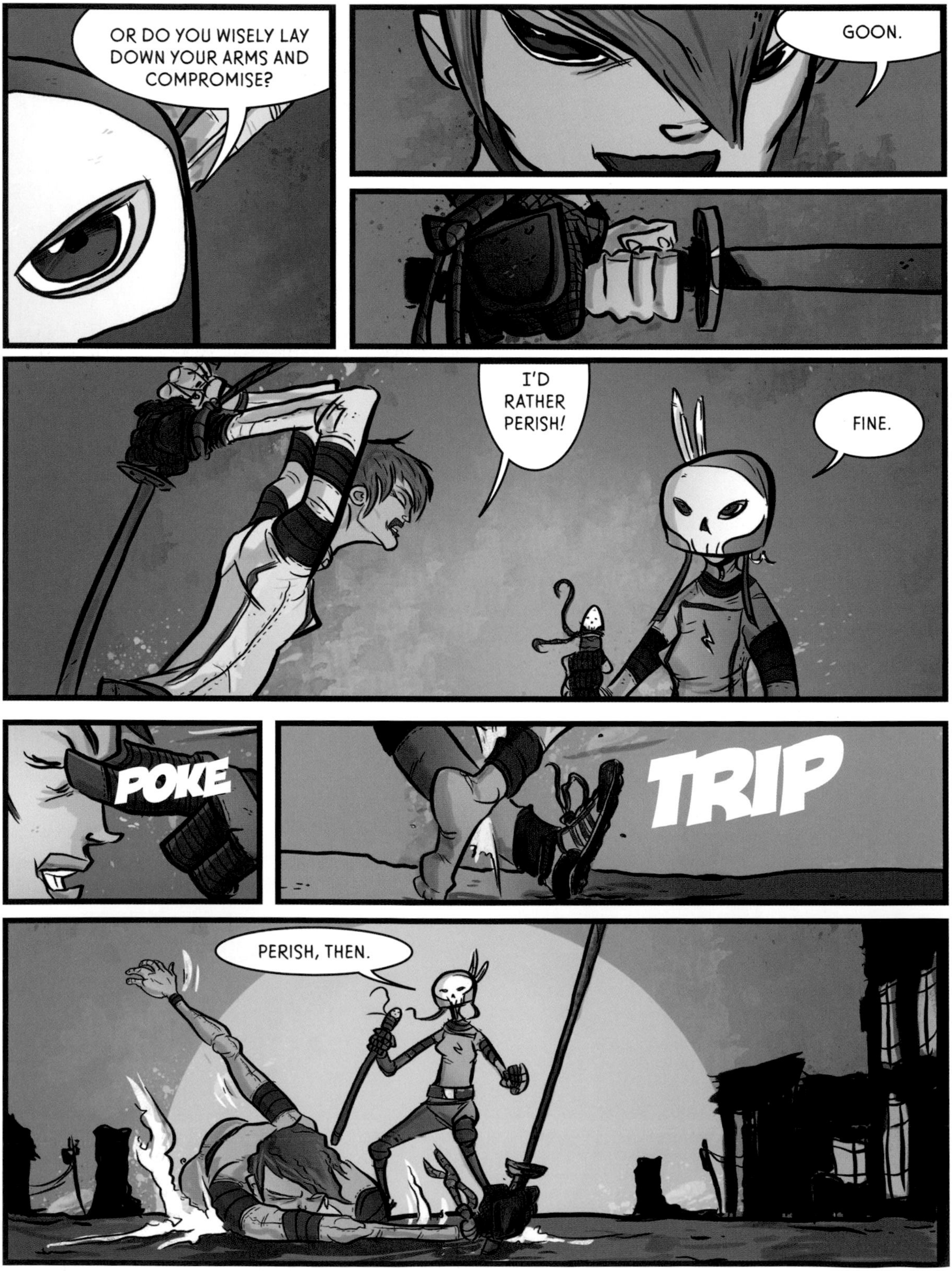
OR DO YOU WISELY LAY DOWN YOUR ARMS AND COMPROMISE?
GOON.
I'D RATHER PERISH!
FINE.
POKE
TRIP
PERISH, THEN.

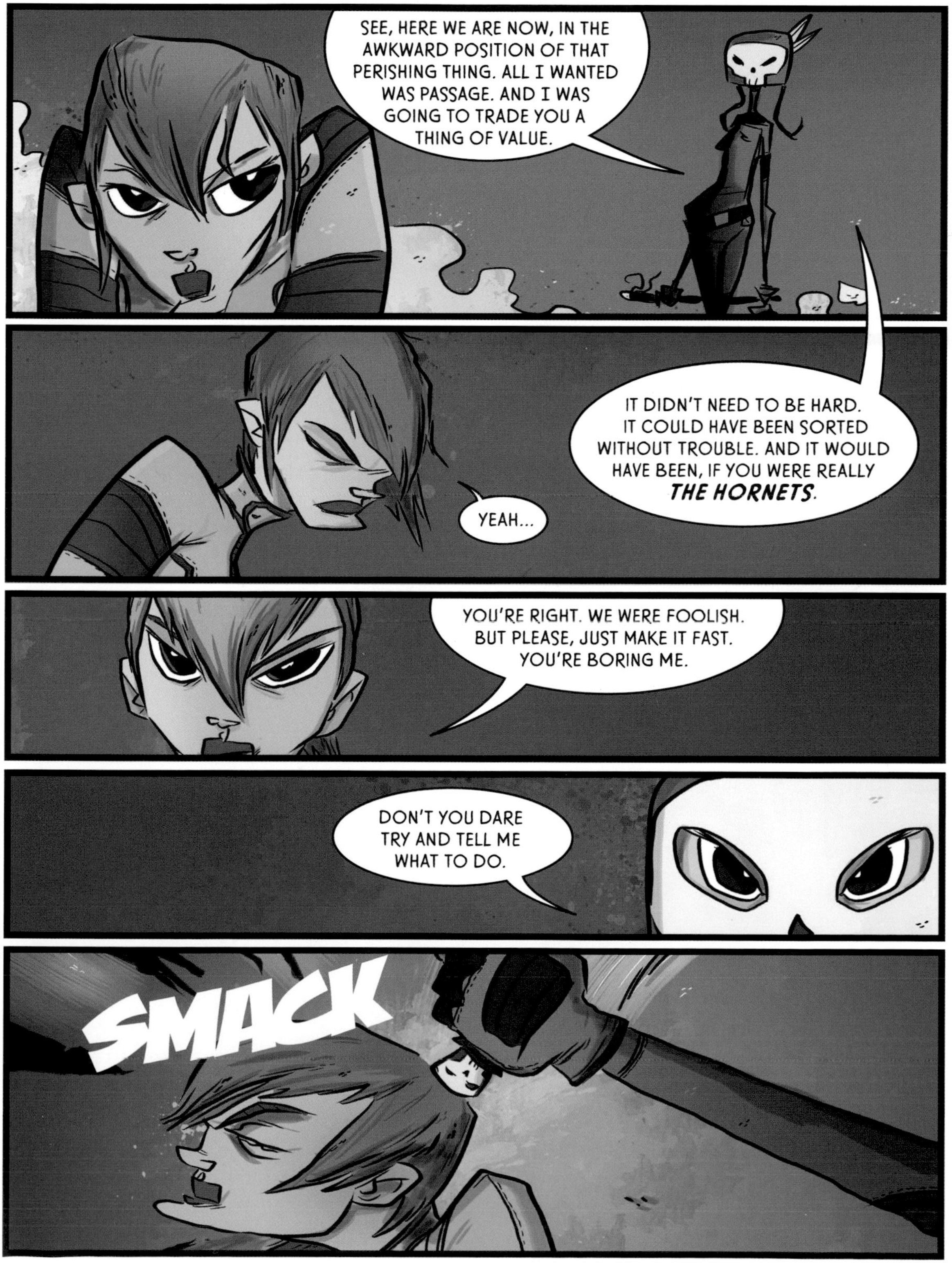
SEE, HERE WE ARE NOW, IN THE AWKWARD POSITION OF THAT PERISHING THING. ALL I WANTED WAS PASSAGE. AND I WAS GOING TO TRADE YOU A THING OF VALUE.
IT DIDN'T NEED TO BE HARD. IT COULD HAVE BEEN SORTED WITHOUT TROUBLE. AND IT WOULD HAVE BEEN, IF YOU WERE REALLY ***THE HORNETS***.
YEAH...
YOU'RE RIGHT. WE WERE FOOLISH. BUT PLEASE, JUST MAKE IT FAST. YOU'RE BORING ME.
DON'T YOU DARE TRY AND TELL ME WHAT TO DO.
SMACK

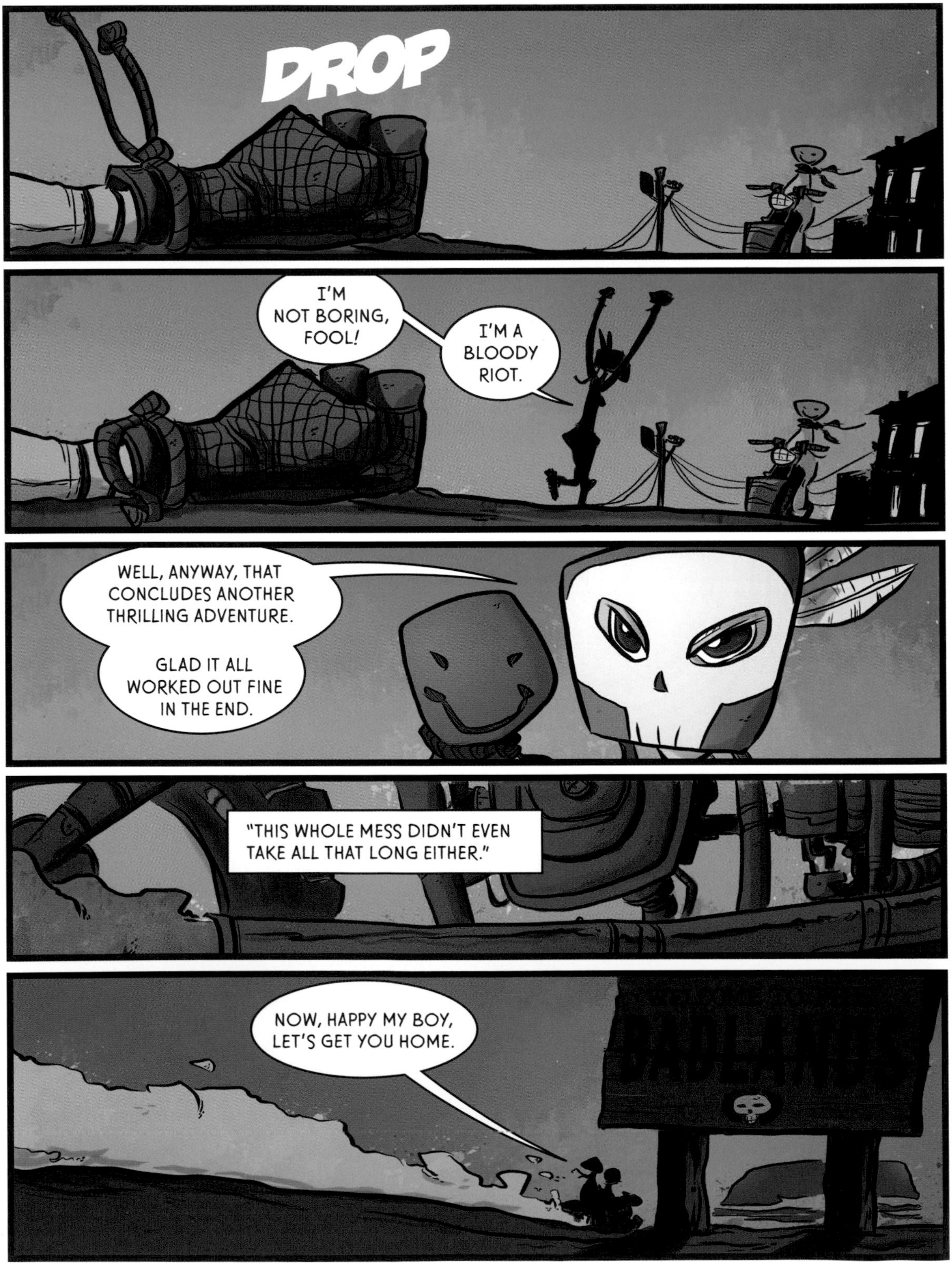
DROP
I'M NOT BORING, FOOL!
I'M A BLOODY RIOT.
WELL, ANYWAY, THAT CONCLUDES ANOTHER THRILLING ADVENTURE.
GLAD IT ALL WORKED OUT FINE IN THE END.
"THIS WHOLE MESS DIDN'T EVEN TAKE ALL THAT LONG EITHER."
NOW, HAPPY MY BOY, LET'S GET YOU HOME.

IRON *and* SKY

CHAPTER ONE

MOTORCYCLE
SAMURAI

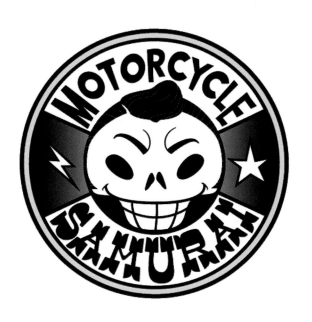

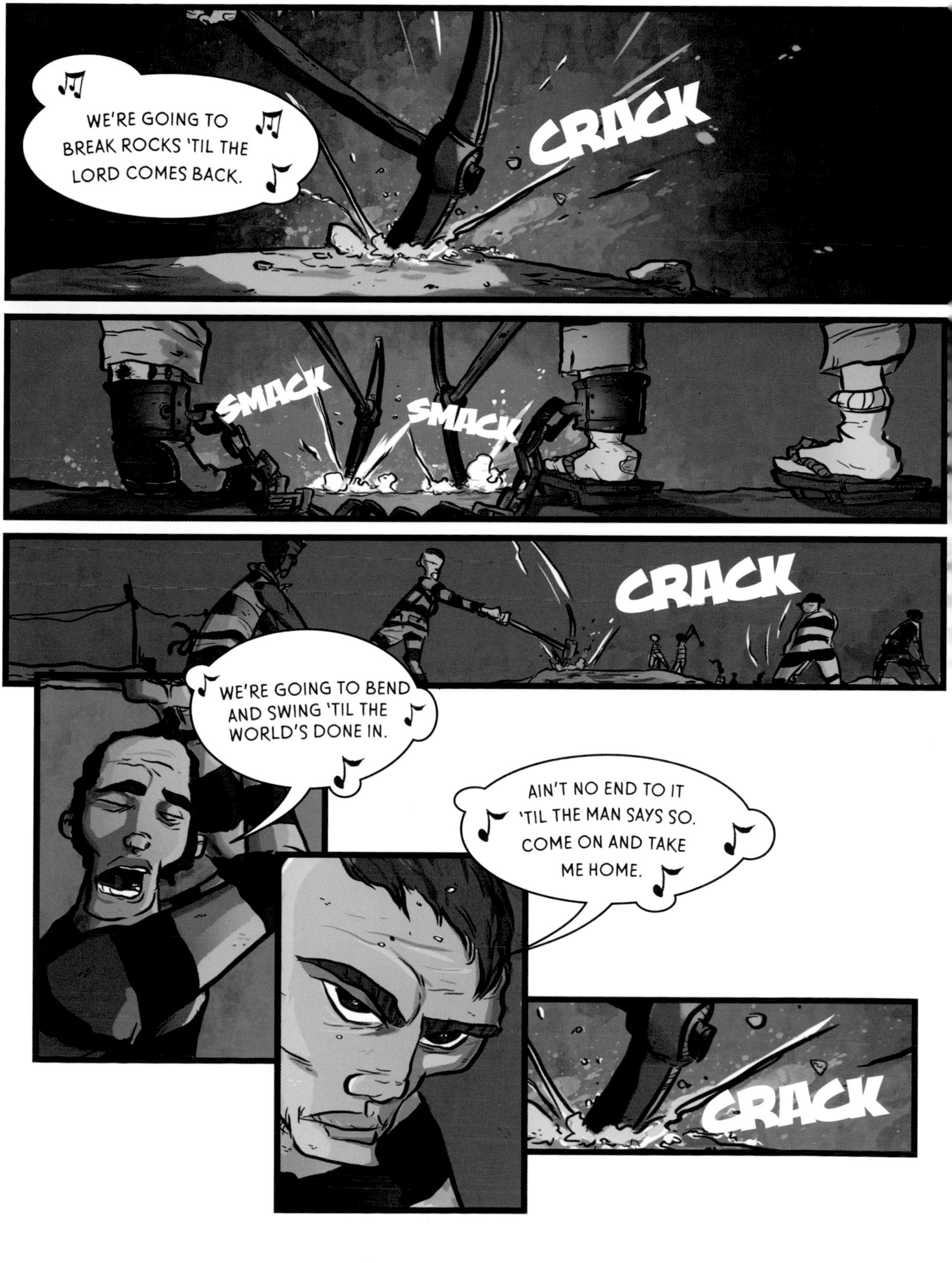
WE'RE GOING TO BREAK ROCKS 'TIL THE LORD COMES BACK.
CRACK
SMACK
SMACK
CRACK
WE'RE GOING TO BEND AND SWING 'TIL THE WORLD'S DONE IN.
AIN'T NO END TO IT 'TIL THE MAN SAYS SO. COME ON AND TAKE ME HOME.
CRACK

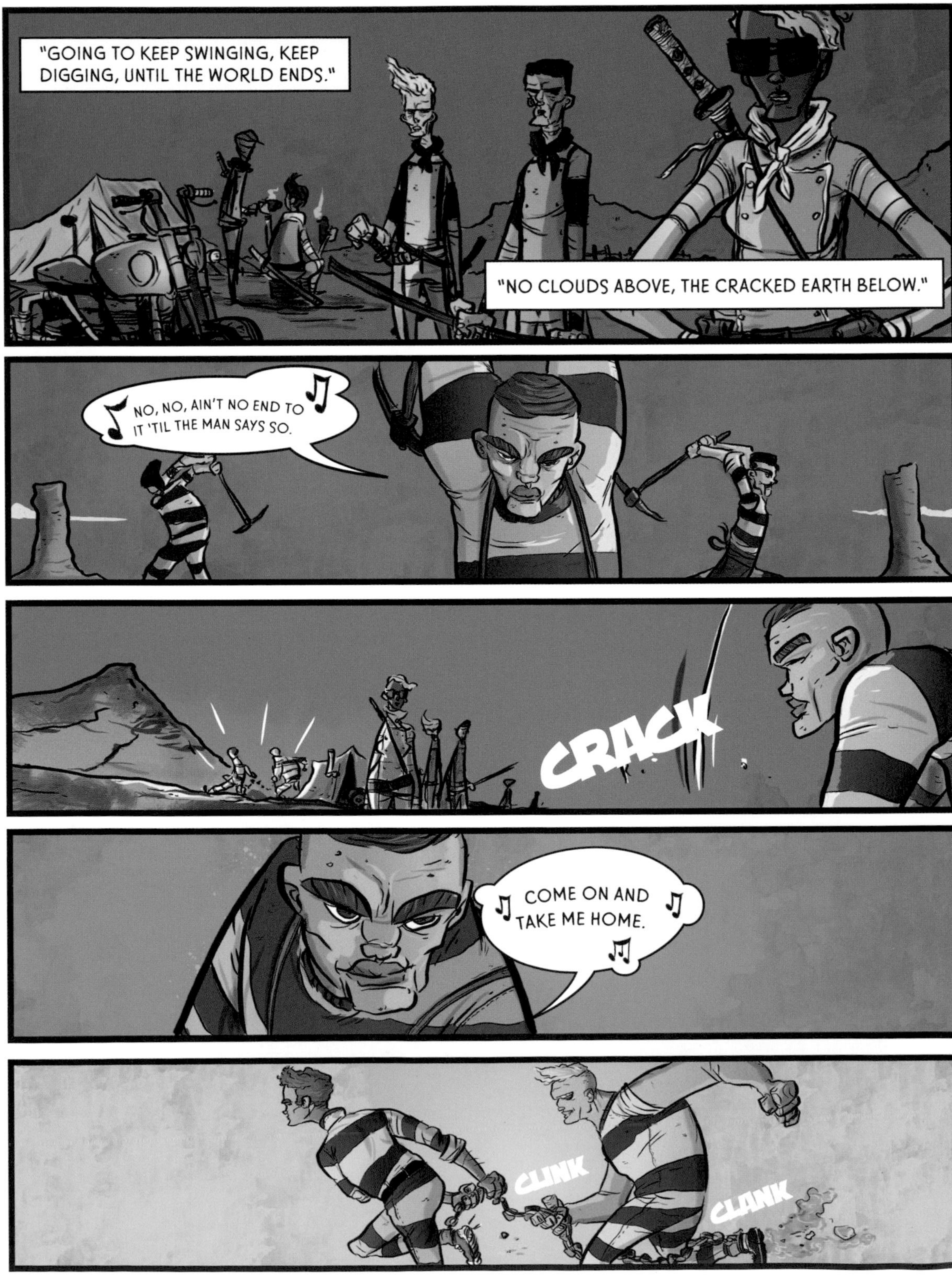
"GOING TO KEEP SWINGING, KEEP DIGGING, UNTIL THE WORLD ENDS."
"NO CLOUDS ABOVE, THE CRACKED EARTH BELOW."
NO, NO, AIN'T NO END TO IT 'TIL THE MAN SAYS SO.
CRACK
COME ON AND TAKE ME HOME.
CLINK
CLANK

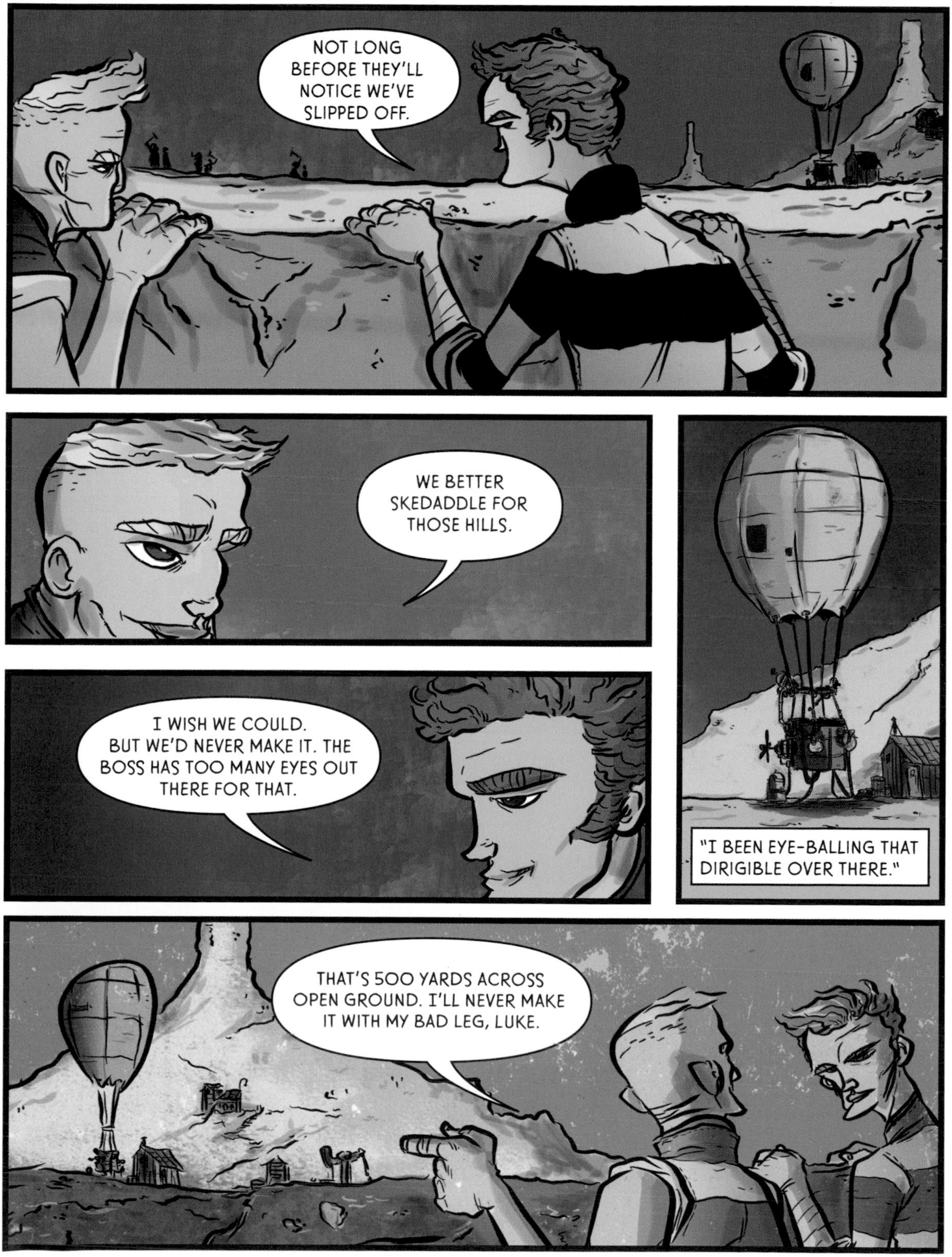
NOT LONG BEFORE THEY'LL NOTICE WE'VE SLIPPED OFF.
WE BETTER SKEDADDLE FOR THOSE HILLS.
I WISH WE COULD. BUT WE'D NEVER MAKE IT. THE BOSS HAS TOO MANY EYES OUT THERE FOR THAT.
"I BEEN EYE-BALLING THAT DIRIGIBLE OVER THERE."
THAT'S 500 YARDS ACROSS OPEN GROUND. I'LL NEVER MAKE IT WITH MY BAD LEG, LUKE.

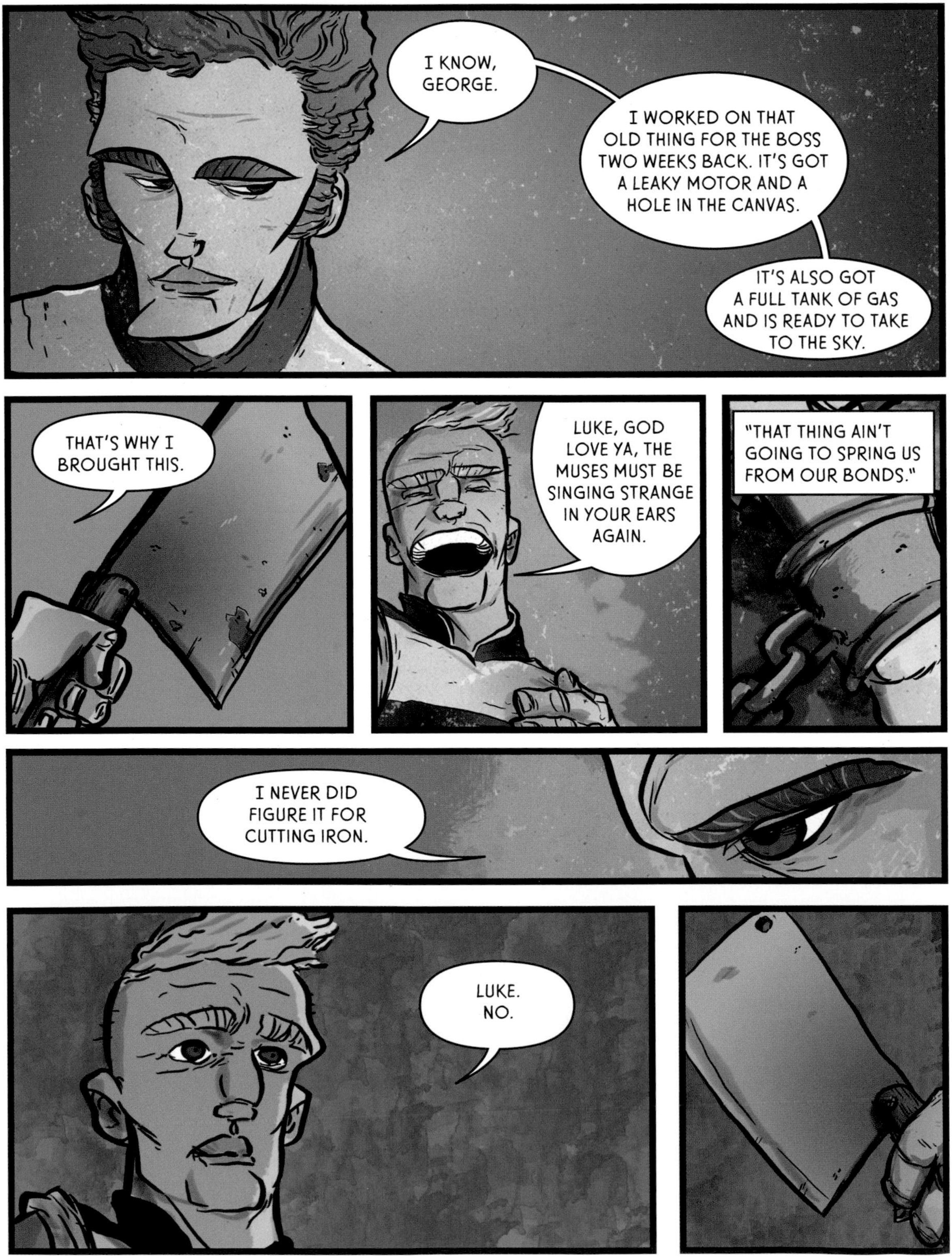
I KNOW, GEORGE.
I WORKED ON THAT OLD THING FOR THE BOSS TWO WEEKS BACK. IT'S GOT A LEAKY MOTOR AND A HOLE IN THE CANVAS.
IT'S ALSO GOT A FULL TANK OF GAS AND IS READY TO TAKE TO THE SKY.
THAT'S WHY I BROUGHT THIS.
LUKE, GOD LOVE YA, THE MUSES MUST BE SINGING STRANGE IN YOUR EARS AGAIN.
"THAT THING AIN'T GOING TO SPRING US FROM OUR BONDS."
I NEVER DID FIGURE IT FOR CUTTING IRON.
LUKE. NO.

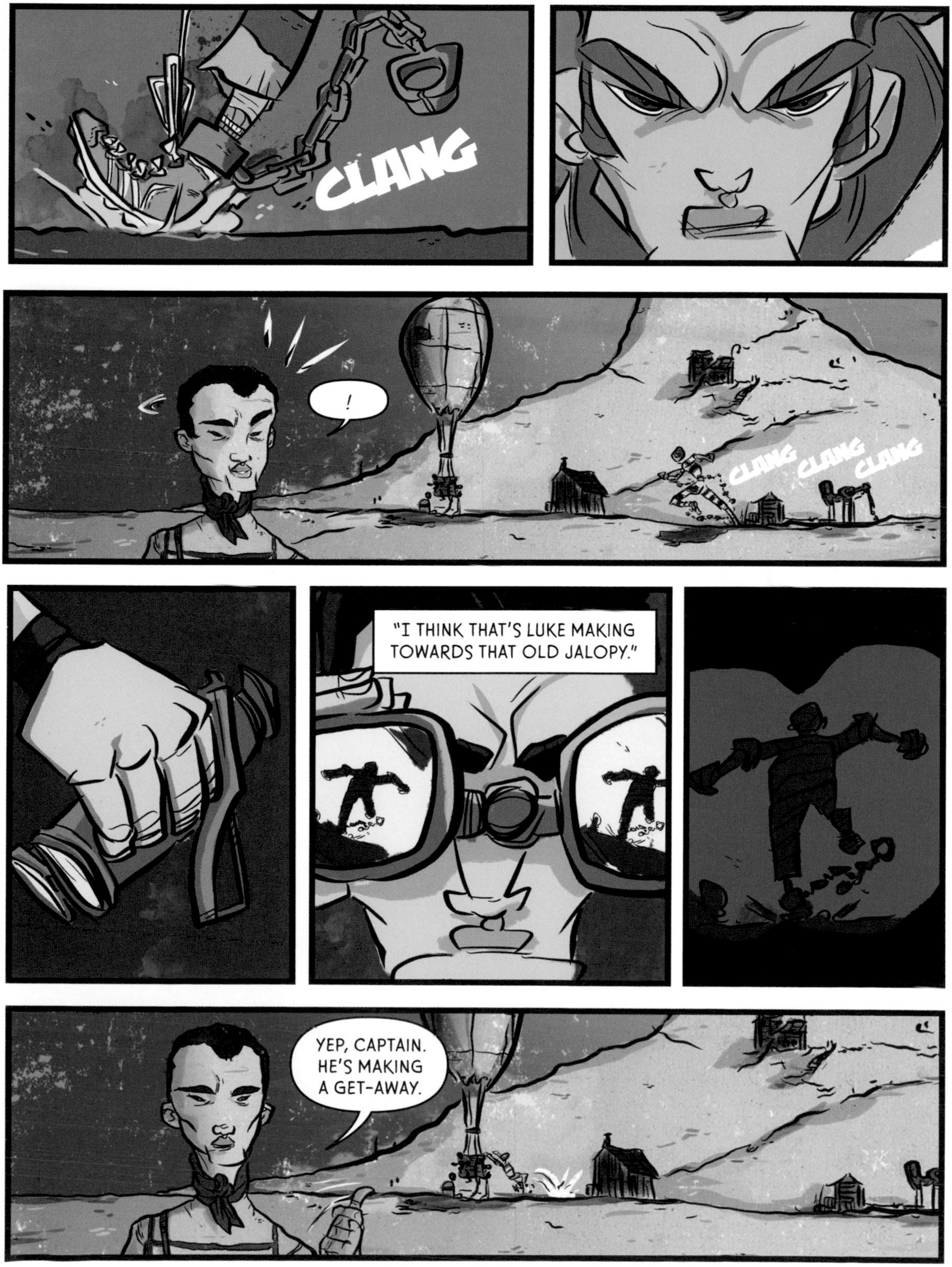
CLANG
!
CLANG
CLANG
CLANG
"I THINK THAT'S LUKE MAKING TOWARDS THAT OLD JALOPY."
YEP, CAPTAIN. HE'S MAKING A GET-AWAY.

"THAT OLD AIR PIRATE MAY MOVE LIKE A JACK-RABBIT..."

"BUT I WOULDN'T WORRY, BOYS."

CRANK

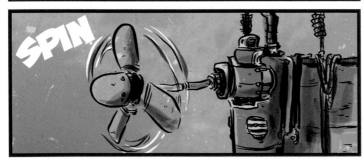

SPIN

"HE'S NOT GETTING AWAY."

"HE'S GOING INTO THE WIND WITH A LOOSE SPARK PLUG, LEAKING VALVES, AND A BUM FLYWHEEL."

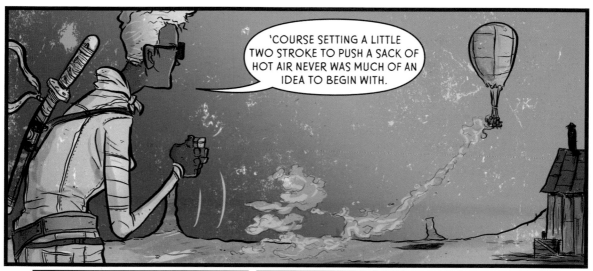

'COURSE SETTING A LITTLE TWO STROKE TO PUSH A SACK OF HOT AIR NEVER WAS MUCH OF AN IDEA TO BEGIN WITH.

FLICK

I REMEMBER THAT THING BROKE DOWN IN THE BATTLE OVER NEW ORLEANS.

TINK

POOF

FOOOSH

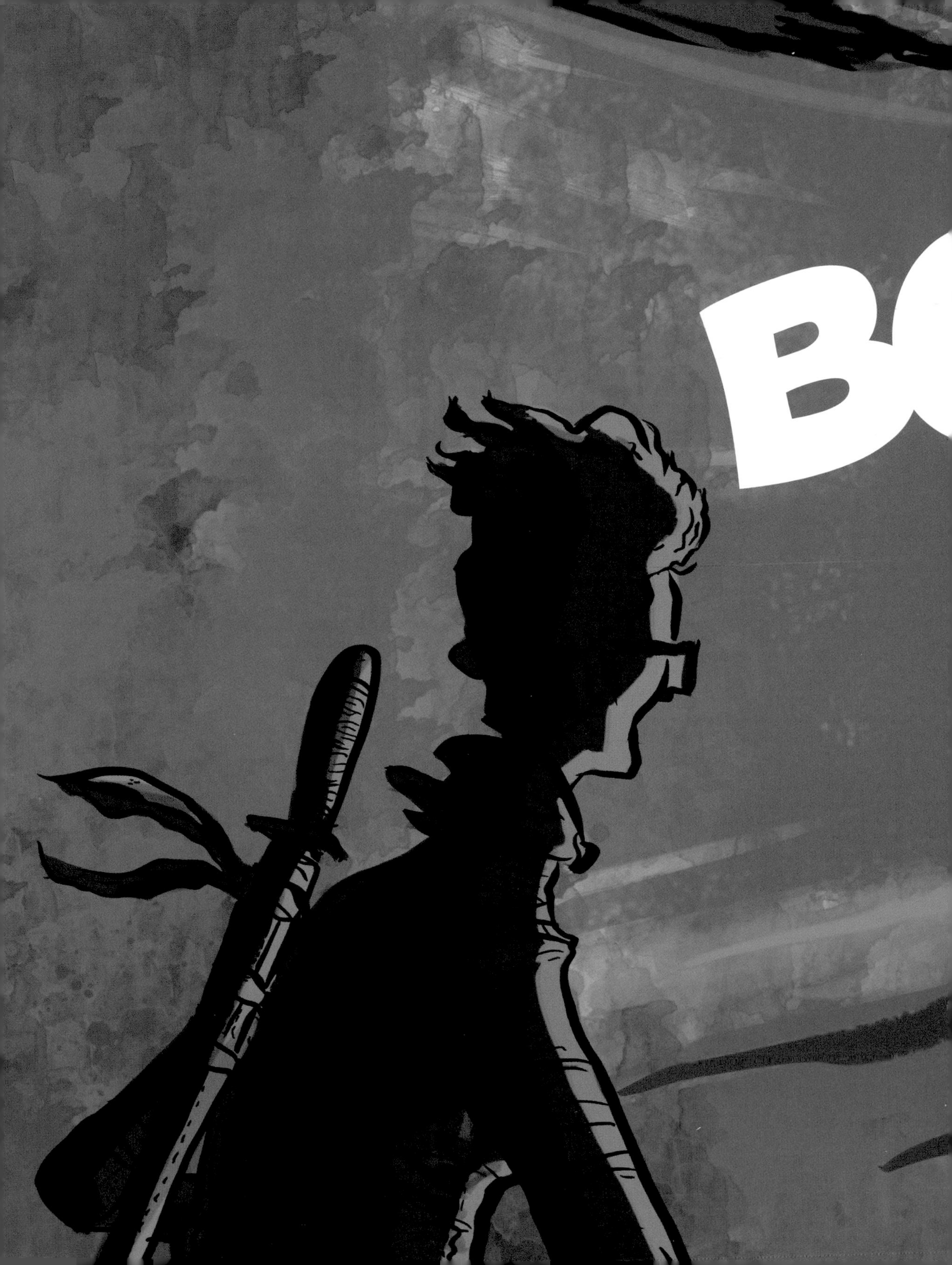

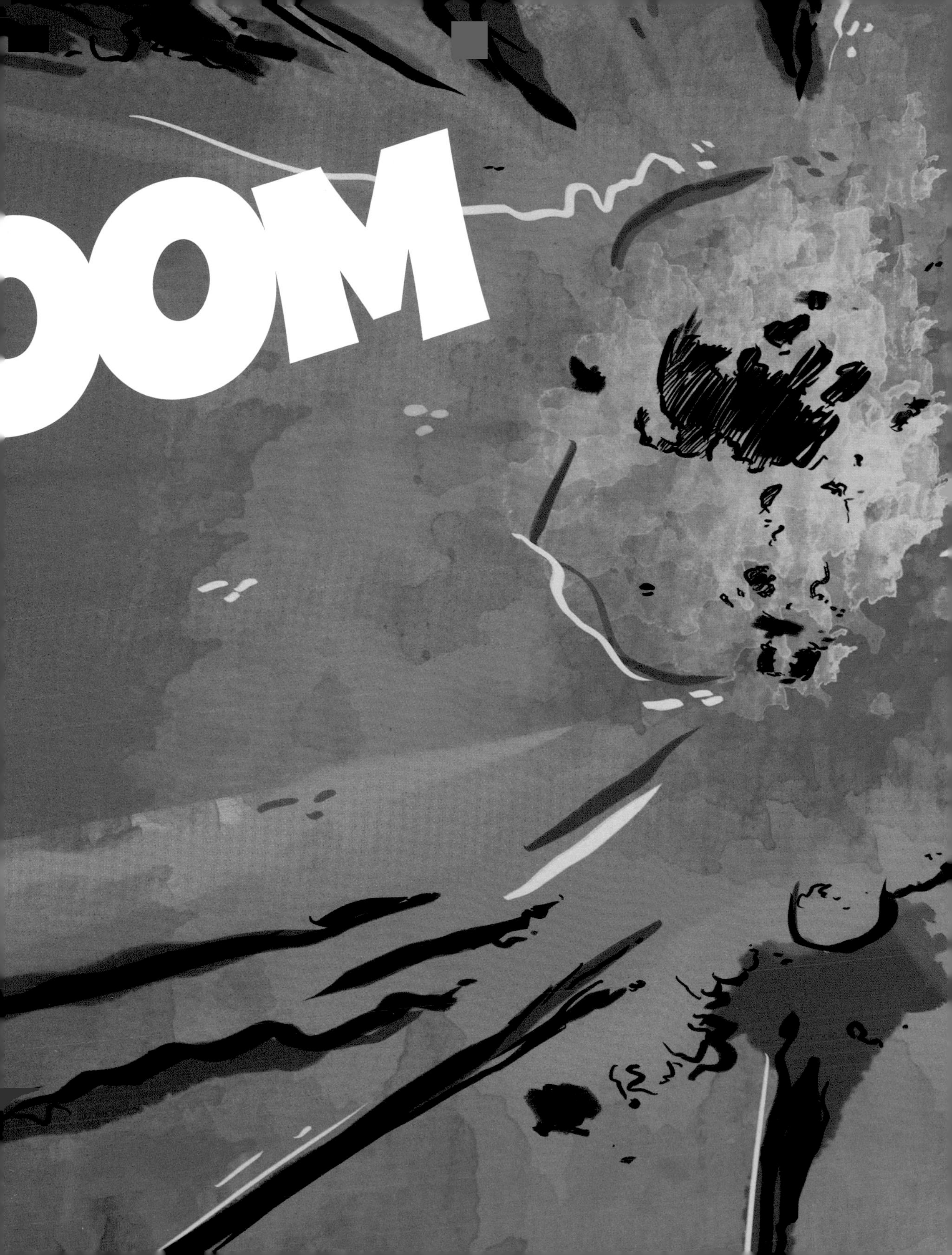
OOM

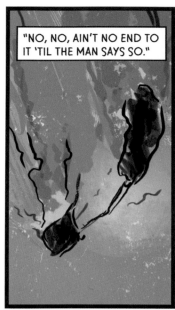

"NO, NO, AIN'T NO END TO IT 'TIL THE MAN SAYS SO."

CRASH

"AIN'T NO END TO IT."

"GOING TO SWING AND DIG 'TIL THE MAN TELLS ME TO."

"AIN'T NO END TO IT."

"BUT EVEN SO SOME DAY SOON I WILL LOOK TO THE SKY."

"WHEN I GET THERE, NOT GOING TO HAVE TO BOW AND SCRAPE."

"NOT GONNA LIFT A THING."

"NOT A THING BUT MY WEARY HEAD."

"A FIERY DEMISE."

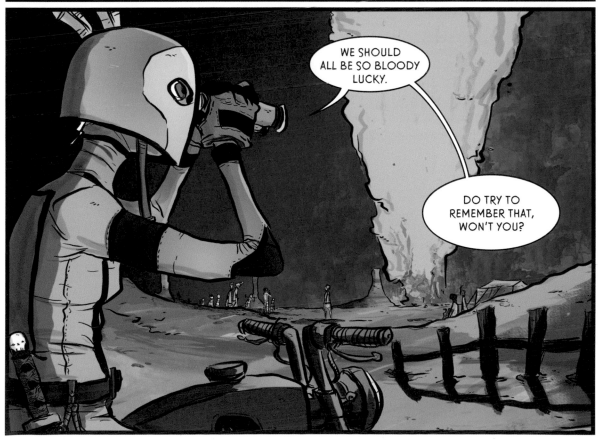

WE SHOULD ALL BE SO BLOODY LUCKY.

DO TRY TO REMEMBER THAT, WON'T YOU?

'CAUSE THINGS ARE ABOUT TO GET INTERESTING. SO BE READY FOR ANYTHING.

YOU GOT THAT?

HAPPY?

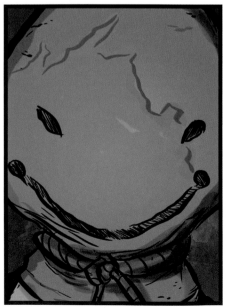

I'M GOING TO TAKE THAT SILENCE AS AGREEMENT ON THE ISSUE OF MAKING A GOOD EXIT.

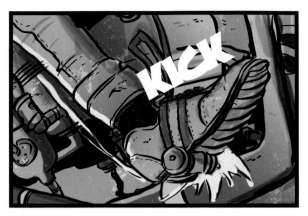

KICK

POOM

TWIST

OH, I WILL ASK YOU TO DO ONE THING.

REMEMBER NOT TO SHOOT YOUR MOUTH OFF WHEN WE GET THERE.

NOW ENTERING TROUBLE
POPULATION 108

POPULATION 108

"OTHERWISE THIS IS GOING TO BE A DAMN SHORT ADVENTURE."

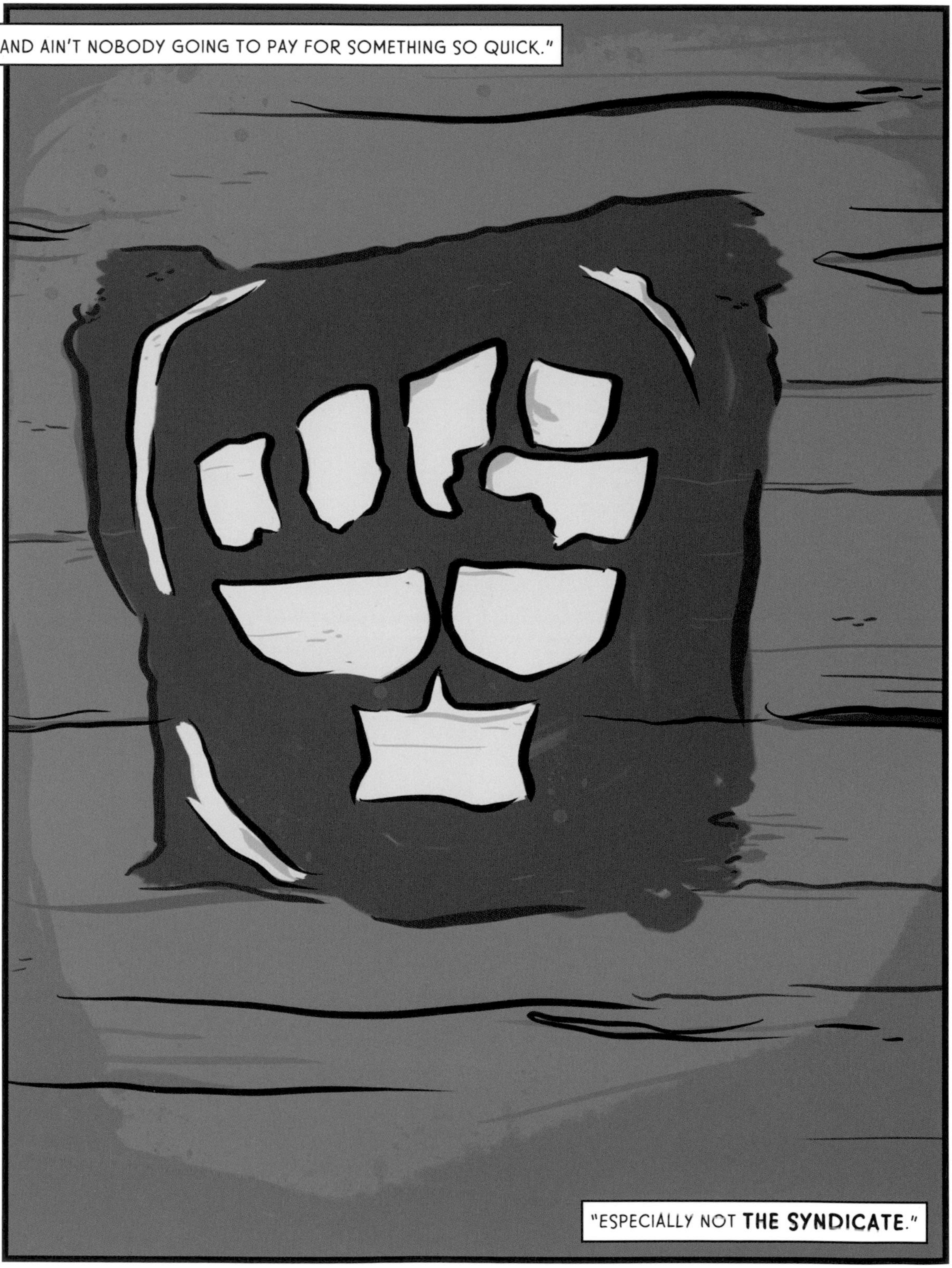
"AND AIN'T NOBODY GOING TO PAY FOR SOMETHING SO QUICK."
"ESPECIALLY NOT **THE SYNDICATE**."

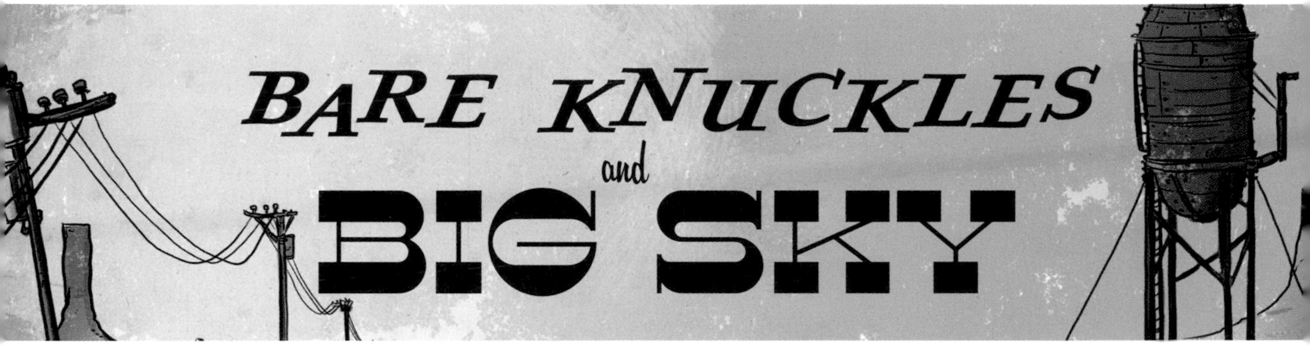
BARE KNUCKLES
and
BIG SKY

CHAPTER TWO

MOTORCYCLE SAMURAI

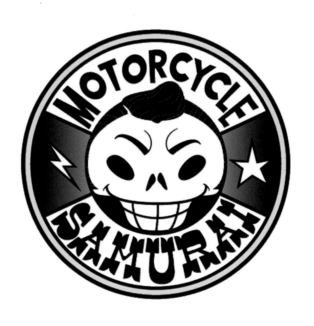

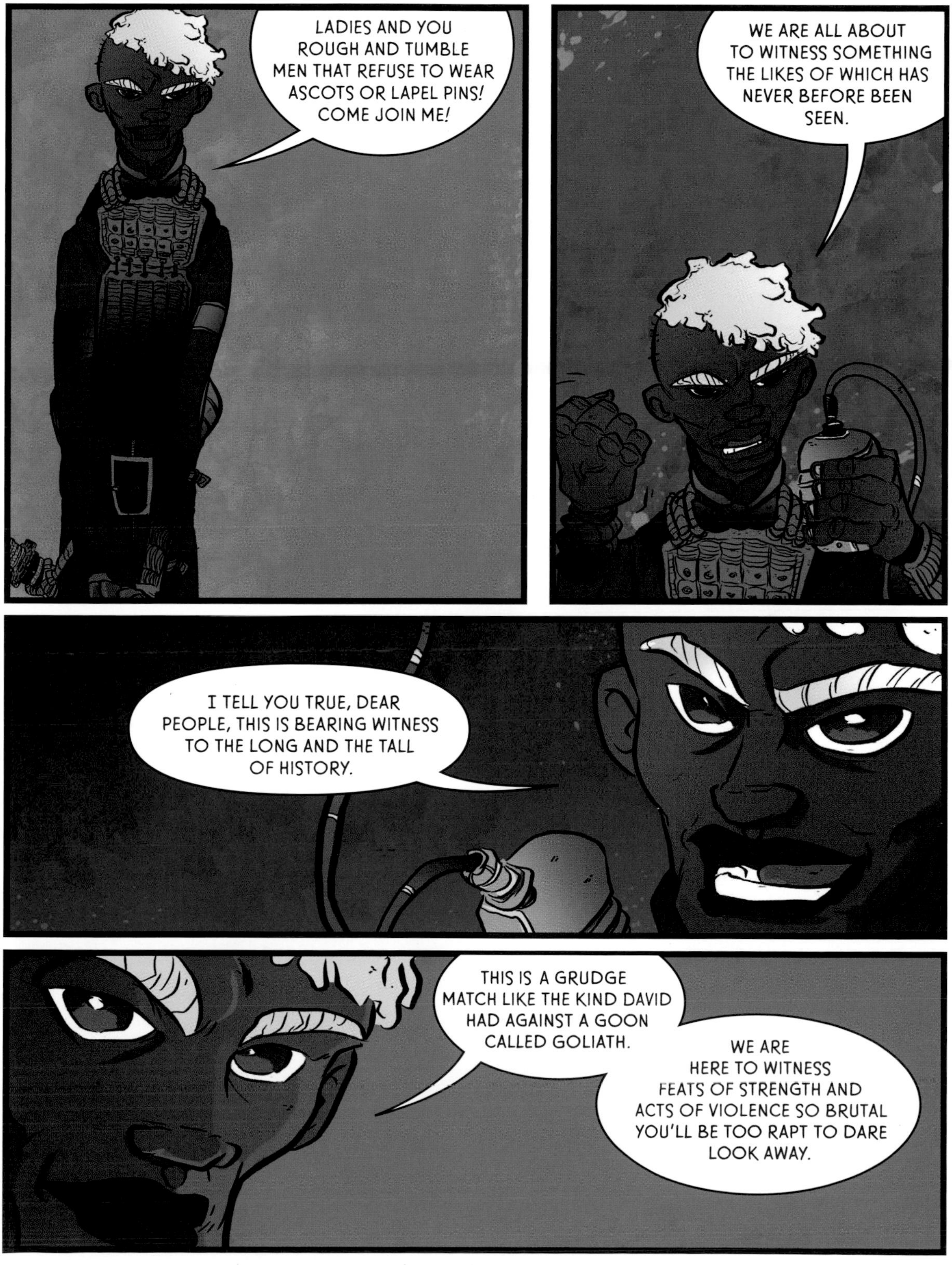
LADIES AND YOU ROUGH AND TUMBLE MEN THAT REFUSE TO WEAR ASCOTS OR LAPEL PINS! COME JOIN ME!
WE ARE ALL ABOUT TO WITNESS SOMETHING THE LIKES OF WHICH HAS NEVER BEFORE BEEN SEEN.
I TELL YOU TRUE, DEAR PEOPLE, THIS IS BEARING WITNESS TO THE LONG AND THE TALL OF HISTORY.
THIS IS A GRUDGE MATCH LIKE THE KIND DAVID HAD AGAINST A GOON CALLED GOLIATH.
WE ARE HERE TO WITNESS FEATS OF STRENGTH AND ACTS OF VIOLENCE SO BRUTAL YOU'LL BE TOO RAPT TO DARE LOOK AWAY.

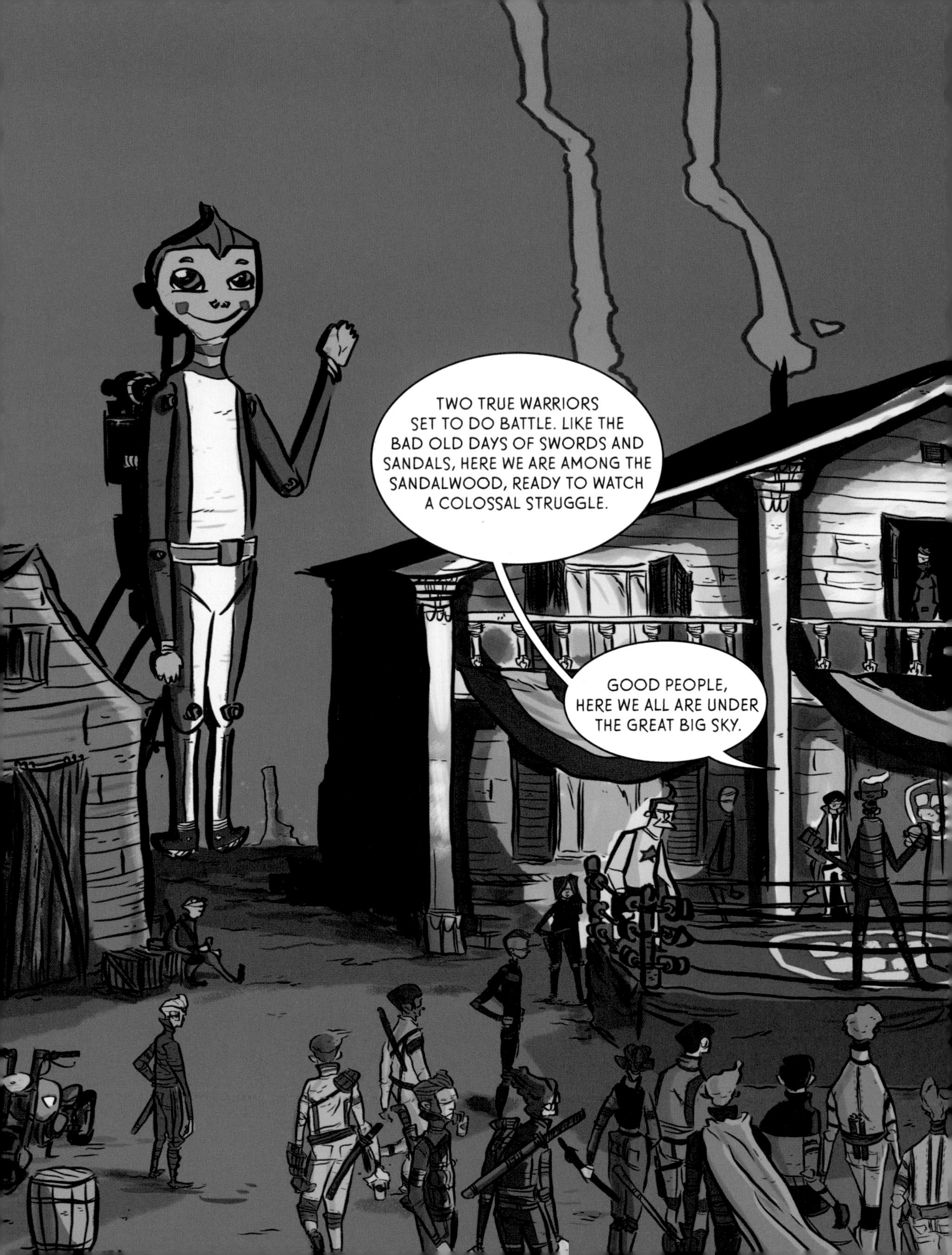
TWO TRUE WARRIORS SET TO DO BATTLE. LIKE THE BAD OLD DAYS OF SWORDS AND SANDALS, HERE WE ARE AMONG THE SANDALWOOD, READY TO WATCH A COLOSSAL STRUGGLE.
GOOD PEOPLE, HERE WE ALL ARE UNDER THE GREAT BIG SKY.

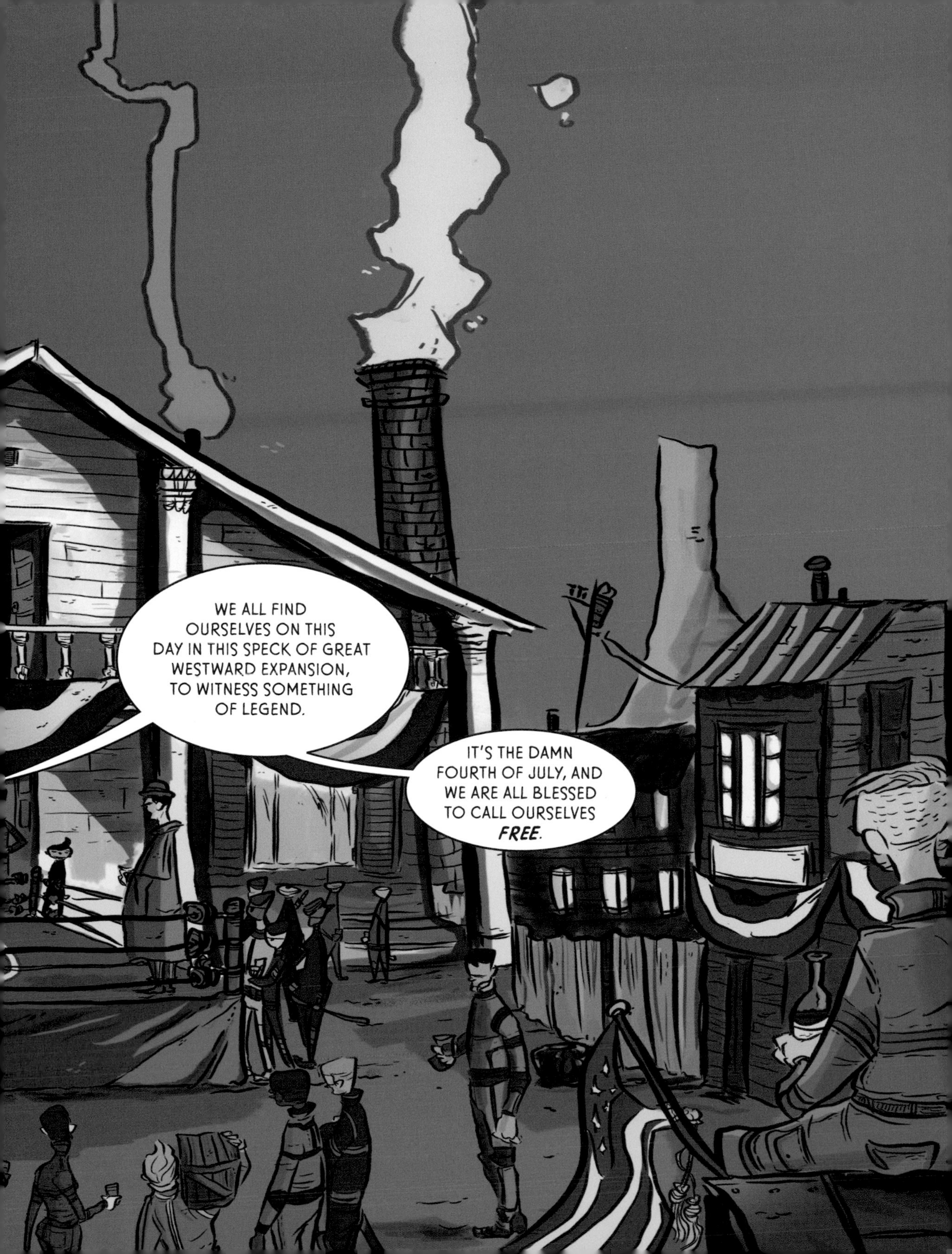
WE ALL FIND OURSELVES ON THIS DAY IN THIS SPECK OF GREAT WESTWARD EXPANSION, TO WITNESS SOMETHING OF LEGEND.
IT'S THE DAMN FOURTH OF JULY, AND WE ARE ALL BLESSED TO CALL OURSELVES *FREE*.

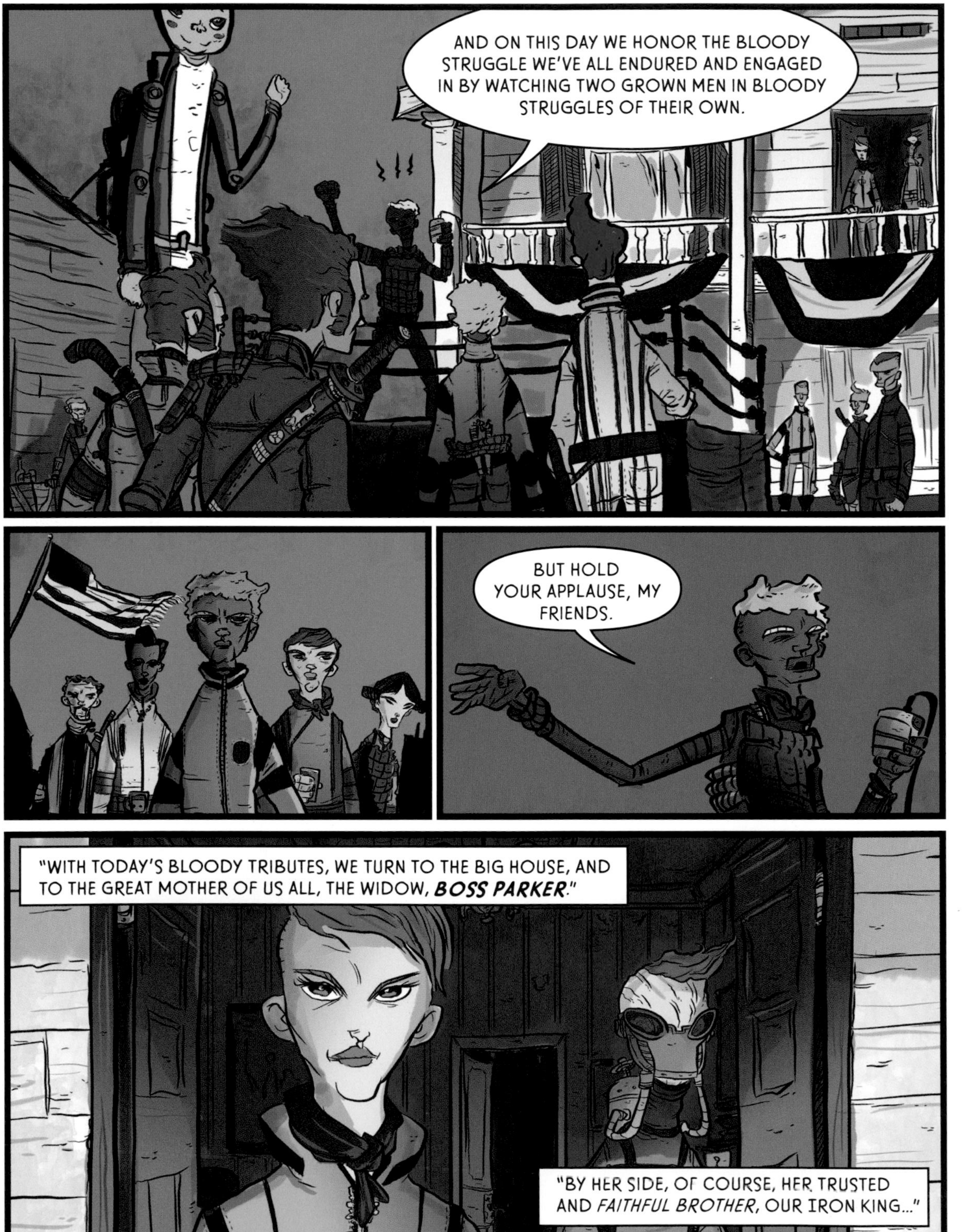
AND ON THIS DAY WE HONOR THE BLOODY STRUGGLE WE'VE ALL ENDURED AND ENGAGED IN BY WATCHING TWO GROWN MEN IN BLOODY STRUGGLES OF THEIR OWN.
BUT HOLD YOUR APPLAUSE, MY FRIENDS.
"WITH TODAY'S BLOODY TRIBUTES, WE TURN TO THE BIG HOUSE, AND TO THE GREAT MOTHER OF US ALL, THE WIDOW, ***BOSS PARKER***."
"BY HER SIDE, OF COURSE, HER TRUSTED AND *FAITHFUL BROTHER*, OUR IRON KING..."

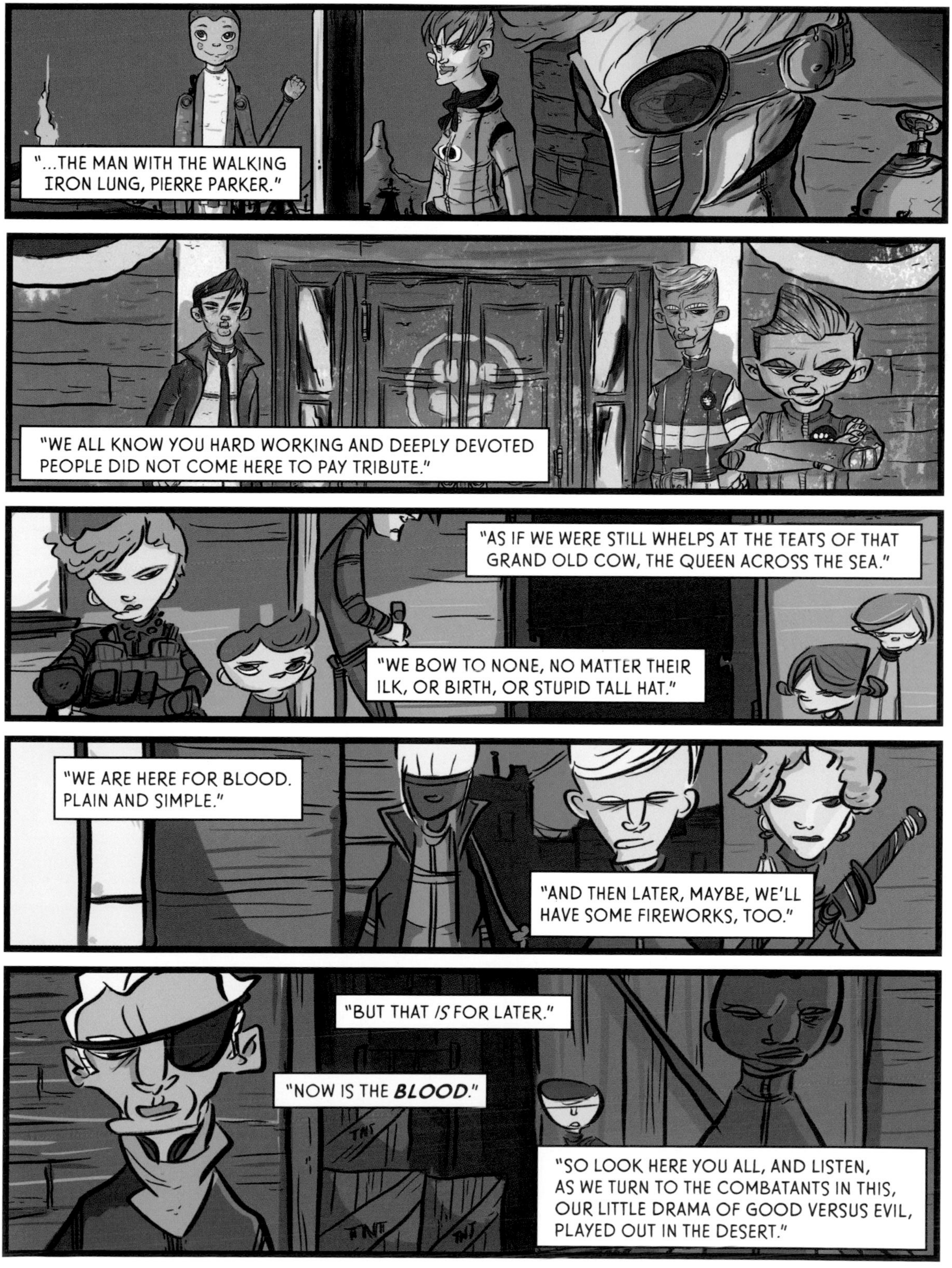
"...THE MAN WITH THE WALKING IRON LUNG, PIERRE PARKER."
"WE ALL KNOW YOU HARD WORKING AND DEEPLY DEVOTED PEOPLE DID NOT COME HERE TO PAY TRIBUTE."
"AS IF WE WERE STILL WHELPS AT THE TEATS OF THAT GRAND OLD COW, THE QUEEN ACROSS THE SEA."
"WE BOW TO NONE, NO MATTER THEIR ILK, OR BIRTH, OR STUPID TALL HAT."
"WE ARE HERE FOR BLOOD. PLAIN AND SIMPLE."
"AND THEN LATER, MAYBE, WE'LL HAVE SOME FIREWORKS, TOO."
"BUT THAT *IS* FOR LATER."
"NOW IS THE ***BLOOD***."
"SO LOOK HERE YOU ALL, AND LISTEN, AS WE TURN TO THE COMBATANTS IN THIS, OUR LITTLE DRAMA OF GOOD VERSUS EVIL, PLAYED OUT IN THE DESERT."
TNT
TNT
TNT

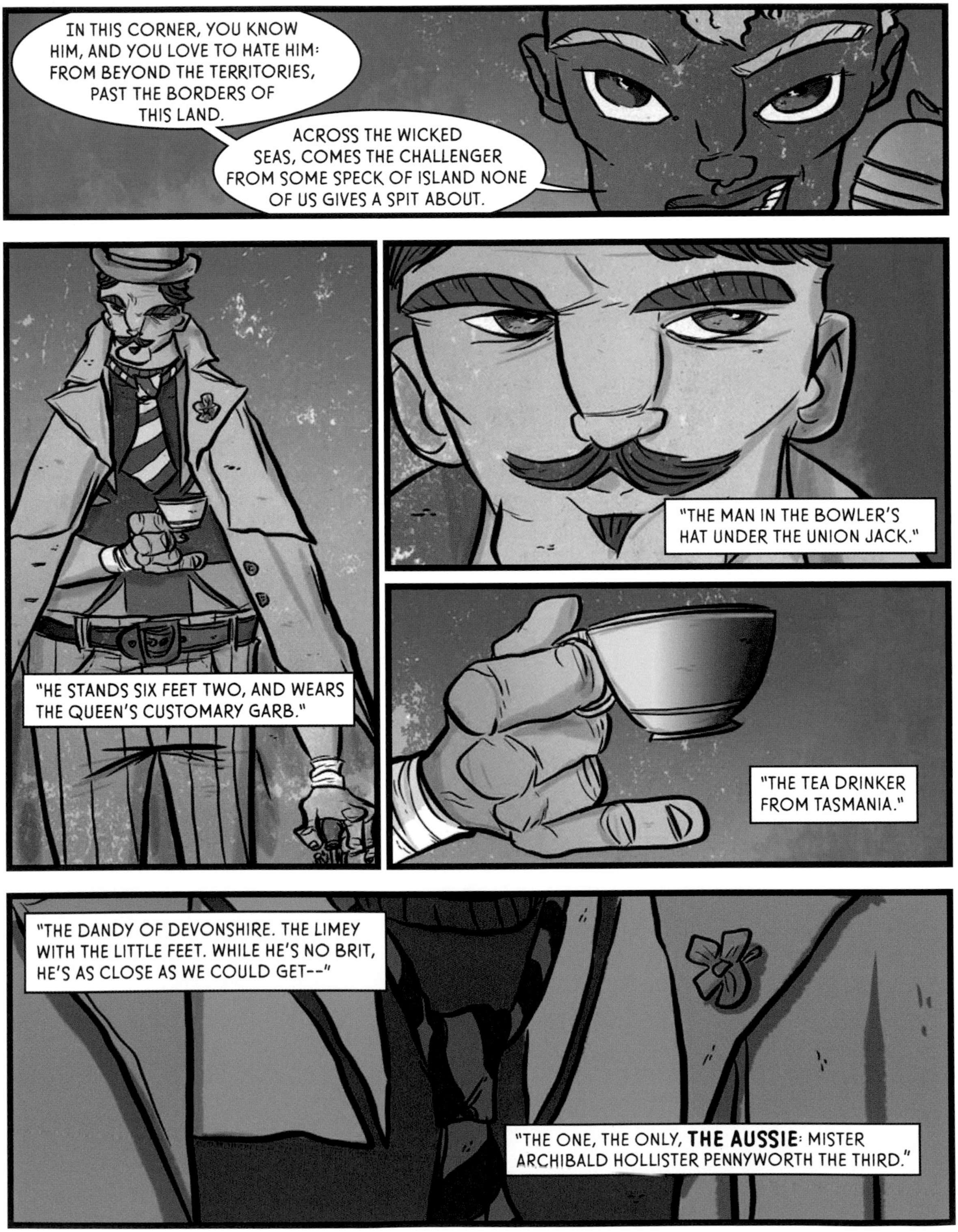
IN THIS CORNER, YOU KNOW HIM, AND YOU LOVE TO HATE HIM: FROM BEYOND THE TERRITORIES, PAST THE BORDERS OF THIS LAND.
ACROSS THE WICKED SEAS, COMES THE CHALLENGER FROM SOME SPECK OF ISLAND NONE OF US GIVES A SPIT ABOUT.
"HE STANDS SIX FEET TWO, AND WEARS THE QUEEN'S CUSTOMARY GARB."
"THE MAN IN THE BOWLER'S HAT UNDER THE UNION JACK."
"THE TEA DRINKER FROM TASMANIA."
"THE DANDY OF DEVONSHIRE. THE LIMEY WITH THE LITTLE FEET. WHILE HE'S NO BRIT, HE'S AS CLOSE AS WE COULD GET--"
"THE ONE, THE ONLY, THE AUSSIE: MISTER ARCHIBALD HOLLISTER PENNYWORTH THE THIRD."

AND OVER HERE IS A MAN THAT CRAWLED OUT OF THE DESERT HALF DEAD AND HOBBLED, BUT WOULDN'T GIVE UP THE WAR.

"A MAN THAT CAME TO TOWN IN A DARK HOUR UNDER A FALLING MOON AND HAS MADE HIMSELF A RIGHT PAIN IN THE ASS."

"HE STANDS FROM TOE TO TIP SIX FOOT THREE."

"BUT WITH HIS HAIR HE'S REALLY SIX FOOT EIGHT."

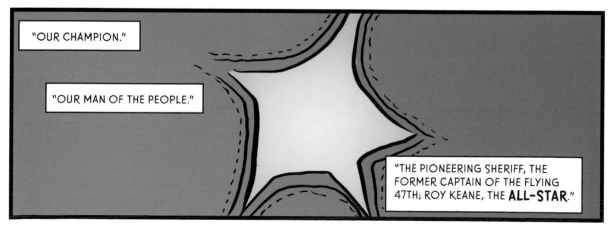

"OUR CHAMPION."

"OUR MAN OF THE PEOPLE."

"THE PIONEERING SHERIFF, THE FORMER CAPTAIN OF THE FLYING 47TH; ROY KEANE, THE **ALL-STAR**."

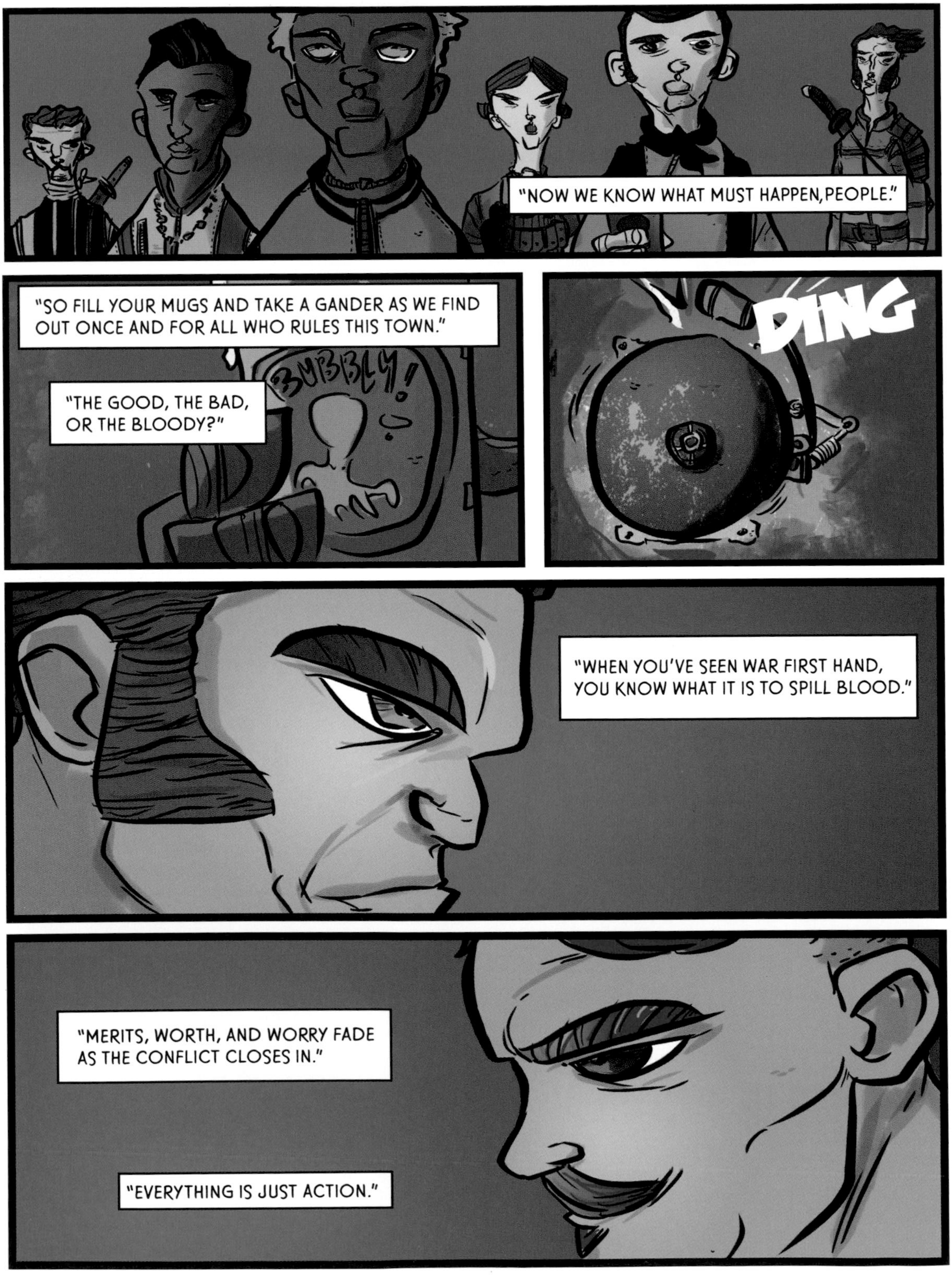
"NOW WE KNOW WHAT MUST HAPPEN, PEOPLE."
"SO FILL YOUR MUGS AND TAKE A GANDER AS WE FIND OUT ONCE AND FOR ALL WHO RULES THIS TOWN."
"THE GOOD, THE BAD, OR THE BLOODY?"
BUBBLY!
DING
"WHEN YOU'VE SEEN WAR FIRST HAND, YOU KNOW WHAT IT IS TO SPILL BLOOD."
"MERITS, WORTH, AND WORRY FADE AS THE CONFLICT CLOSES IN."
"EVERYTHING IS JUST ACTION."

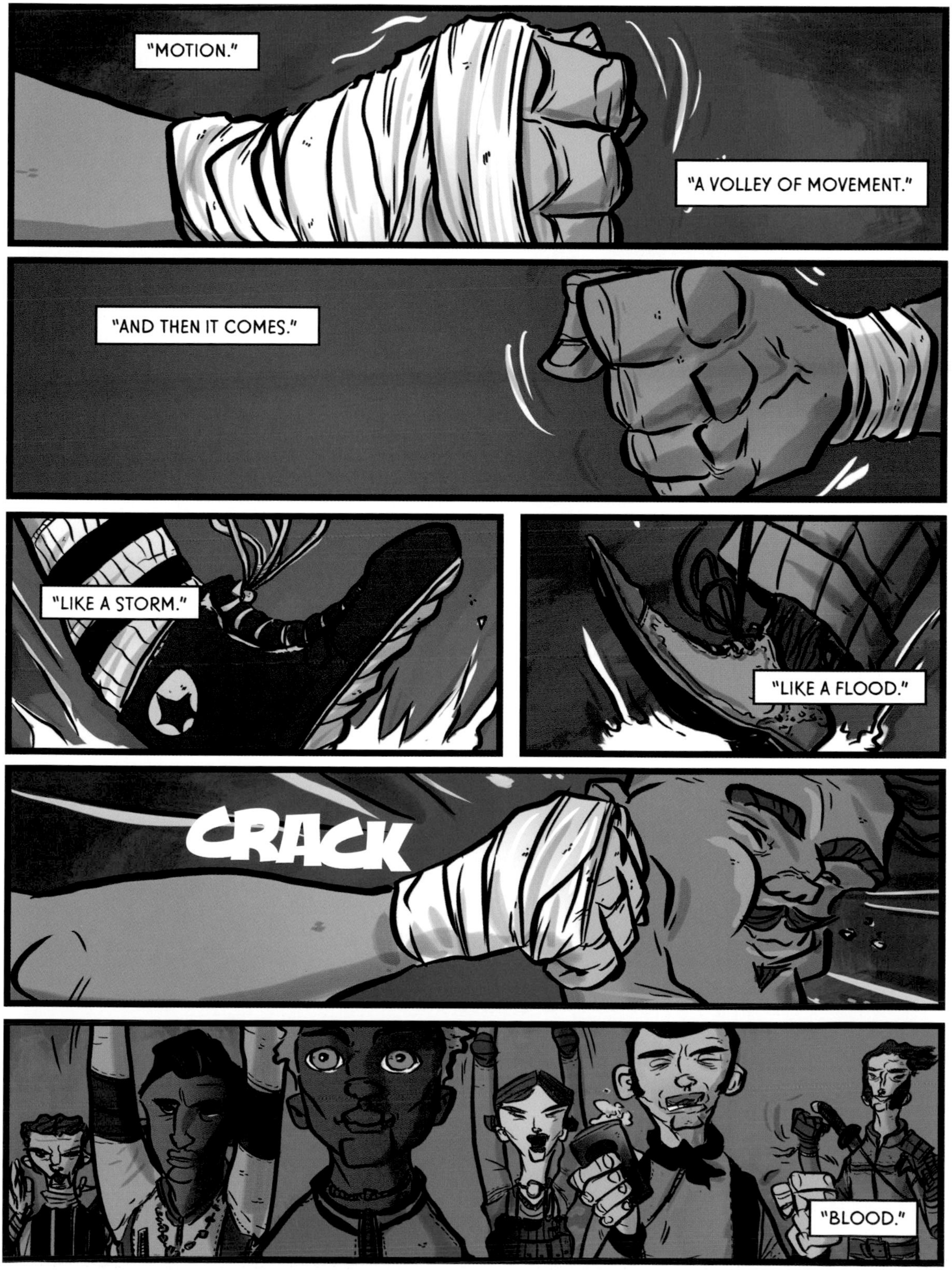
"MOTION."
"A VOLLEY OF MOVEMENT."
"AND THEN IT COMES."
"LIKE A STORM."
"LIKE A FLOOD."
CRACK
"BLOOD."

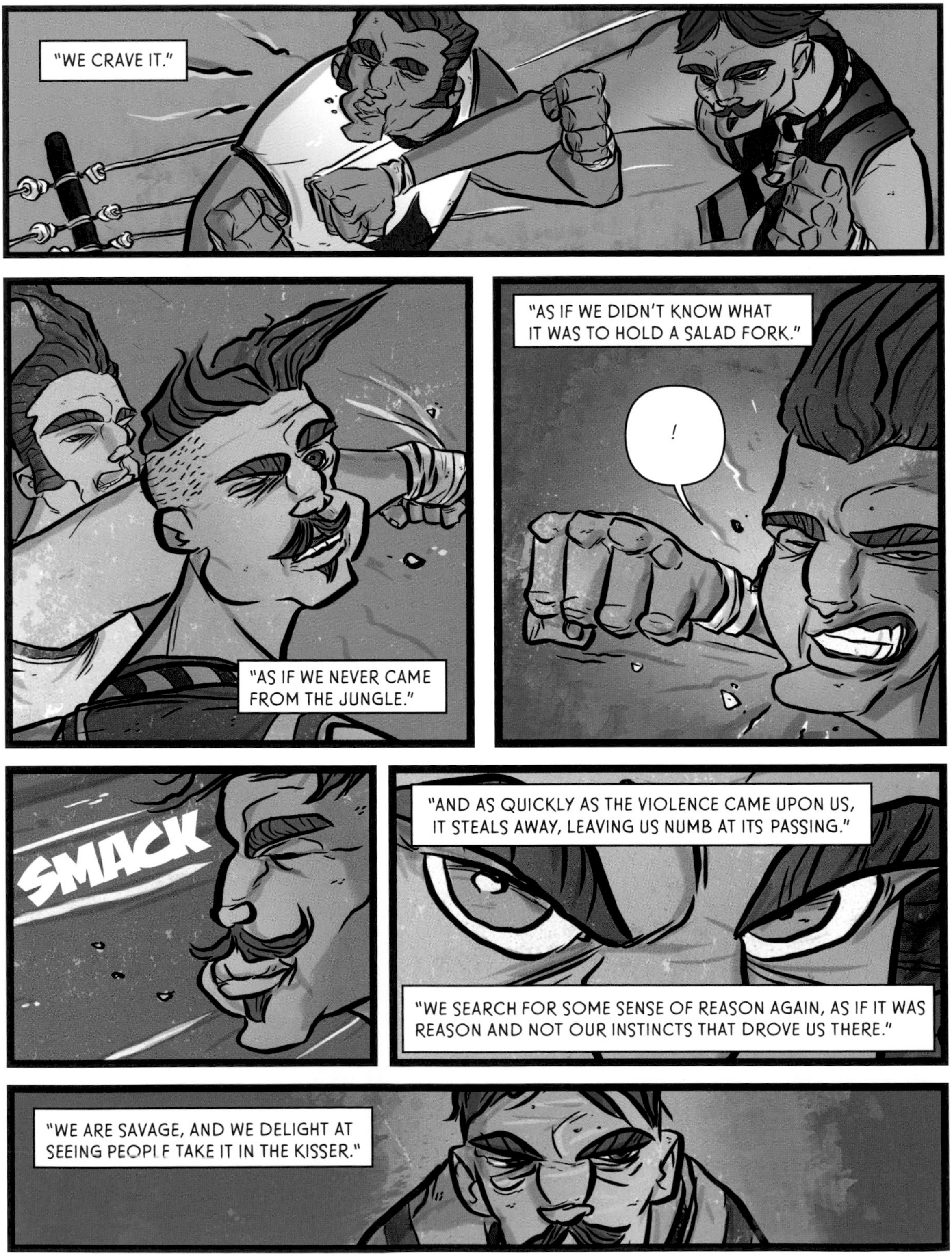
"WE CRAVE IT."
"AS IF WE NEVER CAME FROM THE JUNGLE."
"AS IF WE DIDN'T KNOW WHAT IT WAS TO HOLD A SALAD FORK."
!
SMACK
"AND AS QUICKLY AS THE VIOLENCE CAME UPON US, IT STEALS AWAY, LEAVING US NUMB AT ITS PASSING."
"WE SEARCH FOR SOME SENSE OF REASON AGAIN, AS IF IT WAS REASON AND NOT OUR INSTINCTS THAT DROVE US THERE."
"WE ARE SAVAGE, AND WE DELIGHT AT SEEING PEOPLE TAKE IT IN THE KISSER."

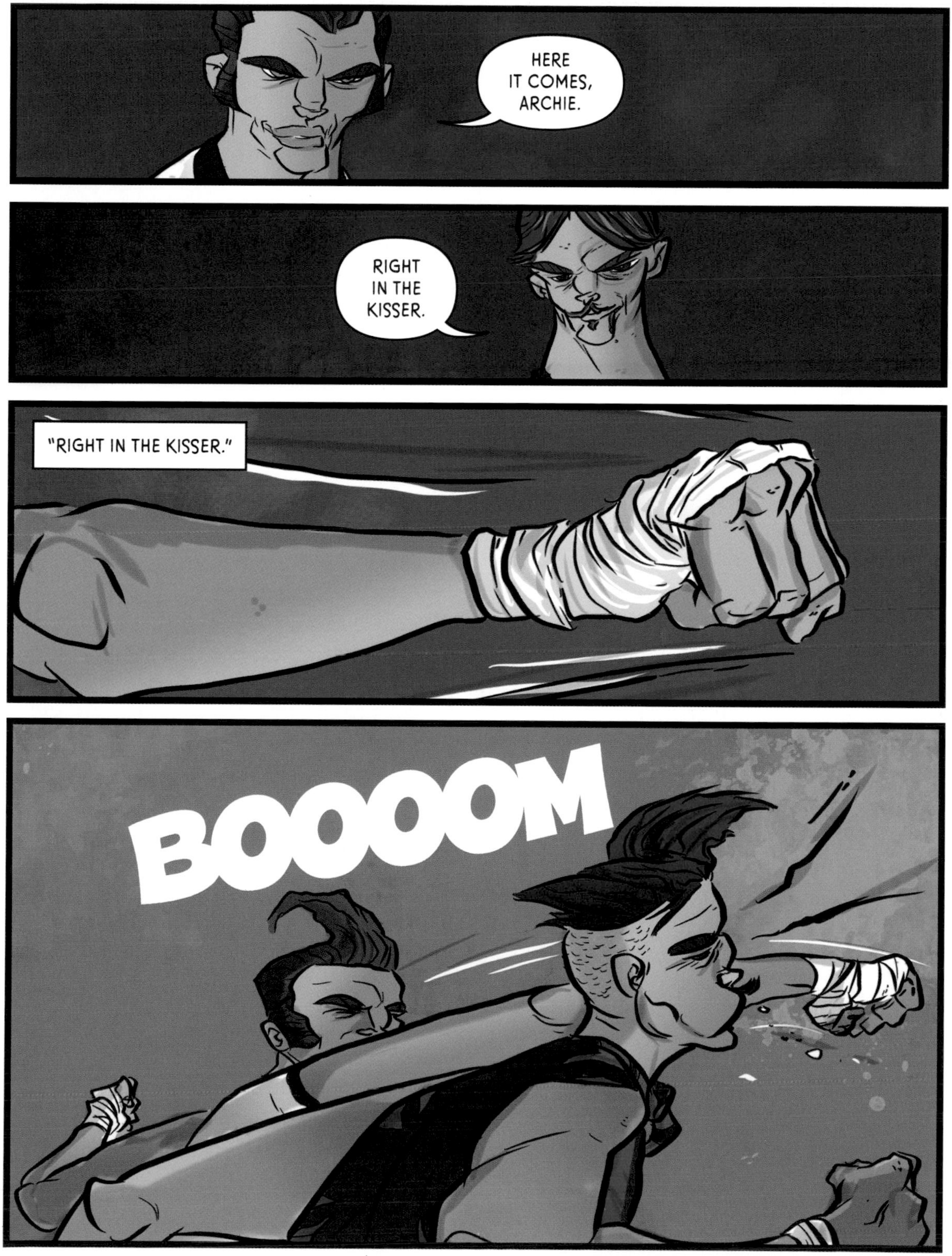
HERE IT COMES, ARCHIE.
RIGHT IN THE KISSER.
"RIGHT IN THE KISSER."
BOOOOM

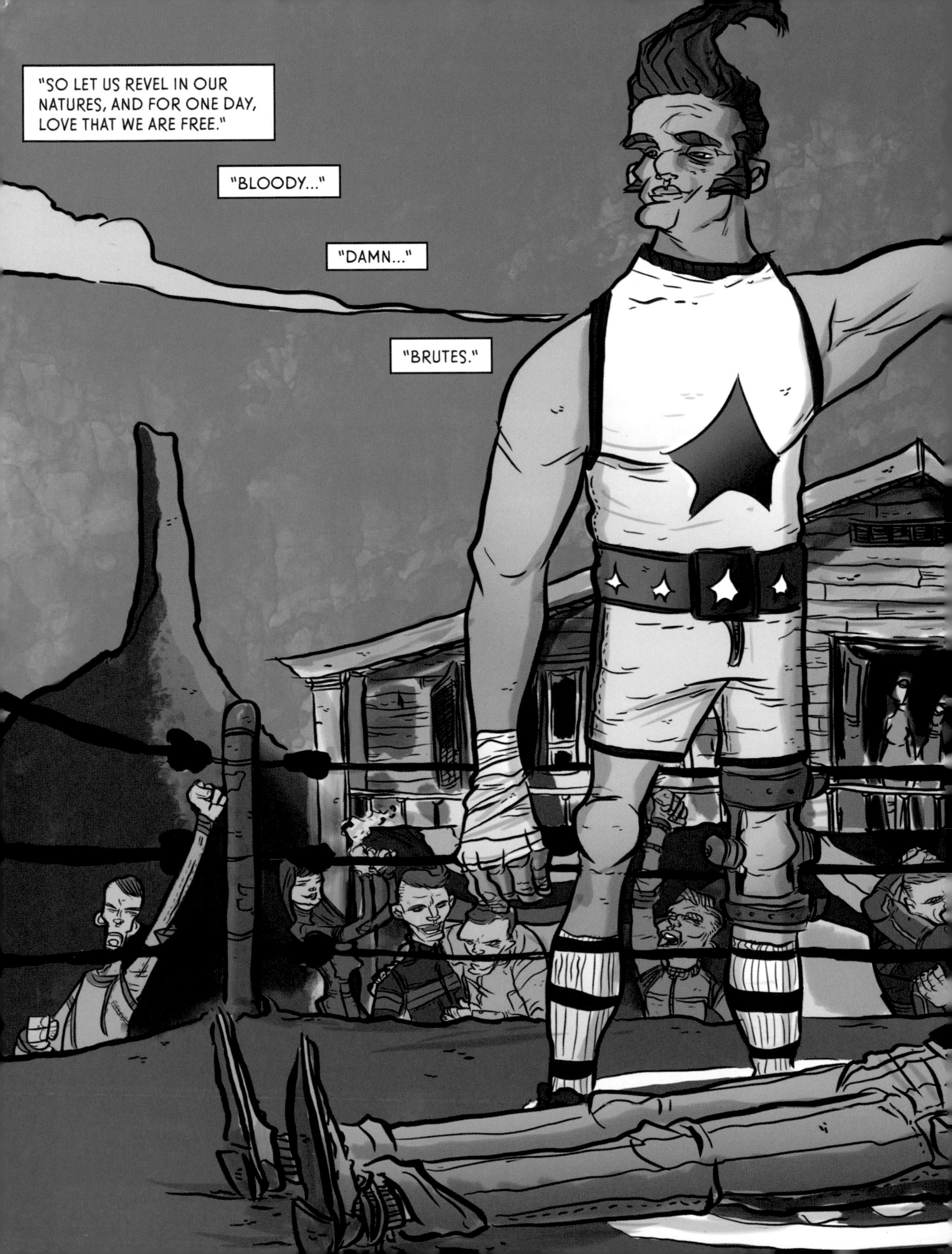
"SO LET US REVEL IN OUR NATURES, AND FOR ONE DAY, LOVE THAT WE ARE FREE."
"BLOODY..."
"DAMN..."
"BRUTES."

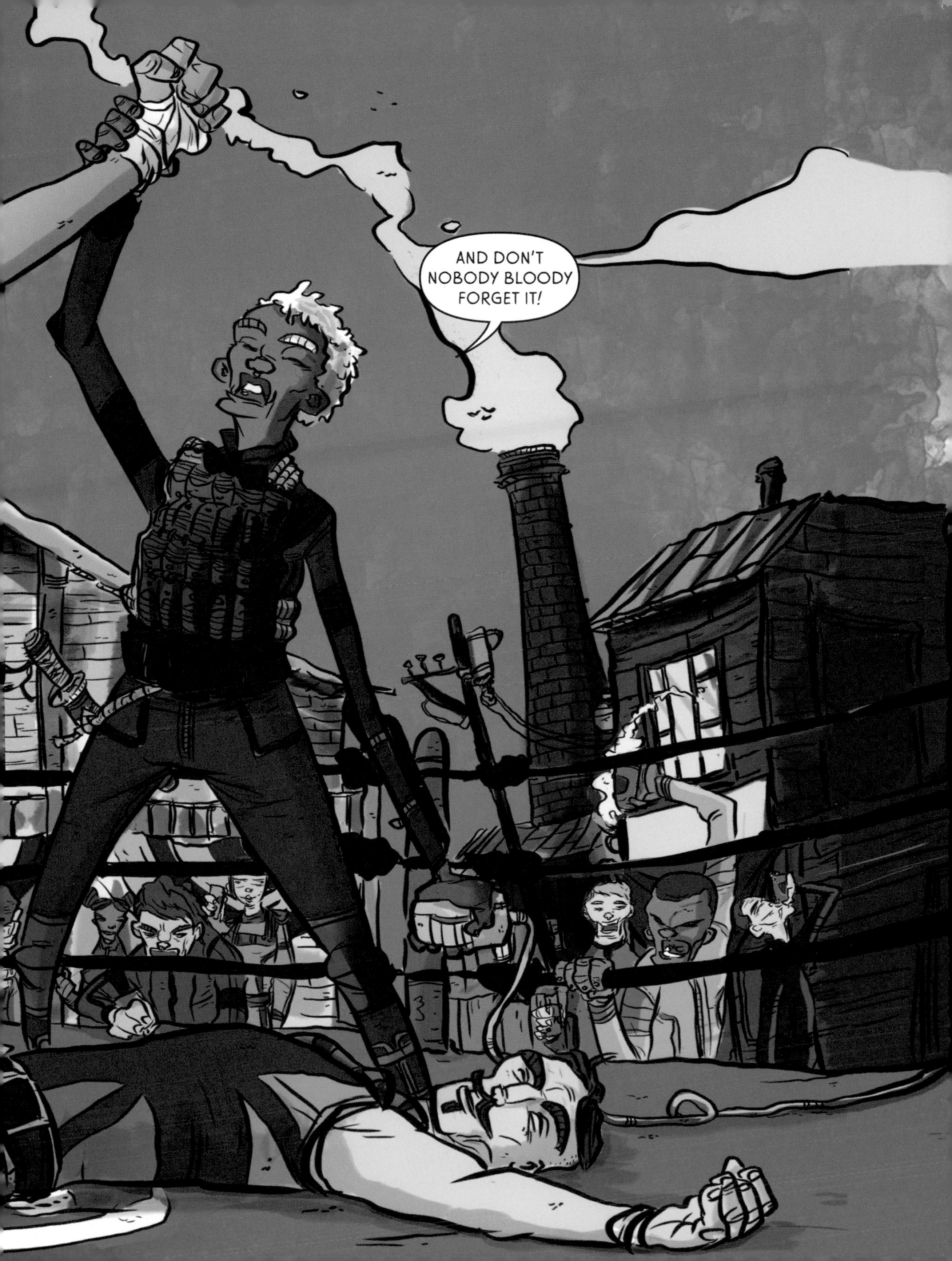
AND DON'T NOBODY BLOODY FORGET IT!

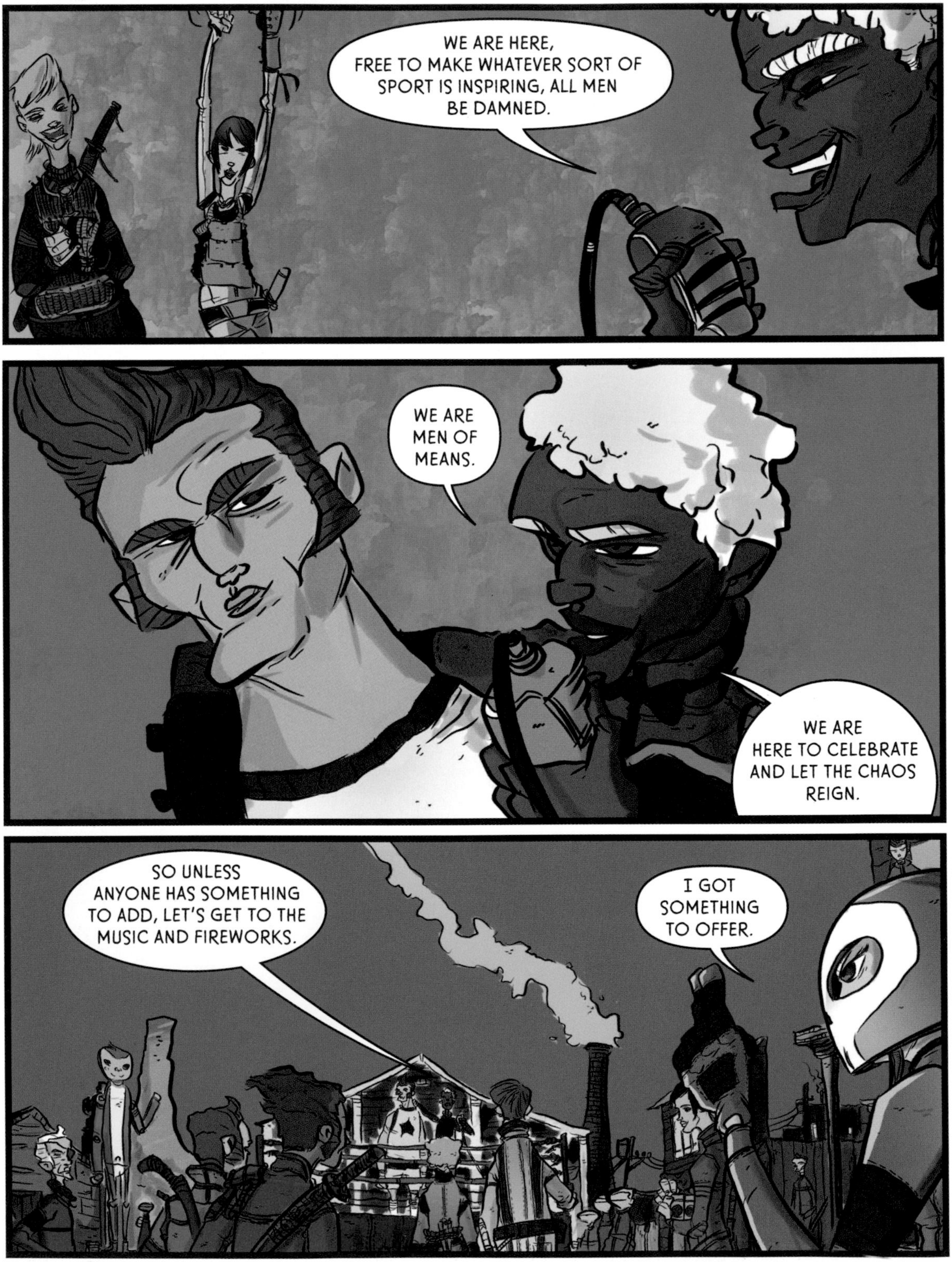
WE ARE HERE, FREE TO MAKE WHATEVER SORT OF SPORT IS INSPIRING, ALL MEN BE DAMNED.
WE ARE MEN OF MEANS.
WE ARE HERE TO CELEBRATE AND LET THE CHAOS REIGN.
SO UNLESS ANYONE HAS SOMETHING TO ADD, LET'S GET TO THE MUSIC AND FIREWORKS.
I GOT SOMETHING TO OFFER.

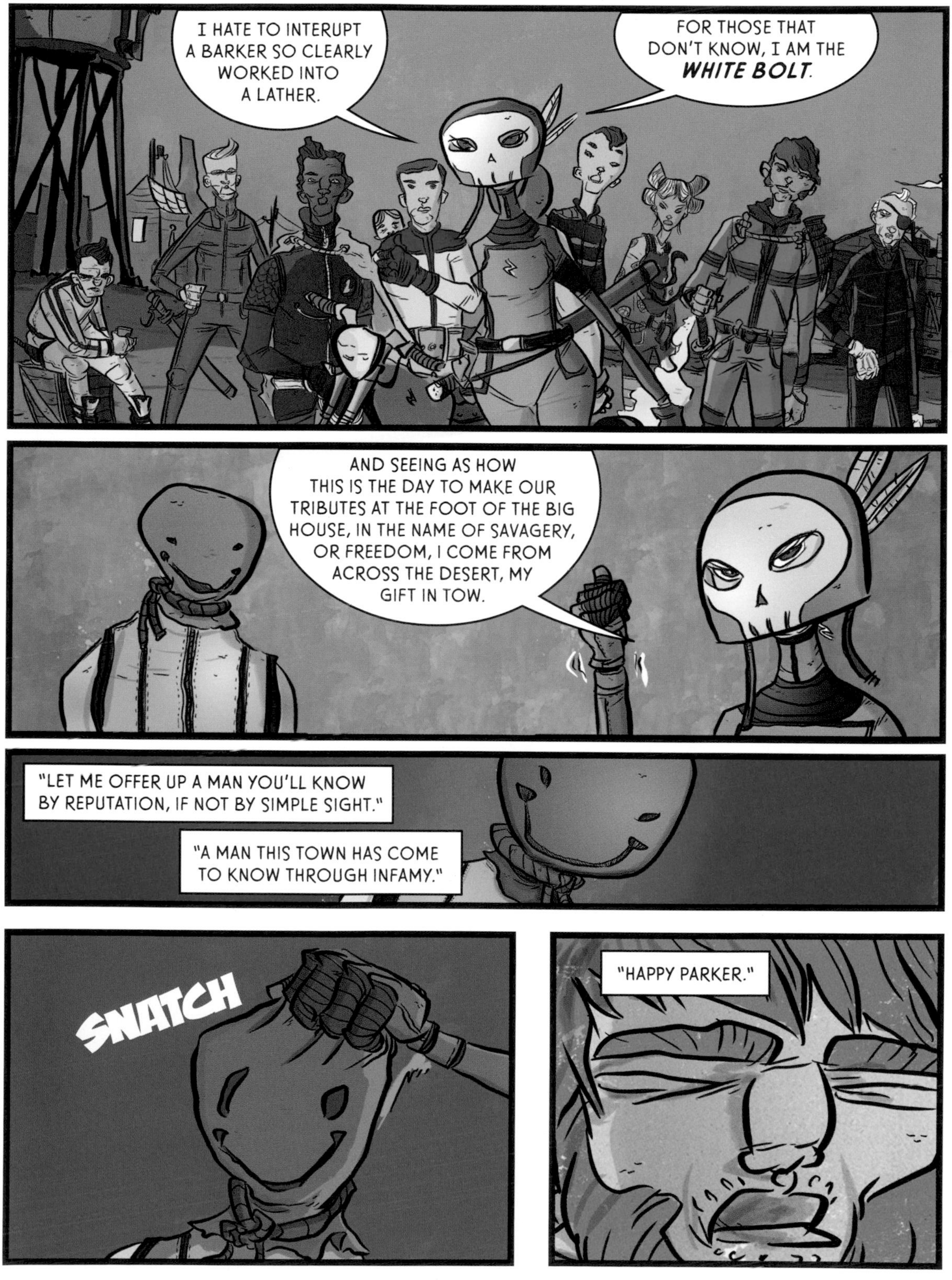
I HATE TO INTERUPT A BARKER SO CLEARLY WORKED INTO A LATHER.
FOR THOSE THAT DON'T KNOW, I AM THE ***WHITE BOLT***.
AND SEEING AS HOW THIS IS THE DAY TO MAKE OUR TRIBUTES AT THE FOOT OF THE BIG HOUSE, IN THE NAME OF SAVAGERY, OR FREEDOM, I COME FROM ACROSS THE DESERT, MY GIFT IN TOW.
"LET ME OFFER UP A MAN YOU'LL KNOW BY REPUTATION, IF NOT BY SIMPLE SIGHT."
"A MAN THIS TOWN HAS COME TO KNOW THROUGH INFAMY."
SNATCH
"HAPPY PARKER."

"THE FUGITIVE SOUGHT FOR KILLING THE LAST SHERIFF OF YOUR TOWN."

"HE'S BROTHER OF THE MATRIARCH OF THIS HAMLET, THE OWNER OF THE BIG HOUSE AND BOSS OF THIS LITTLE TOWN, BOSS FRANCES PARKER."

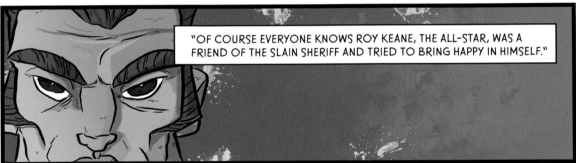

"OF COURSE EVERYONE KNOWS ROY KEANE, THE ALL-STAR, WAS A FRIEND OF THE SLAIN SHERIFF AND TRIED TO BRING HAPPY IN HIMSELF."

SO HERE I STAND, HAVING HAULED THE FUGITIVE *HAPPY* BEFORE YOU THROUGH STRIFE AND STRUGGLE, JUST SO HE COULD STAND FOR WHAT HE'S DONE.

THAT AND I WANT THE BOUNTY DUE ON HIS LITTLE GINGER HEAD.

"MAYBE I'M JUST CRAZY THINKING *EVERYONE* HERE WOULD BE GLAD TO SEE ME HAUL OL' HAPPY BACK TO TOWN."

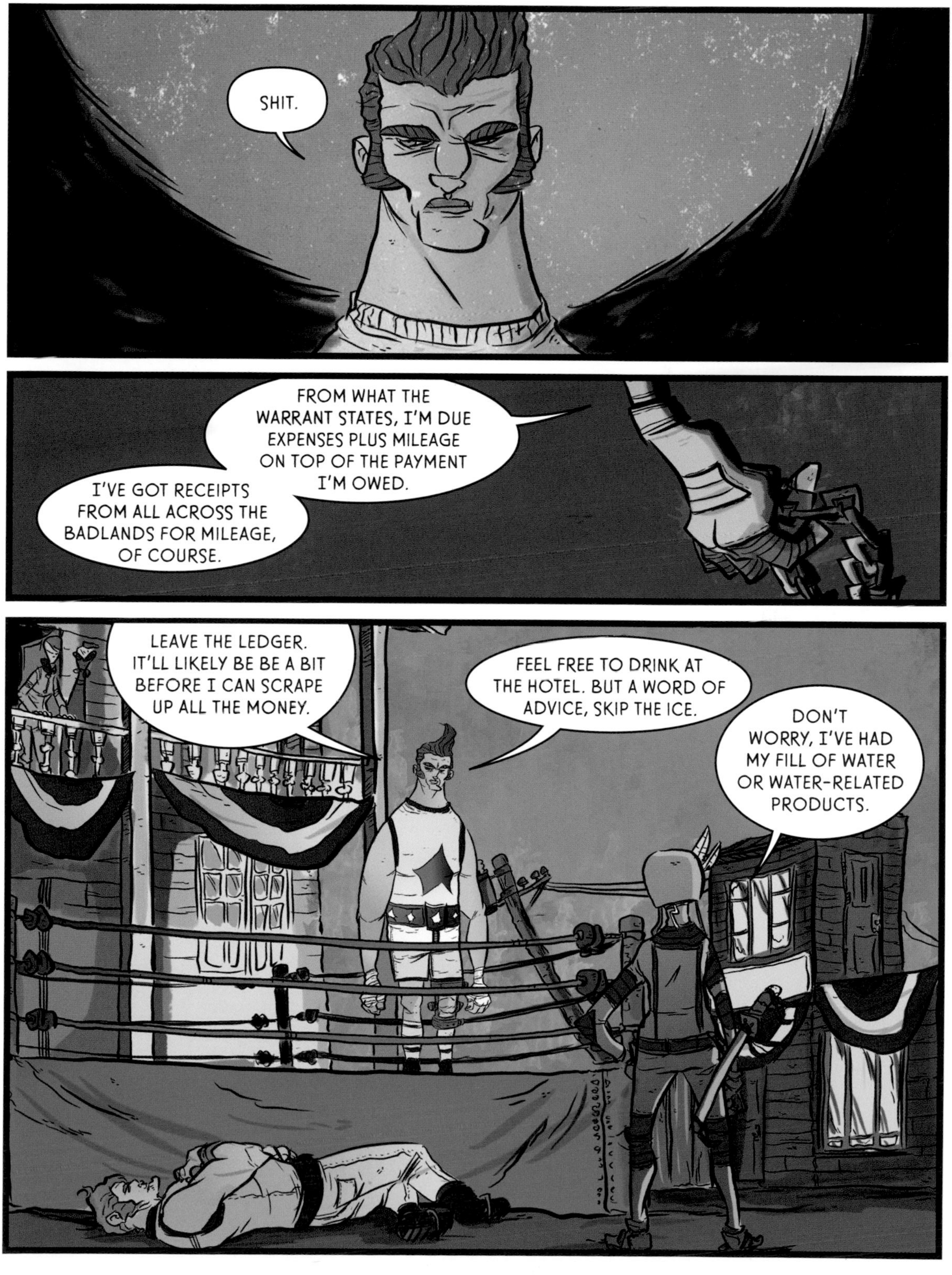
SHIT.
FROM WHAT THE WARRANT STATES, I'M DUE EXPENSES PLUS MILEAGE ON TOP OF THE PAYMENT I'M OWED.
I'VE GOT RECEIPTS FROM ALL ACROSS THE BADLANDS FOR MILEAGE, OF COURSE.
LEAVE THE LEDGER. IT'LL LIKELY BE BE A BIT BEFORE I CAN SCRAPE UP ALL THE MONEY.
FEEL FREE TO DRINK AT THE HOTEL. BUT A WORD OF ADVICE, SKIP THE ICE.
DON'T WORRY, I'VE HAD MY FILL OF WATER OR WATER-RELATED PRODUCTS.

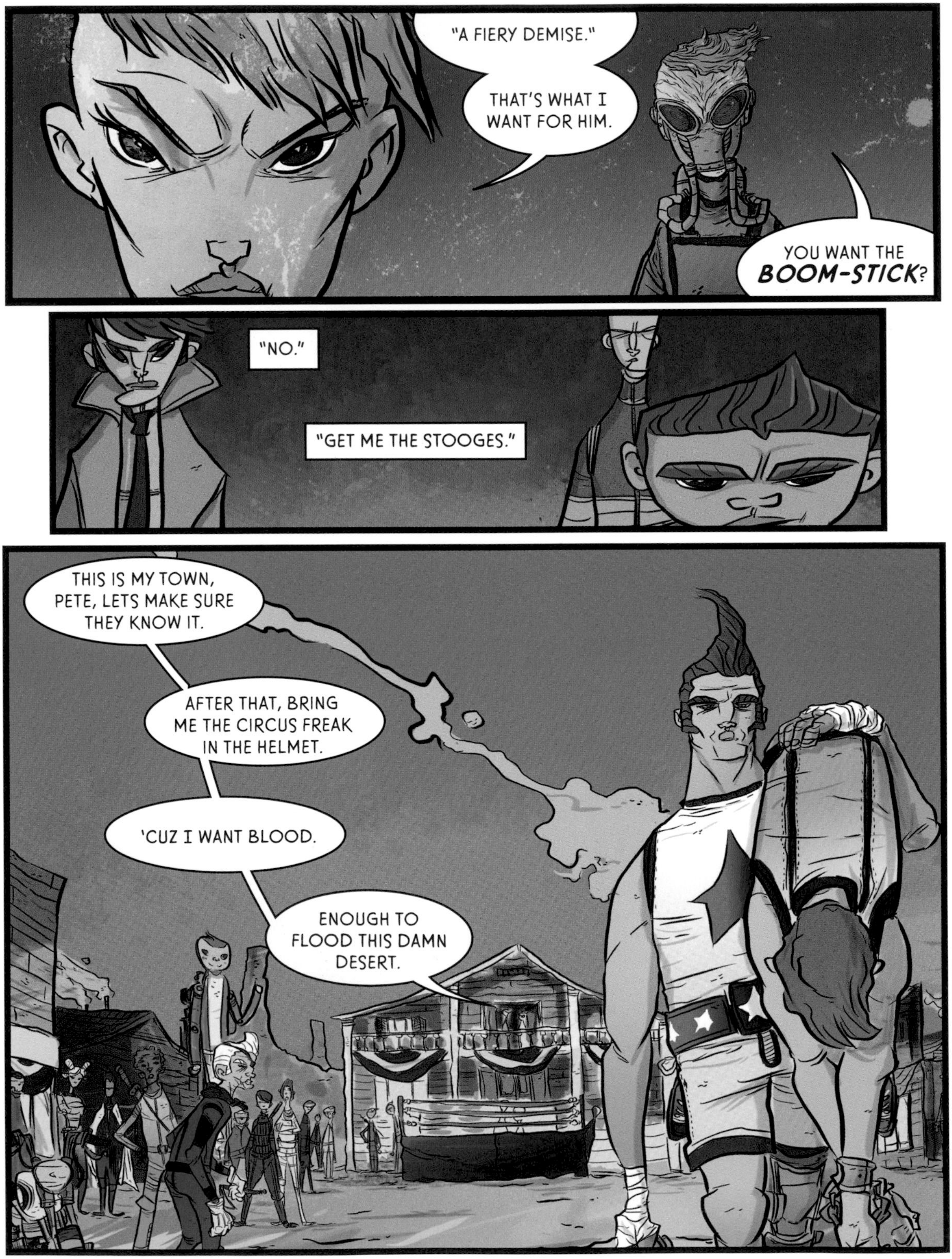
"A FIERY DEMISE."
THAT'S WHAT I WANT FOR HIM.
YOU WANT THE **BOOM-STICK**?
"NO."
"GET ME THE STOOGES."
THIS IS MY TOWN, PETE, LETS MAKE SURE THEY KNOW IT.
AFTER THAT, BRING ME THE CIRCUS FREAK IN THE HELMET.
'CUZ I WANT BLOOD.
ENOUGH TO FLOOD THIS DAMN DESERT.

SHOWDOWN
at
SUNDOWN

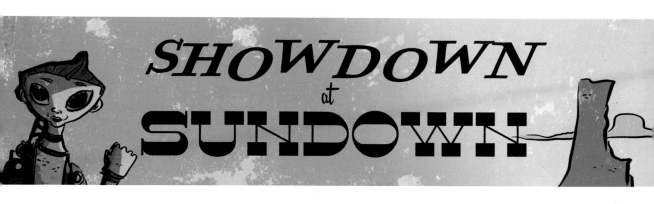

CHAPTER THREE

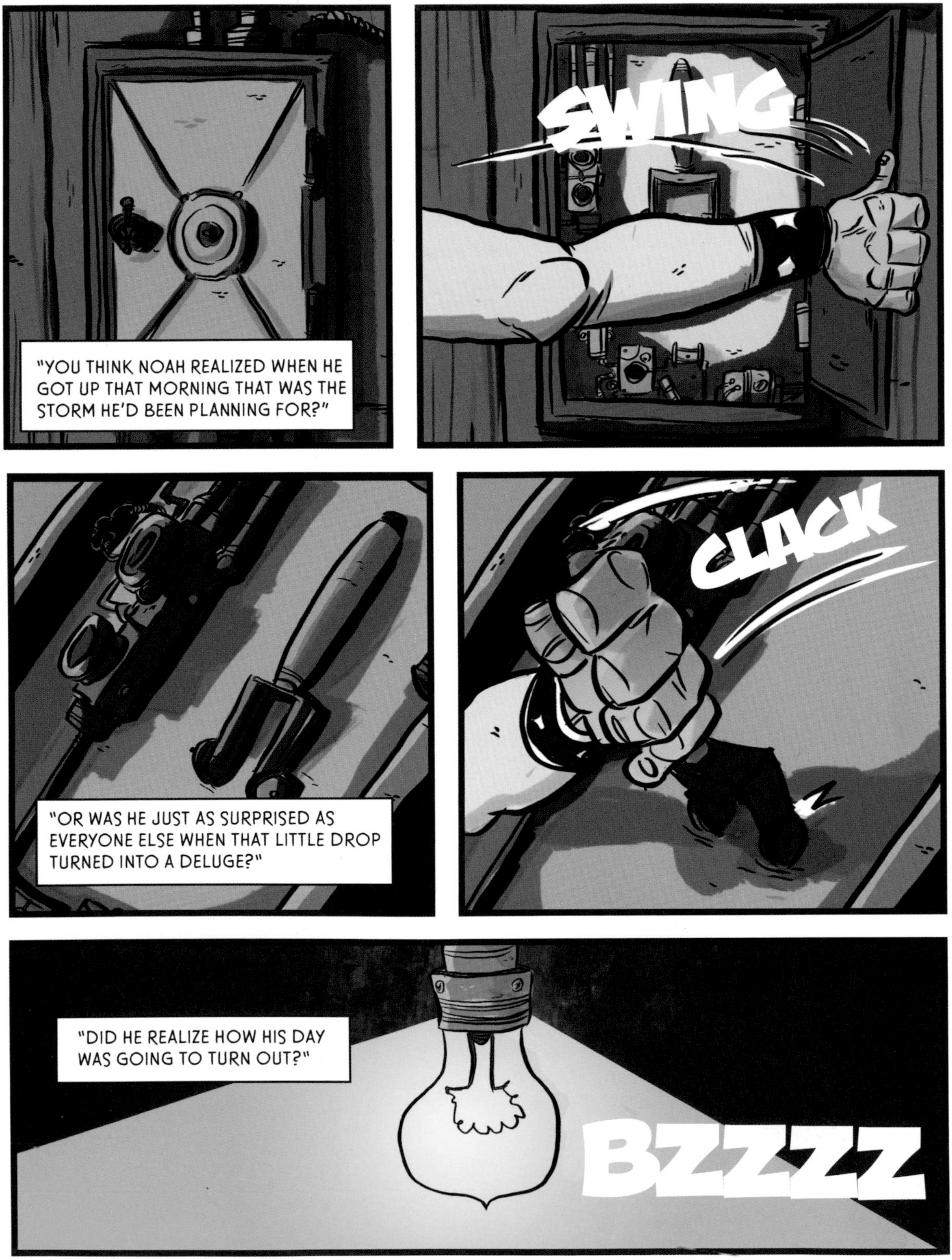
"YOU THINK NOAH REALIZED WHEN HE GOT UP THAT MORNING THAT WAS THE STORM HE'D BEEN PLANNING FOR?"
SWING
"OR WAS HE JUST AS SURPRISED AS EVERYONE ELSE WHEN THAT LITTLE DROP TURNED INTO A DELUGE?"
CLACK
"DID HE REALIZE HOW HIS DAY WAS GOING TO TURN OUT?"
BZZZZ

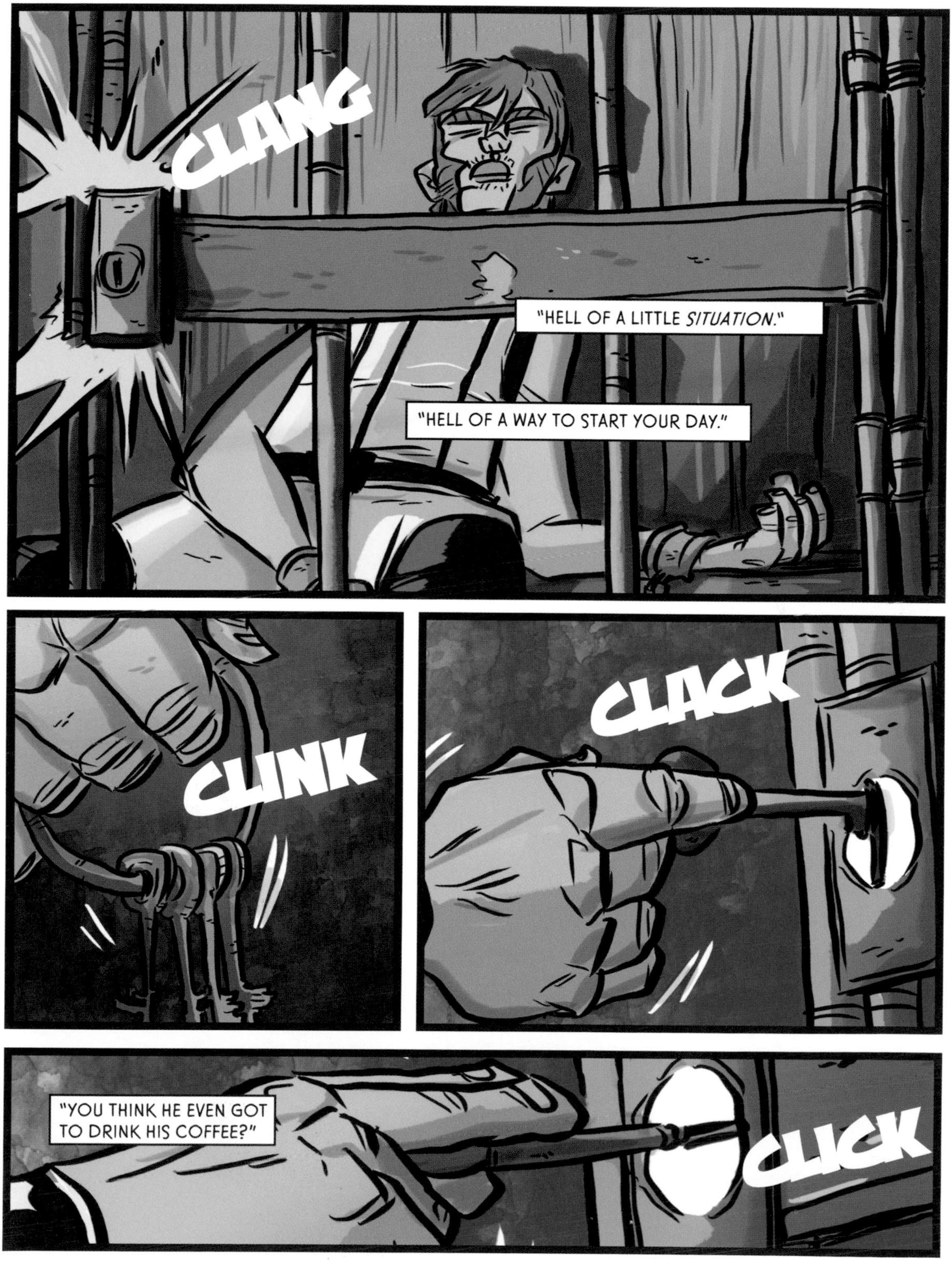
CLANG
"HELL OF A LITTLE *SITUATION*."
"HELL OF A WAY TO START YOUR DAY."
CLINK
CLACK
"YOU THINK HE EVEN GOT TO DRINK HIS COFFEE?"
CLICK

CINCH

ZIP

SNAP

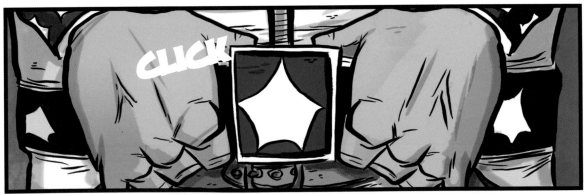

CLICK

WELL, I'M BLOODY TELLING YOU, THIS IS ONE OF THOSE TYPE OF MOMENTS.

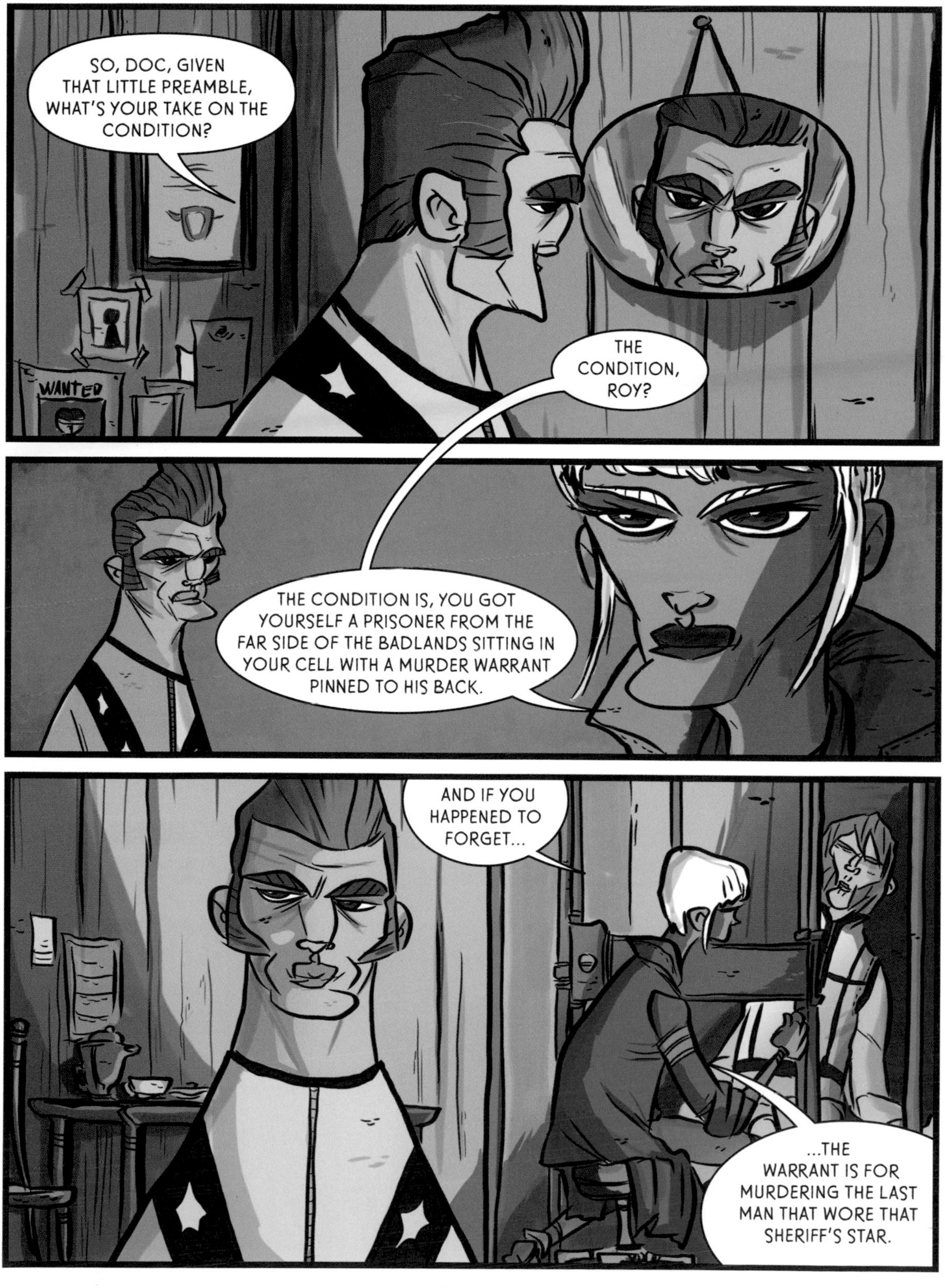

SO, DOC, GIVEN THAT LITTLE PREAMBLE, WHAT'S YOUR TAKE ON THE CONDITION?
WANTED
THE CONDITION, ROY?
THE CONDITION IS, YOU GOT YOURSELF A PRISONER FROM THE FAR SIDE OF THE BADLANDS SITTING IN YOUR CELL WITH A MURDER WARRANT PINNED TO HIS BACK.
AND IF YOU HAPPENED TO FORGET...
...THE WARRANT IS FOR MURDERING THE LAST MAN THAT WORE THAT SHERIFF'S STAR.

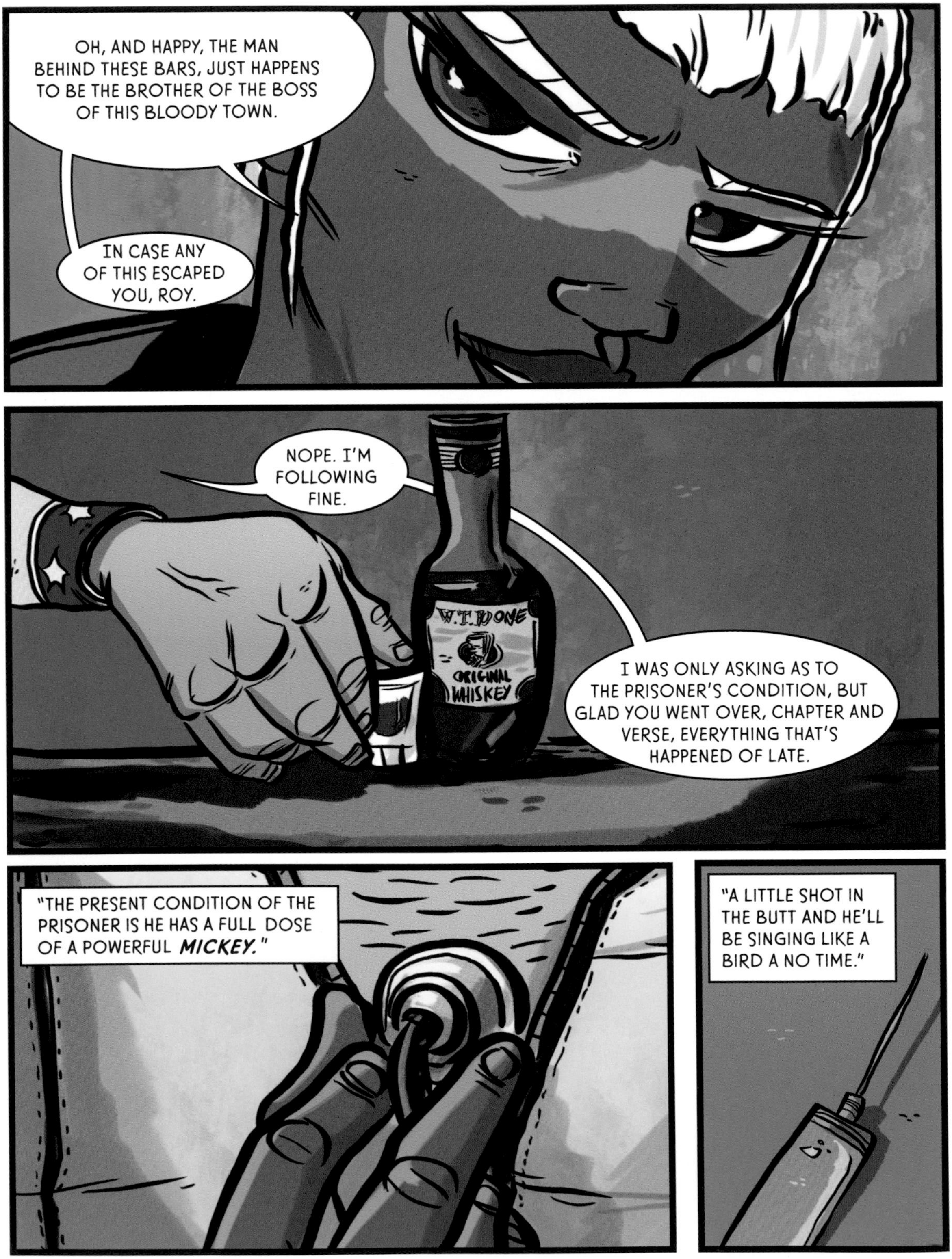
OH, AND HAPPY, THE MAN BEHIND THESE BARS, JUST HAPPENS TO BE THE BROTHER OF THE BOSS OF THIS BLOODY TOWN.
IN CASE ANY OF THIS ESCAPED YOU, ROY.
NOPE. I'M FOLLOWING FINE.
W.T. DONE ORIGINAL WHISKEY
I WAS ONLY ASKING AS TO THE PRISONER'S CONDITION, BUT GLAD YOU WENT OVER, CHAPTER AND VERSE, EVERYTHING THAT'S HAPPENED OF LATE.
"THE PRESENT CONDITION OF THE PRISONER IS HE HAS A FULL DOSE OF A POWERFUL *MICKEY.*"
"A LITTLE SHOT IN THE BUTT AND HE'LL BE SINGING LIKE A BIRD A NO TIME."

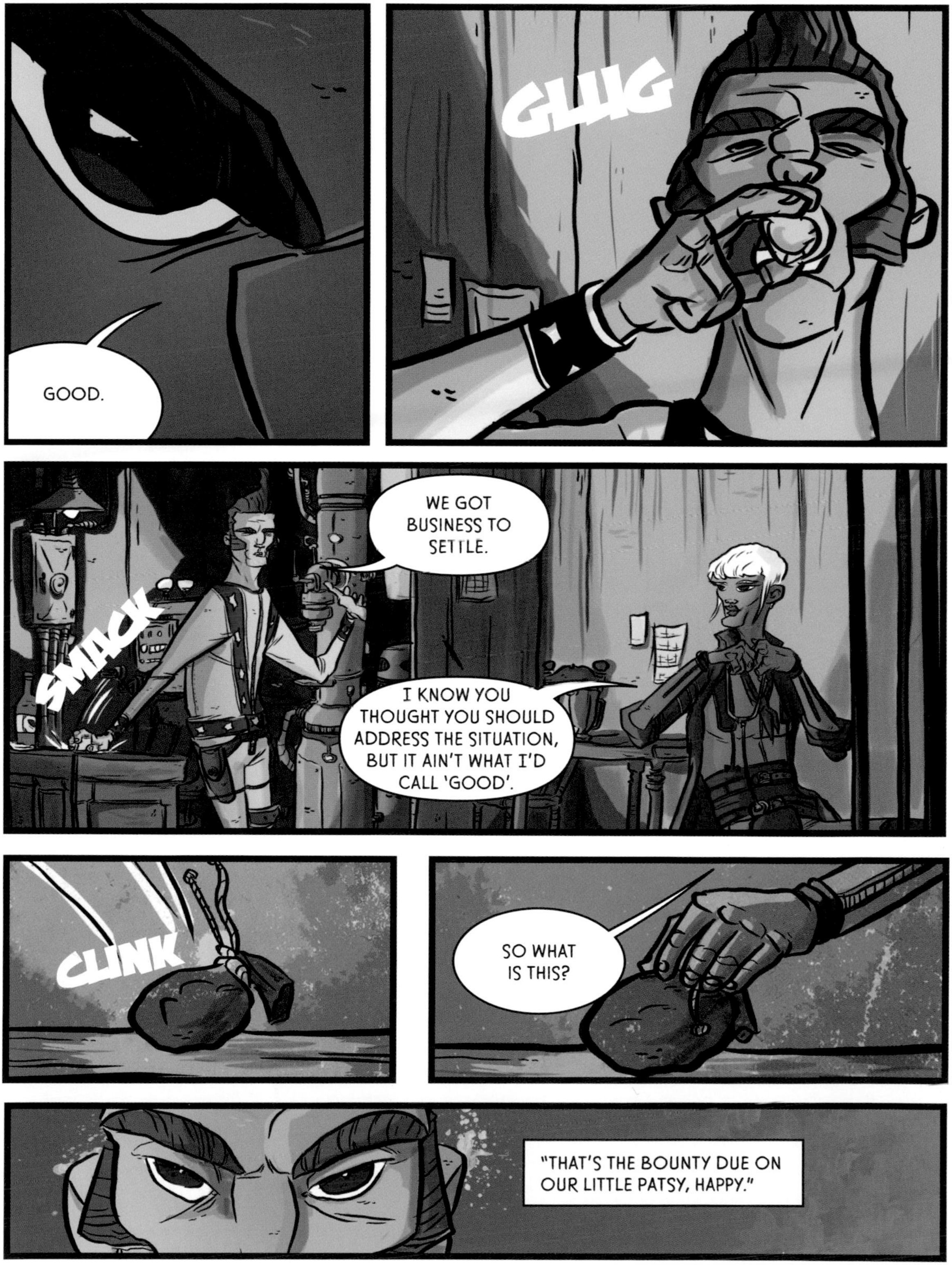
GOOD.
GLUG
WE GOT BUSINESS TO SETTLE.
SMACK
I KNOW YOU THOUGHT YOU SHOULD ADDRESS THE SITUATION, BUT IT AIN'T WHAT I'D CALL 'GOOD'.
CLINK
SO WHAT IS THIS?
"THAT'S THE BOUNTY DUE ON OUR LITTLE PATSY, HAPPY."

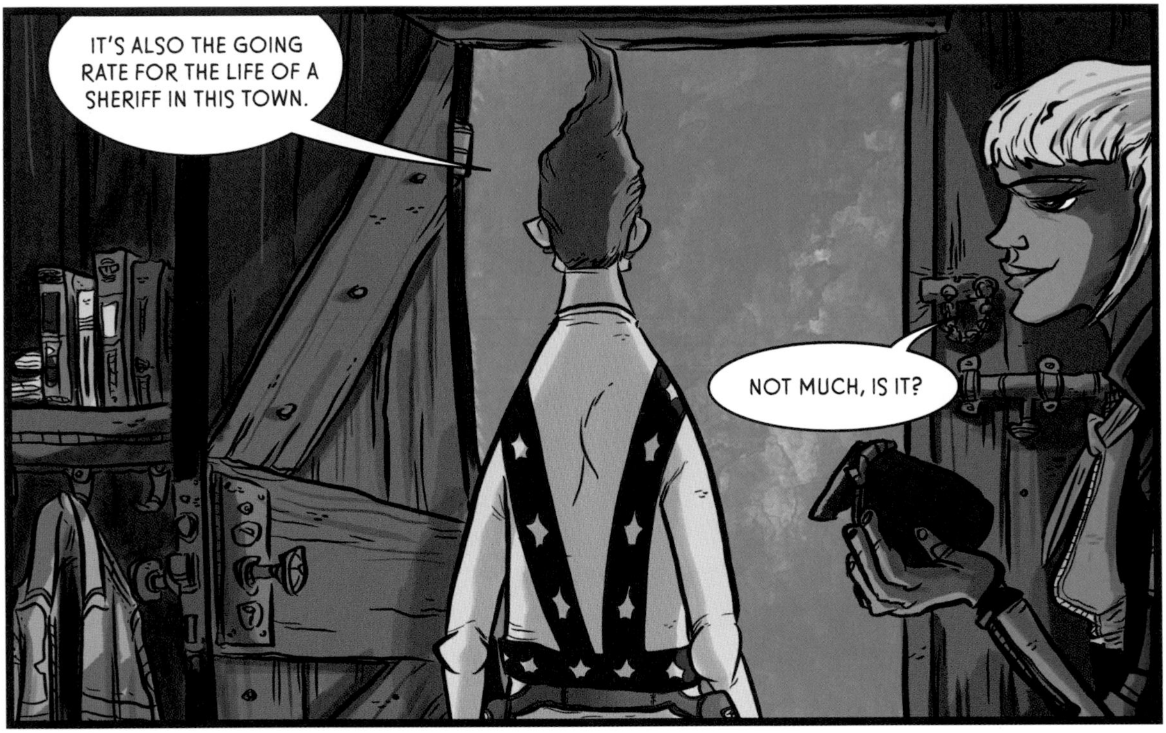
IT'S ALSO THE GOING RATE FOR THE LIFE OF A SHERIFF IN THIS TOWN.
NOT MUCH, IS IT?

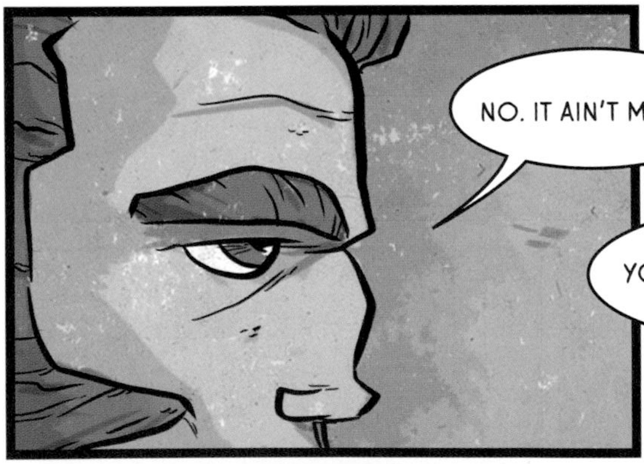
NO. IT AIN'T MUCH.
IT'S NOT OFTEN YOU KNOW EXACTLY WHAT YOUR LIFE IS WORTH.
I CAN THANK *BOSS PARKER* FOR THAT INSIGHT.

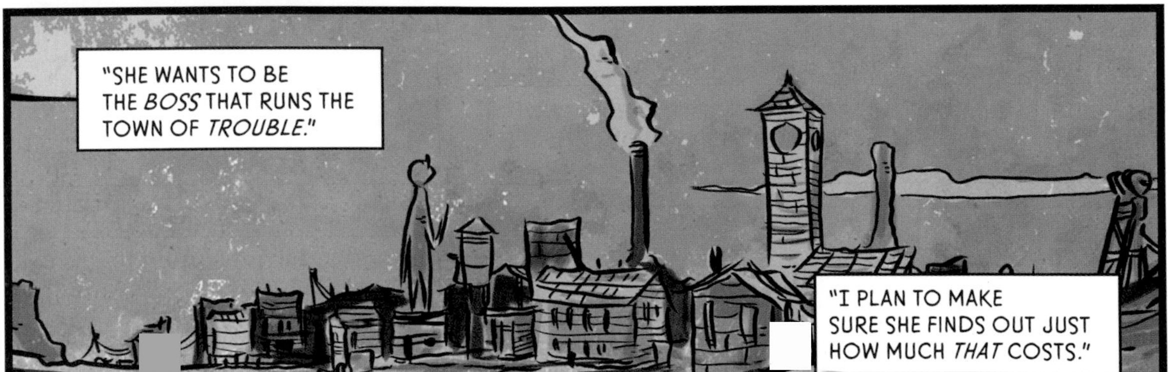
"SHE WANTS TO BE THE *BOSS* THAT RUNS THE TOWN OF *TROUBLE*."
"I PLAN TO MAKE SURE SHE FINDS OUT JUST HOW MUCH *THAT* COSTS."

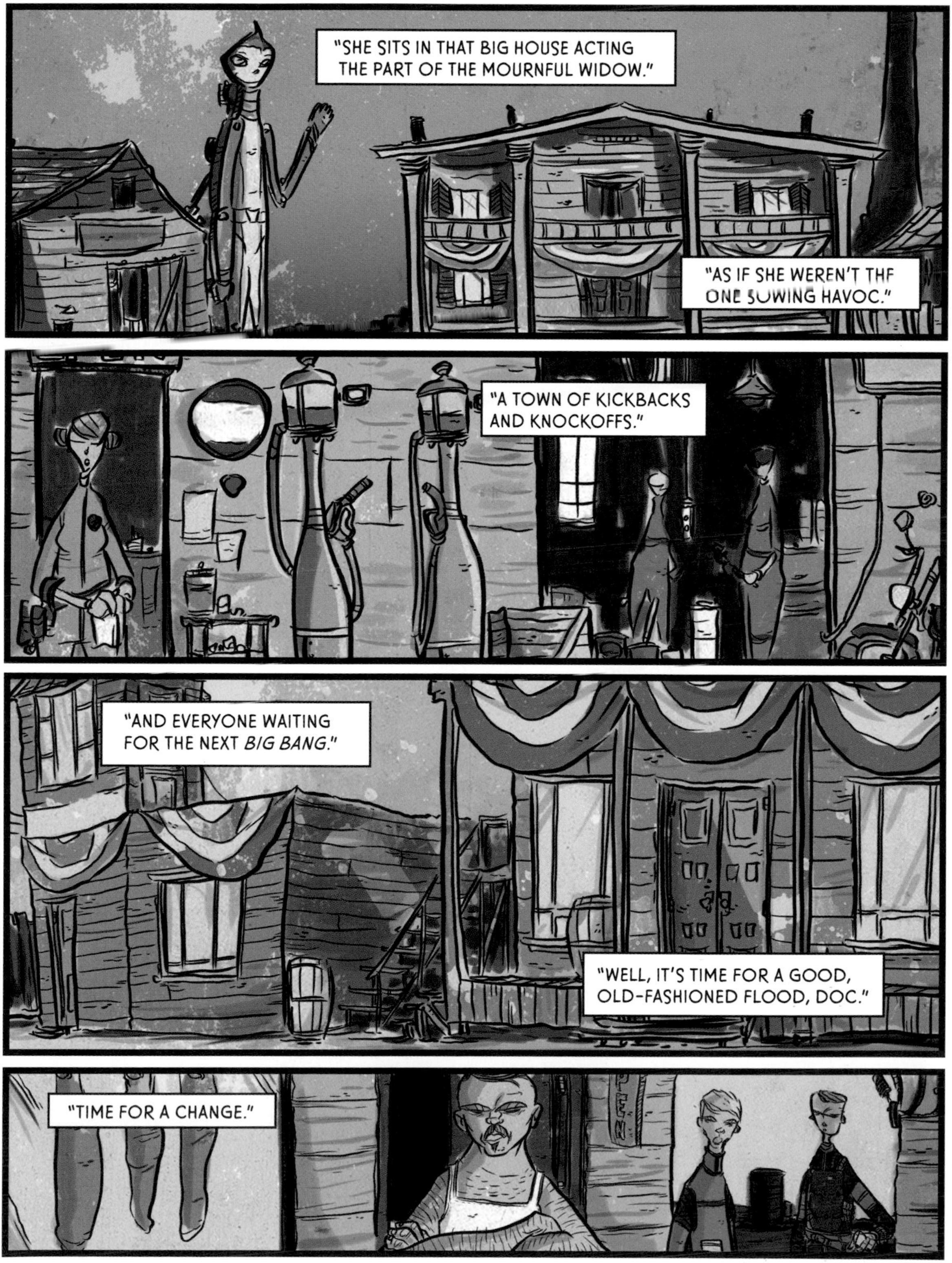
"SHE SITS IN THAT BIG HOUSE ACTING THE PART OF THE MOURNFUL WIDOW."
"AS IF SHE WEREN'T THE ONE SOWING HAVOC."
"A TOWN OF KICKBACKS AND KNOCKOFFS."
"AND EVERYONE WAITING FOR THE NEXT *BIG BANG*."
"WELL, IT'S TIME FOR A GOOD, OLD-FASHIONED FLOOD, DOC."
"TIME FOR A CHANGE."

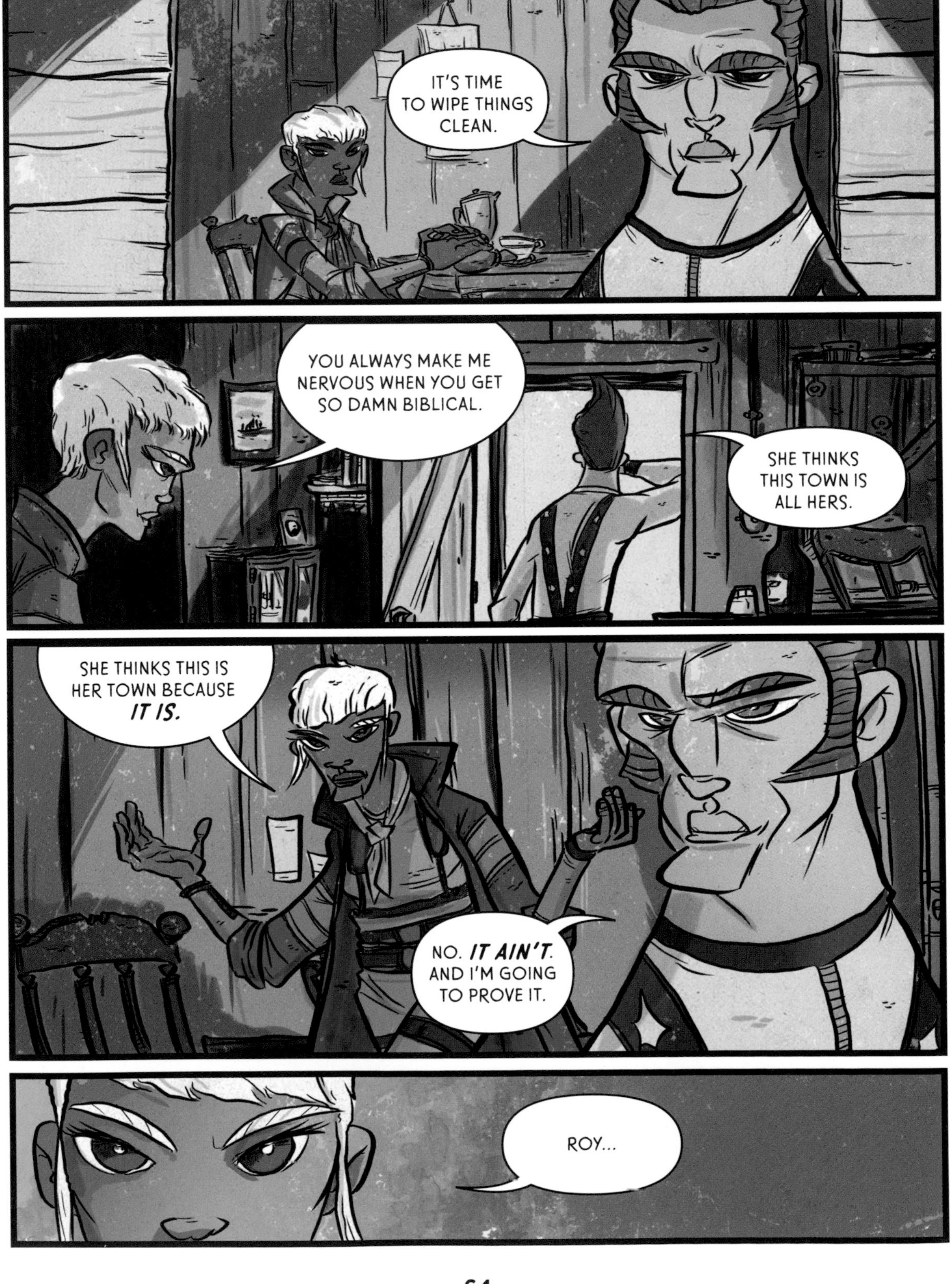
IT'S TIME TO WIPE THINGS CLEAN.
YOU ALWAYS MAKE ME NERVOUS WHEN YOU GET SO DAMN BIBLICAL.
SHE THINKS THIS TOWN IS ALL HERS.
SHE THINKS THIS IS HER TOWN BECAUSE *IT IS.*
NO. *IT AIN'T.* AND I'M GOING TO PROVE IT.
ROY...

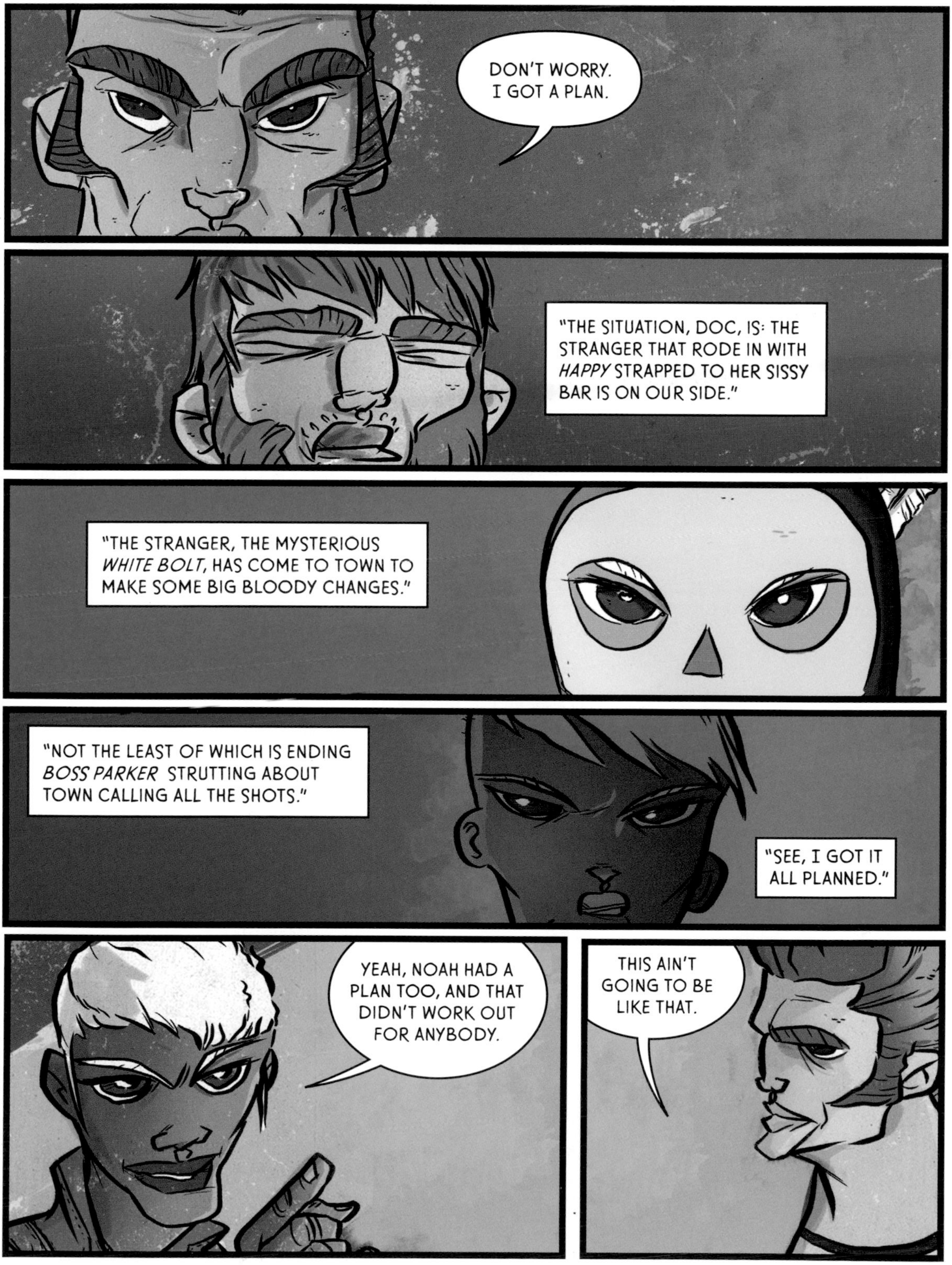
DON'T WORRY. I GOT A PLAN.
"THE SITUATION, DOC, IS: THE STRANGER THAT RODE IN WITH *HAPPY* STRAPPED TO HER SISSY BAR IS ON OUR SIDE."
"THE STRANGER, THE MYSTERIOUS *WHITE BOLT*, HAS COME TO TOWN TO MAKE SOME BIG BLOODY CHANGES."
"NOT THE LEAST OF WHICH IS ENDING *BOSS PARKER* STRUTTING ABOUT TOWN CALLING ALL THE SHOTS."
"SEE, I GOT IT ALL PLANNED."
YEAH, NOAH HAD A PLAN TOO, AND THAT DIDN'T WORK OUT FOR ANYBODY.
THIS AIN'T GOING TO BE LIKE THAT.

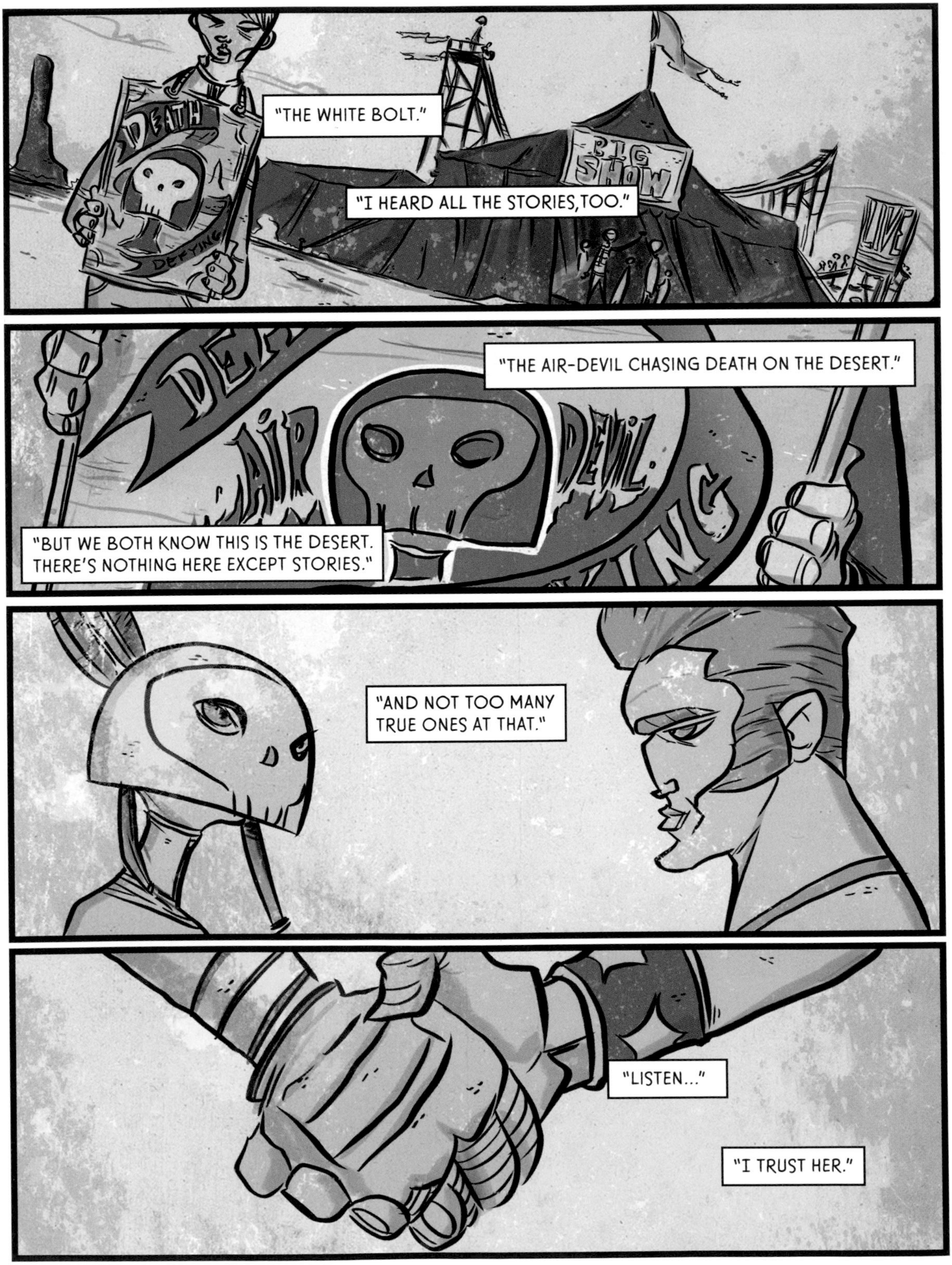
"THE WHITE BOLT."
DEATH
DEFYING
BIG SHOW
"I HEARD ALL THE STORIES, TOO."
LIVE
"THE AIR-DEVIL CHASING DEATH ON THE DESERT."
AIR DEVIL
"BUT WE BOTH KNOW THIS IS THE DESERT. THERE'S NOTHING HERE EXCEPT STORIES."
"AND NOT TOO MANY TRUE ONES AT THAT."
"LISTEN..."
"I TRUST HER."

"OH...LORD HELP US ALL, ROY."

"YOU TRUST HER."

"I HOPE THIS WORKS OUT BETTER THAN THE LAST TIME YOU TOOK TO TRUSTING ANYONE."

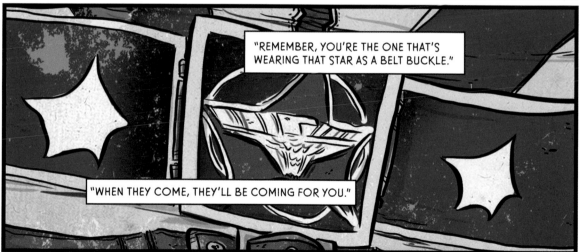

"REMEMBER, YOU'RE THE ONE THAT'S WEARING THAT STAR AS A BELT BUCKLE."

"WHEN THEY COME, THEY'LL BE COMING FOR YOU."

AND, WELL, HERE *THEY* COME NOW.

THE STOOGES.

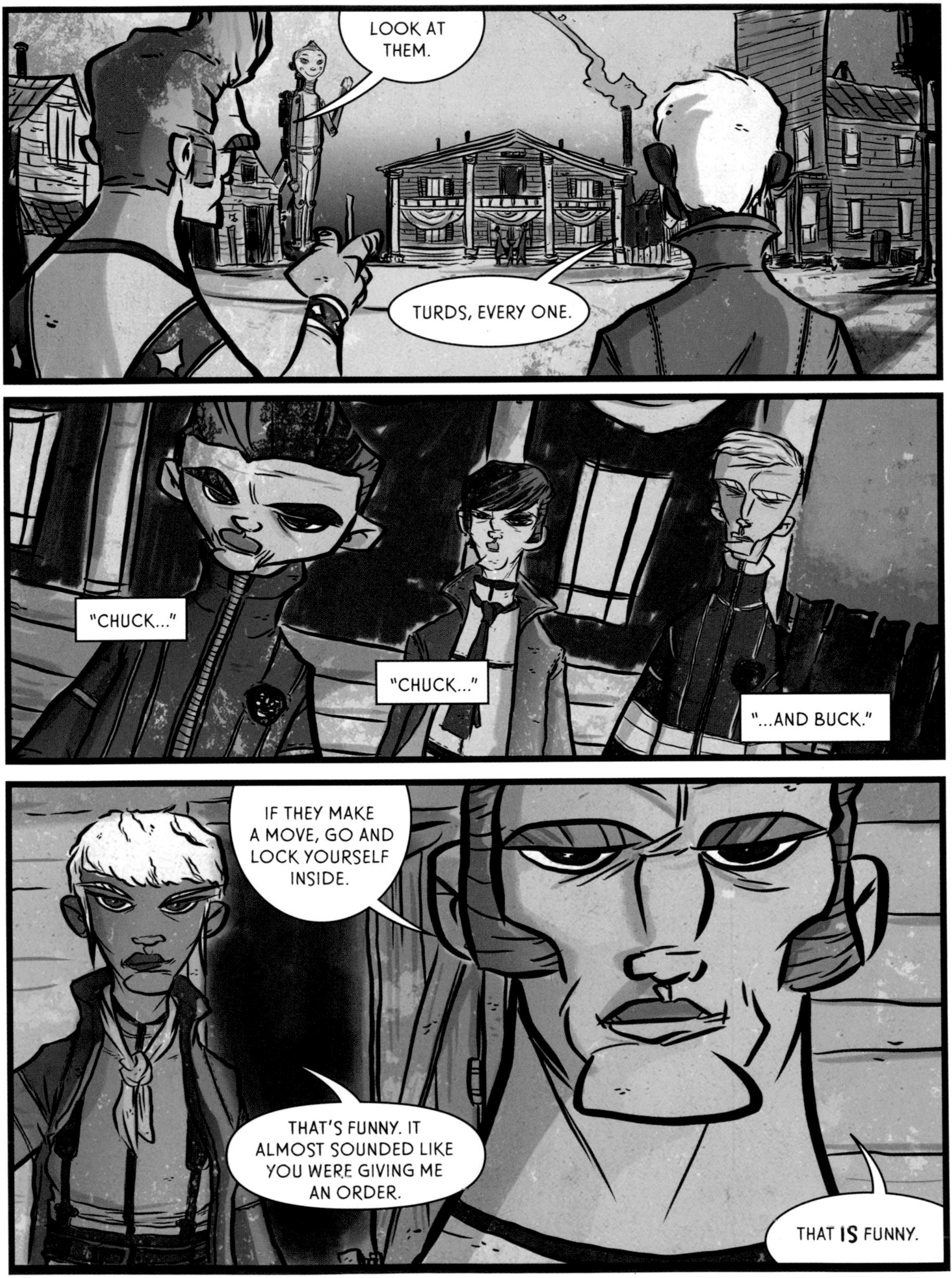
LOOK AT THEM.
TURDS, EVERY ONE.
"CHUCK..."
"CHUCK..."
"...AND BUCK."
IF THEY MAKE A MOVE, GO AND LOCK YOURSELF INSIDE.
THAT'S FUNNY. IT ALMOST SOUNDED LIKE YOU WERE GIVING ME AN ORDER.
THAT IS FUNNY.

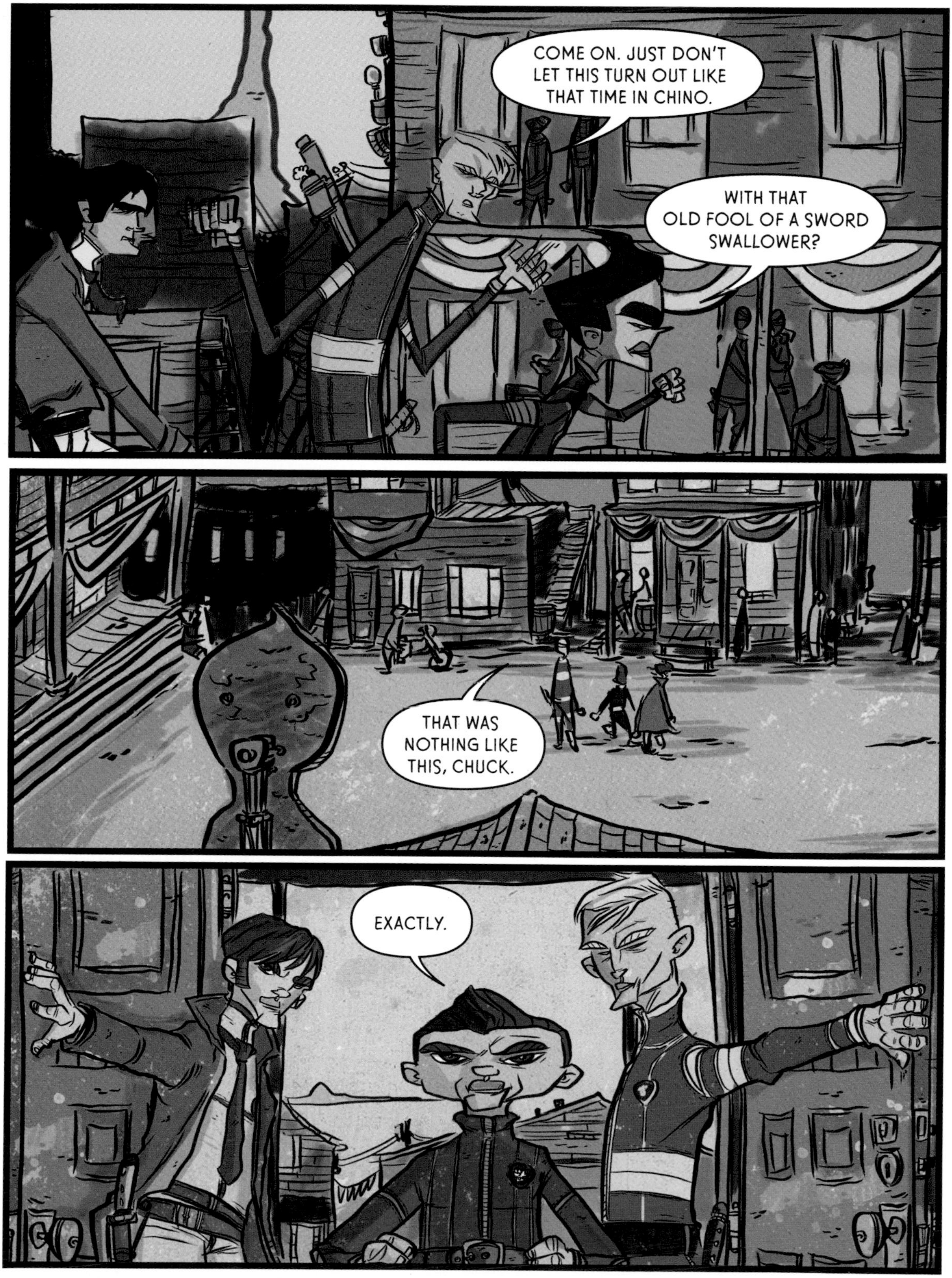
COME ON. JUST DON'T LET THIS TURN OUT LIKE THAT TIME IN CHINO.
WITH THAT OLD FOOL OF A SWORD SWALLOWER?
THAT WAS NOTHING LIKE THIS, CHUCK.
EXACTLY.

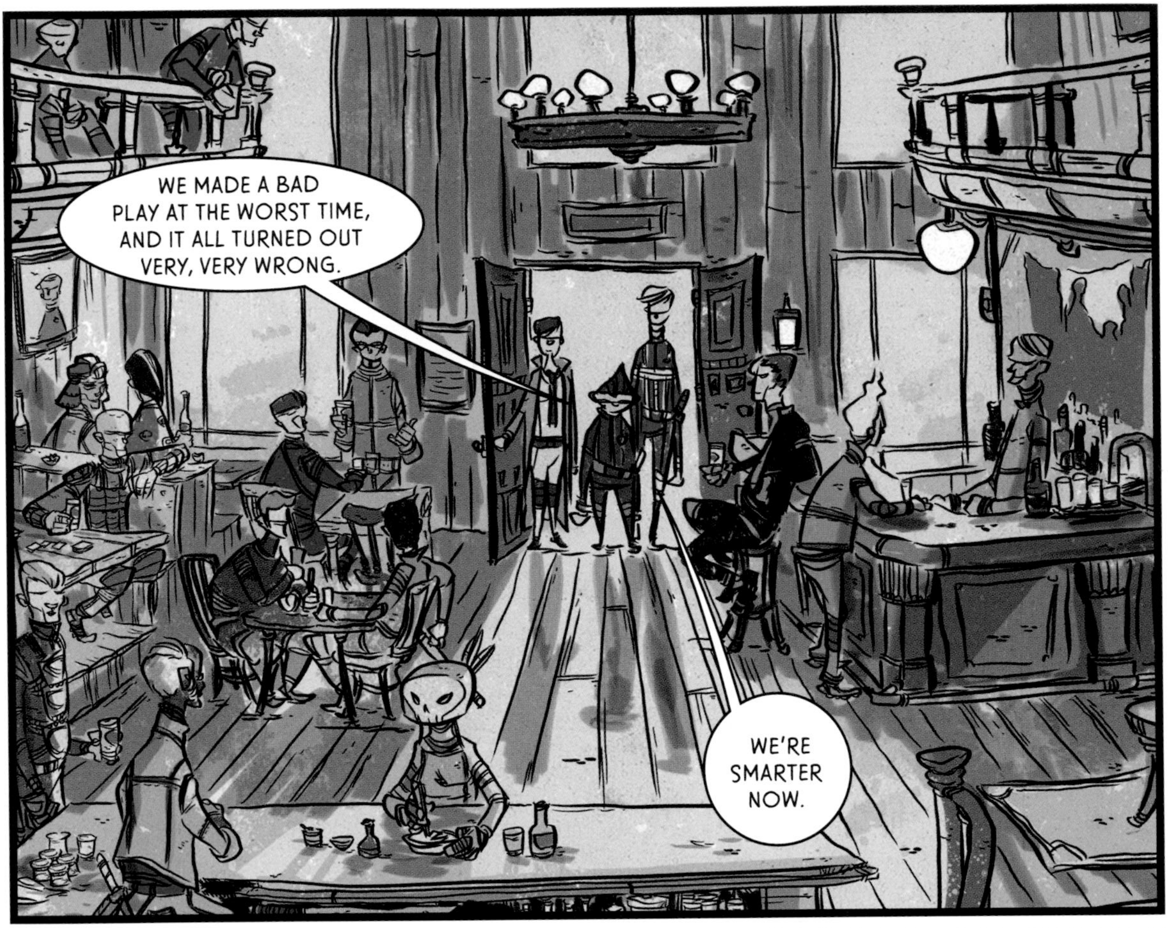
WE MADE A BAD PLAY AT THE WORST TIME, AND IT ALL TURNED OUT VERY, VERY WRONG.
WE'RE SMARTER NOW.

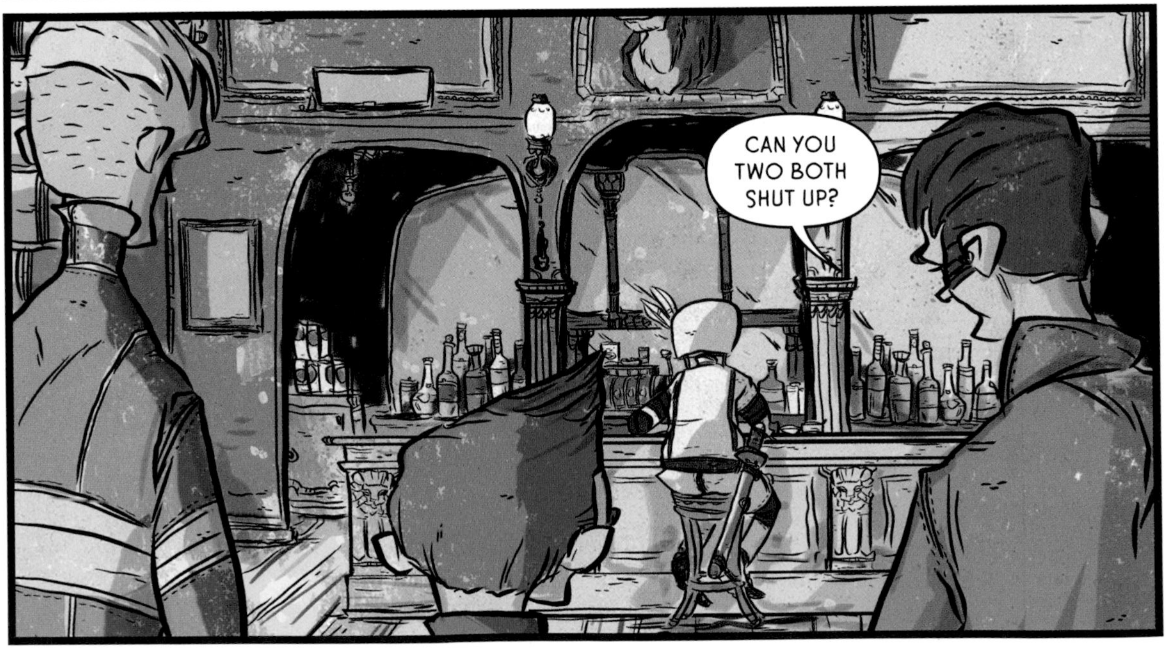
CAN YOU TWO BOTH SHUT UP?

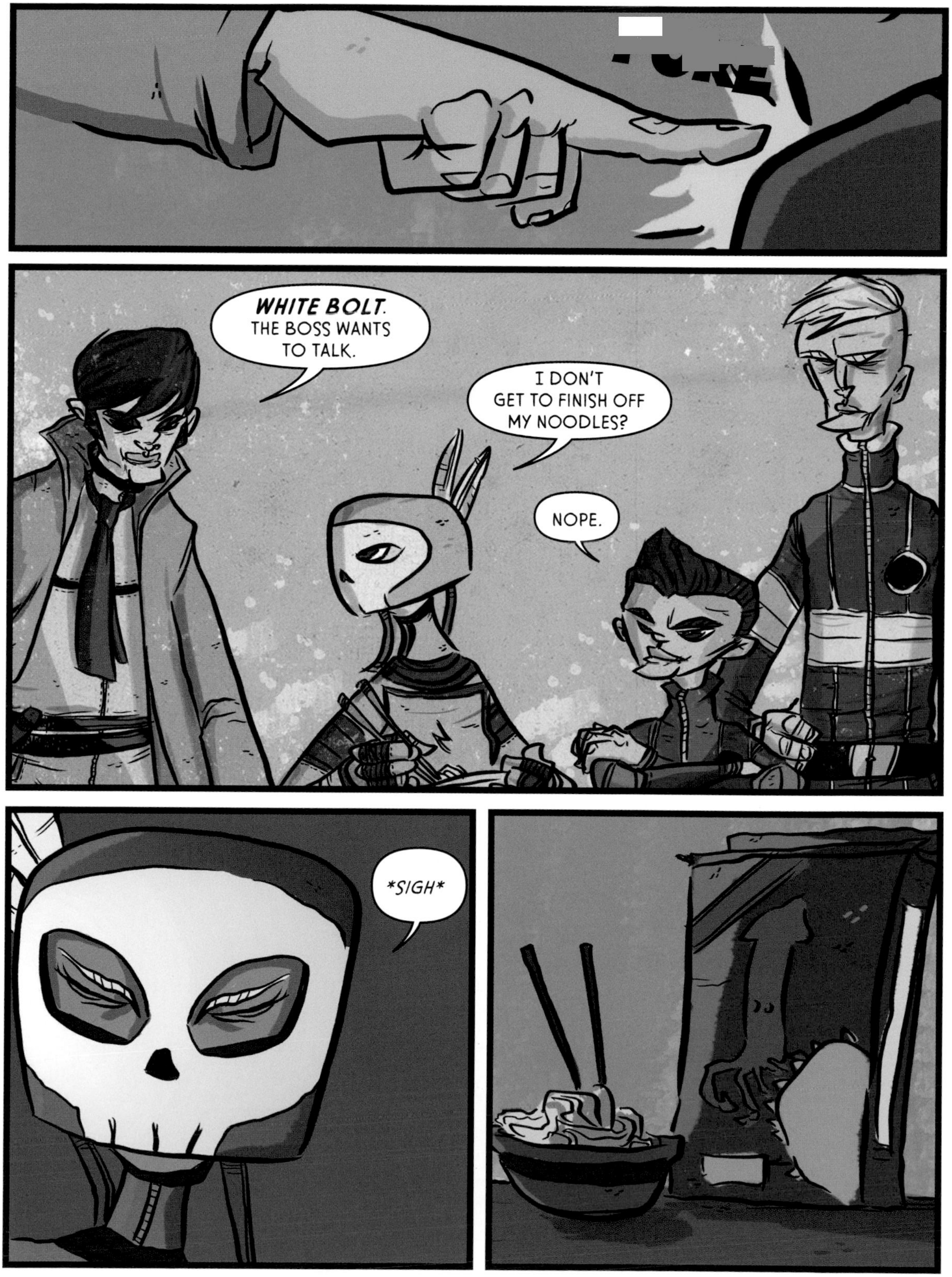
WHITE BOLT.
THE BOSS WANTS TO TALK.
I DON'T GET TO FINISH OFF MY NOODLES?
NOPE.
SIGH

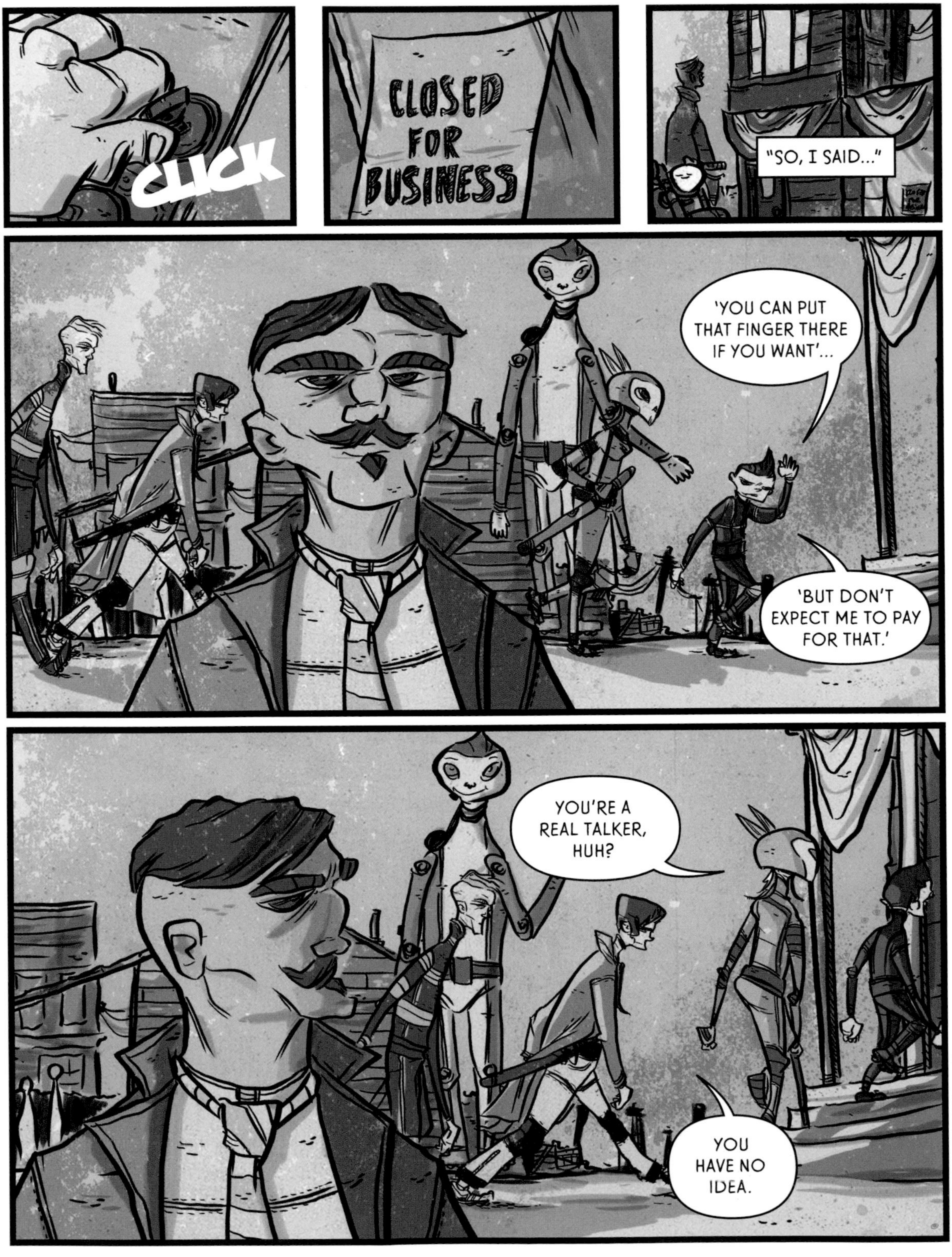
CLICK
CLOSED FOR BUSINESS
"SO, I SAID..."
'YOU CAN PUT THAT FINGER THERE IF YOU WANT'...
'BUT DON'T EXPECT ME TO PAY FOR THAT.'
YOU'RE A REAL TALKER, HUH?
YOU HAVE NO IDEA.

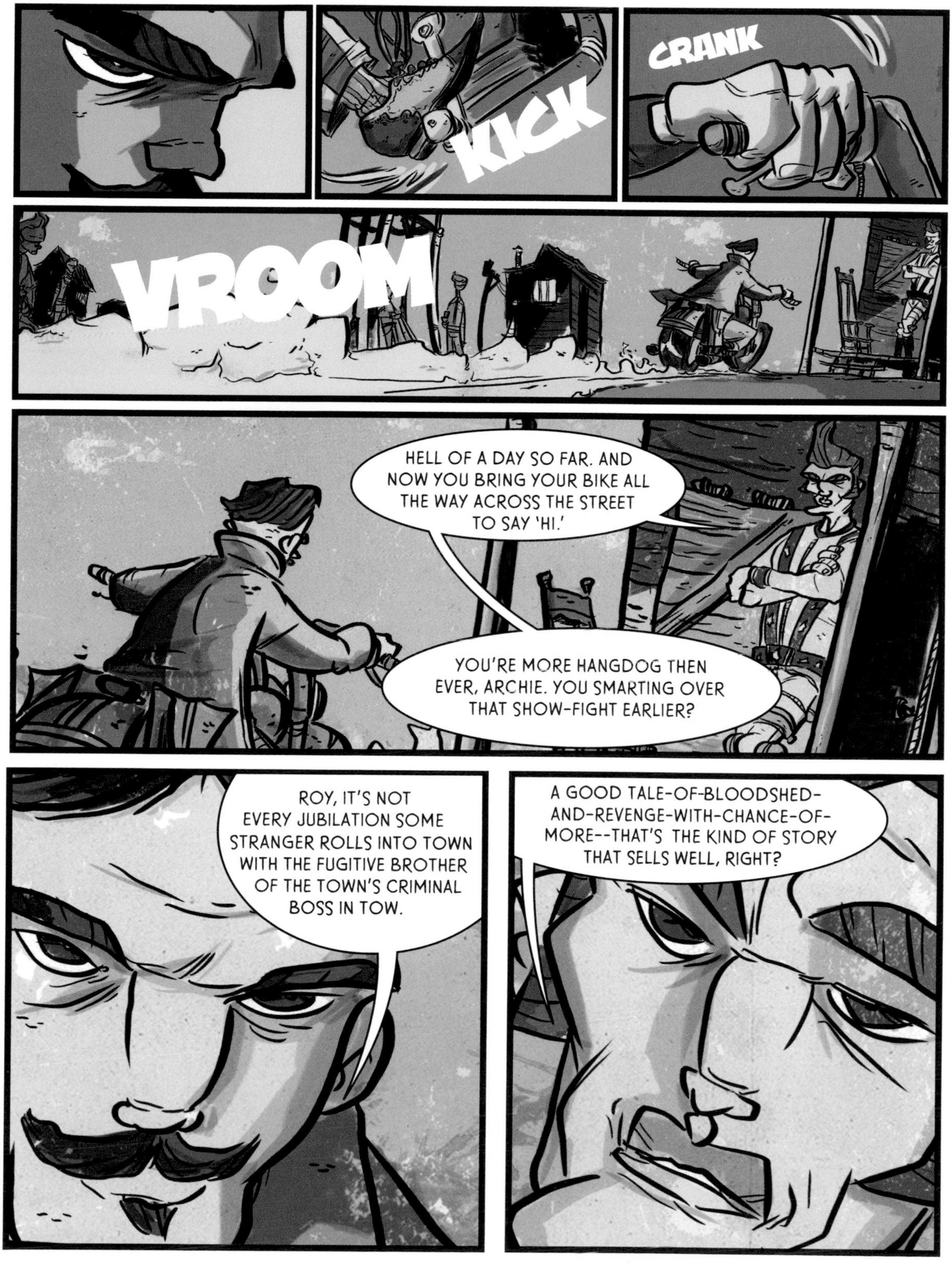
KICK
CRANK
VROOM
HELL OF A DAY SO FAR. AND NOW YOU BRING YOUR BIKE ALL THE WAY ACROSS THE STREET TO SAY 'HI.'
YOU'RE MORE HANGDOG THEN EVER, ARCHIE. YOU SMARTING OVER THAT SHOW-FIGHT EARLIER?
ROY, IT'S NOT EVERY JUBILATION SOME STRANGER ROLLS INTO TOWN WITH THE FUGITIVE BROTHER OF THE TOWN'S CRIMINAL BOSS IN TOW.
A GOOD TALE-OF-BLOODSHED-AND-REVENGE-WITH-CHANCE-OF-MORE--THAT'S THE KIND OF STORY THAT SELLS WELL, RIGHT?

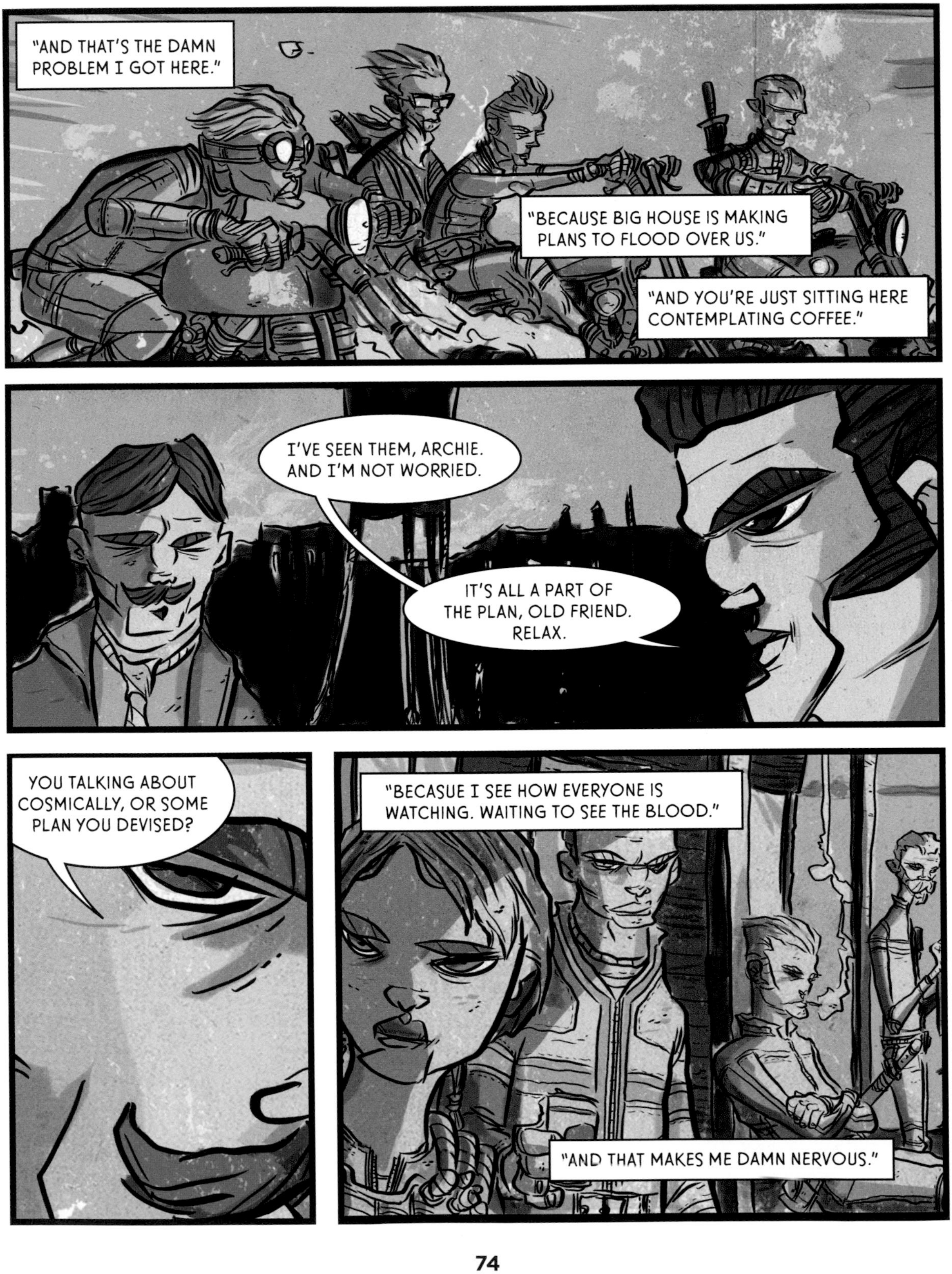
"AND THAT'S THE DAMN PROBLEM I GOT HERE."
"BECAUSE BIG HOUSE IS MAKING PLANS TO FLOOD OVER US."
"AND YOU'RE JUST SITTING HERE CONTEMPLATING COFFEE."
I'VE SEEN THEM, ARCHIE. AND I'M NOT WORRIED.
IT'S ALL A PART OF THE PLAN, OLD FRIEND. RELAX.
YOU TALKING ABOUT COSMICALLY, OR SOME PLAN YOU DEVISED?
"BECASUE I SEE HOW EVERYONE IS WATCHING. WAITING TO SEE THE BLOOD."
"AND THAT MAKES ME DAMN NERVOUS."

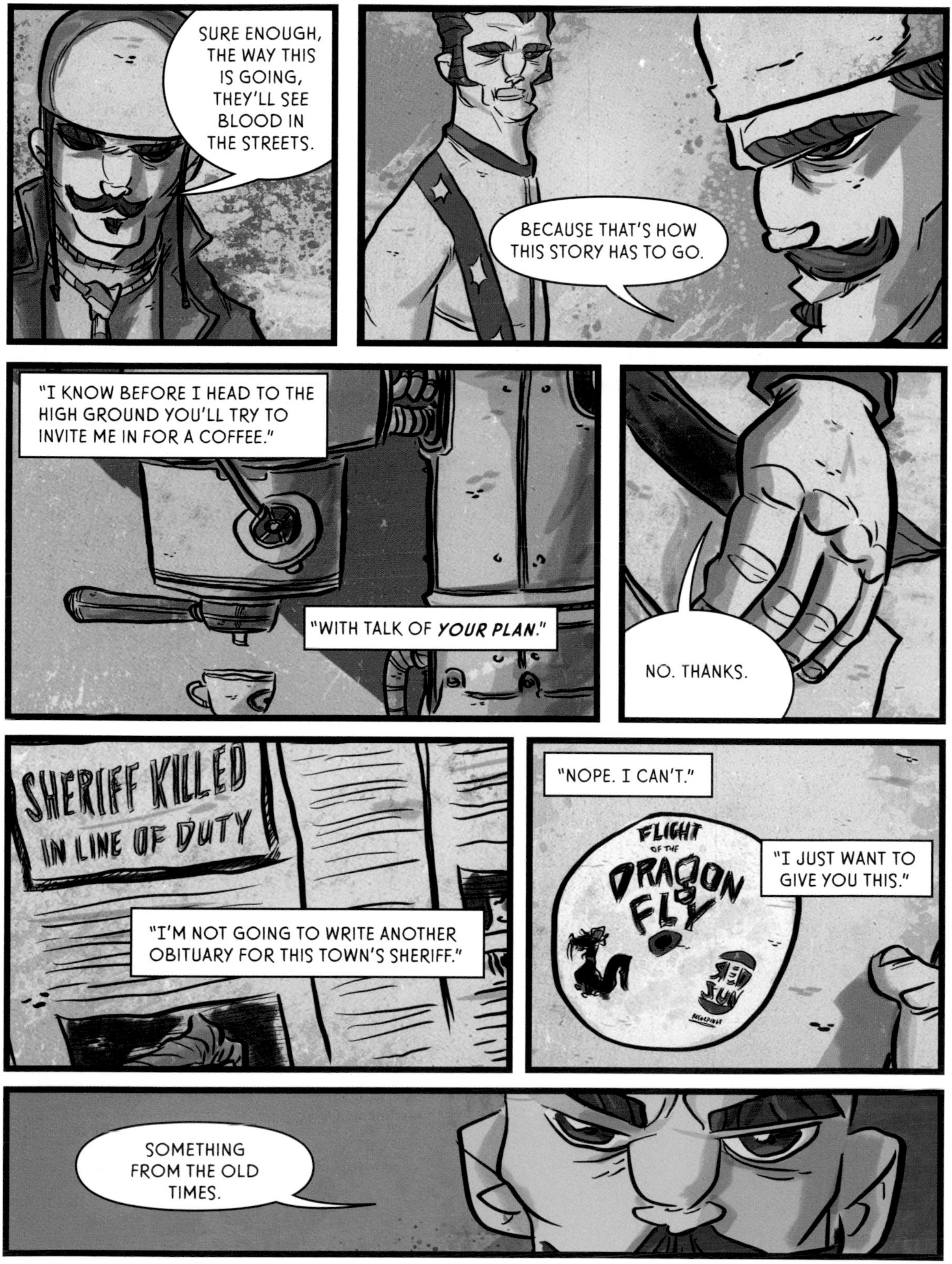

SURE ENOUGH, THE WAY THIS IS GOING, THEY'LL SEE BLOOD IN THE STREETS.
BECAUSE THAT'S HOW THIS STORY HAS TO GO.
"I KNOW BEFORE I HEAD TO THE HIGH GROUND YOU'LL TRY TO INVITE ME IN FOR A COFFEE."
"WITH TALK OF *YOUR PLAN*."
NO. THANKS.
SHERIFF KILLED IN LINE OF DUTY
"I'M NOT GOING TO WRITE ANOTHER OBITUARY FOR THIS TOWN'S SHERIFF."
"NOPE. I CAN'T."
FLIGHT OF THE DRAGON FLY
RED SUN
"I JUST WANT TO GIVE YOU THIS."
SOMETHING FROM THE OLD TIMES.

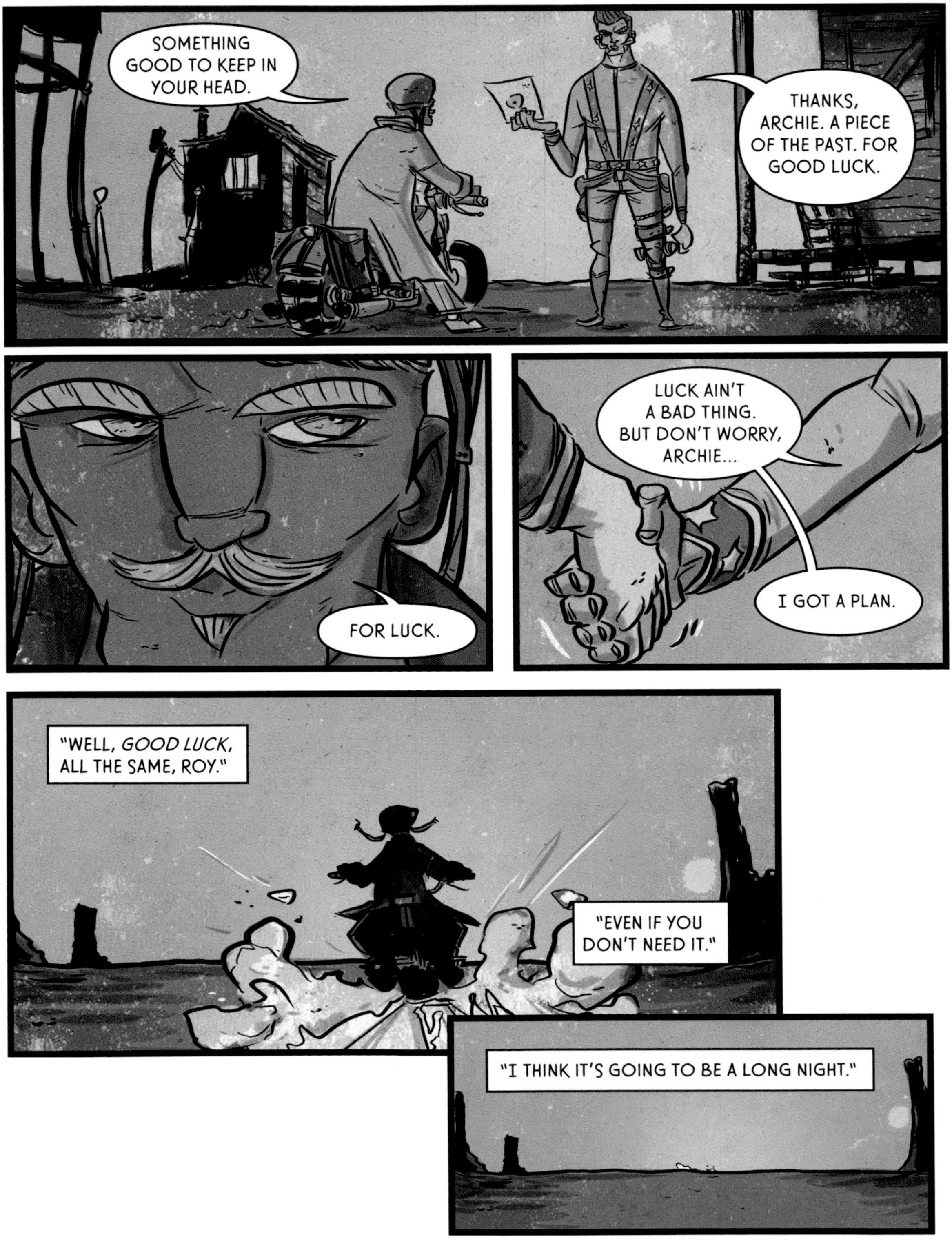

SOMETHING GOOD TO KEEP IN YOUR HEAD.
THANKS, ARCHIE. A PIECE OF THE PAST. FOR GOOD LUCK.
FOR LUCK.
LUCK AIN'T A BAD THING. BUT DON'T WORRY, ARCHIE...
I GOT A PLAN.
"WELL, *GOOD LUCK*, ALL THE SAME, ROY."
"EVEN IF YOU DON'T NEED IT."
"I THINK IT'S GOING TO BE A LONG NIGHT."

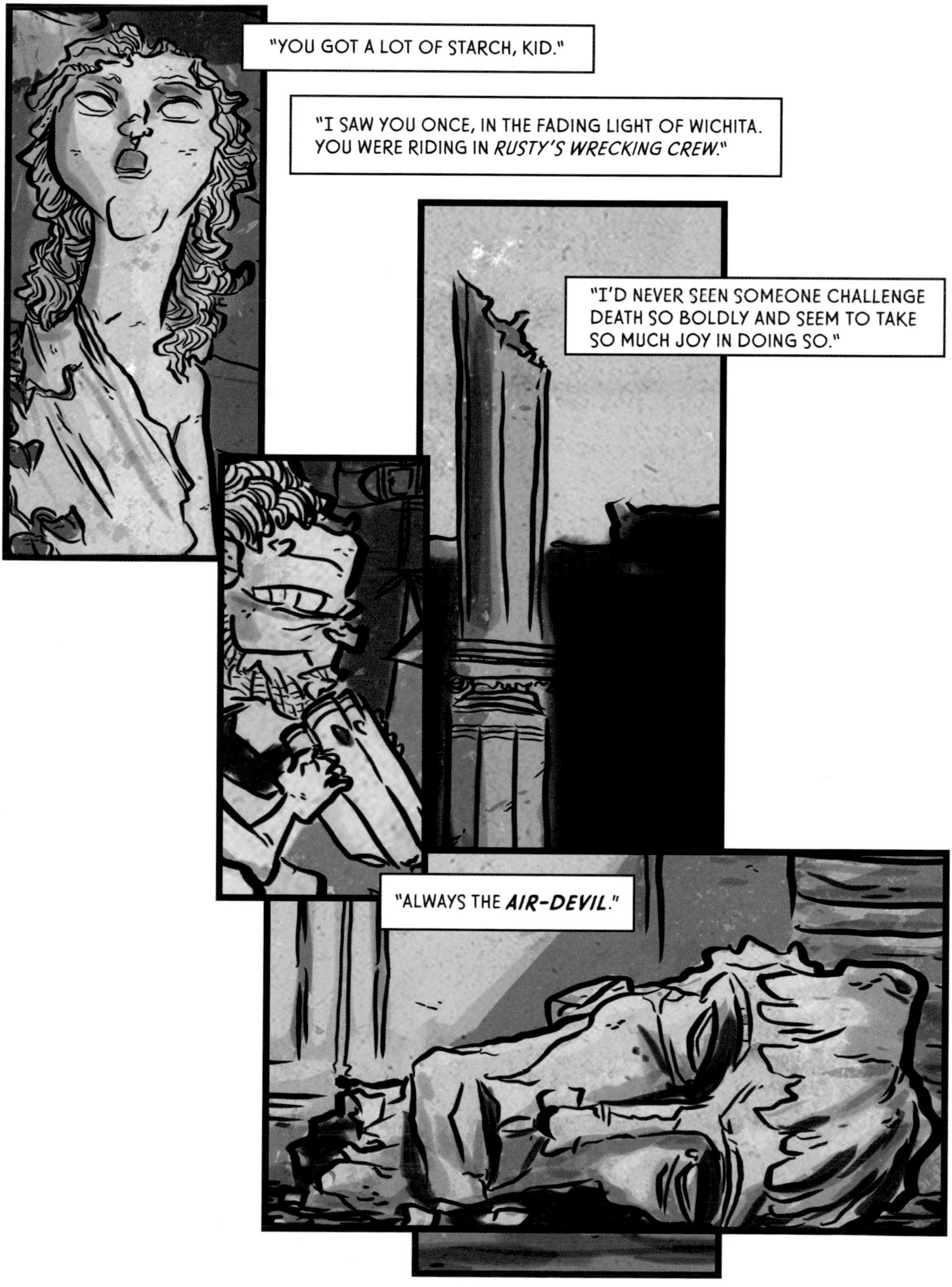
"YOU GOT A LOT OF STARCH, KID."
"I SAW YOU ONCE, IN THE FADING LIGHT OF WICHITA. YOU WERE RIDING IN *RUSTY'S WRECKING CREW*."
"I'D NEVER SEEN SOMEONE CHALLENGE DEATH SO BOLDLY AND SEEM TO TAKE SO MUCH JOY IN DOING SO."
"ALWAYS THE ***AIR-DEVIL***."

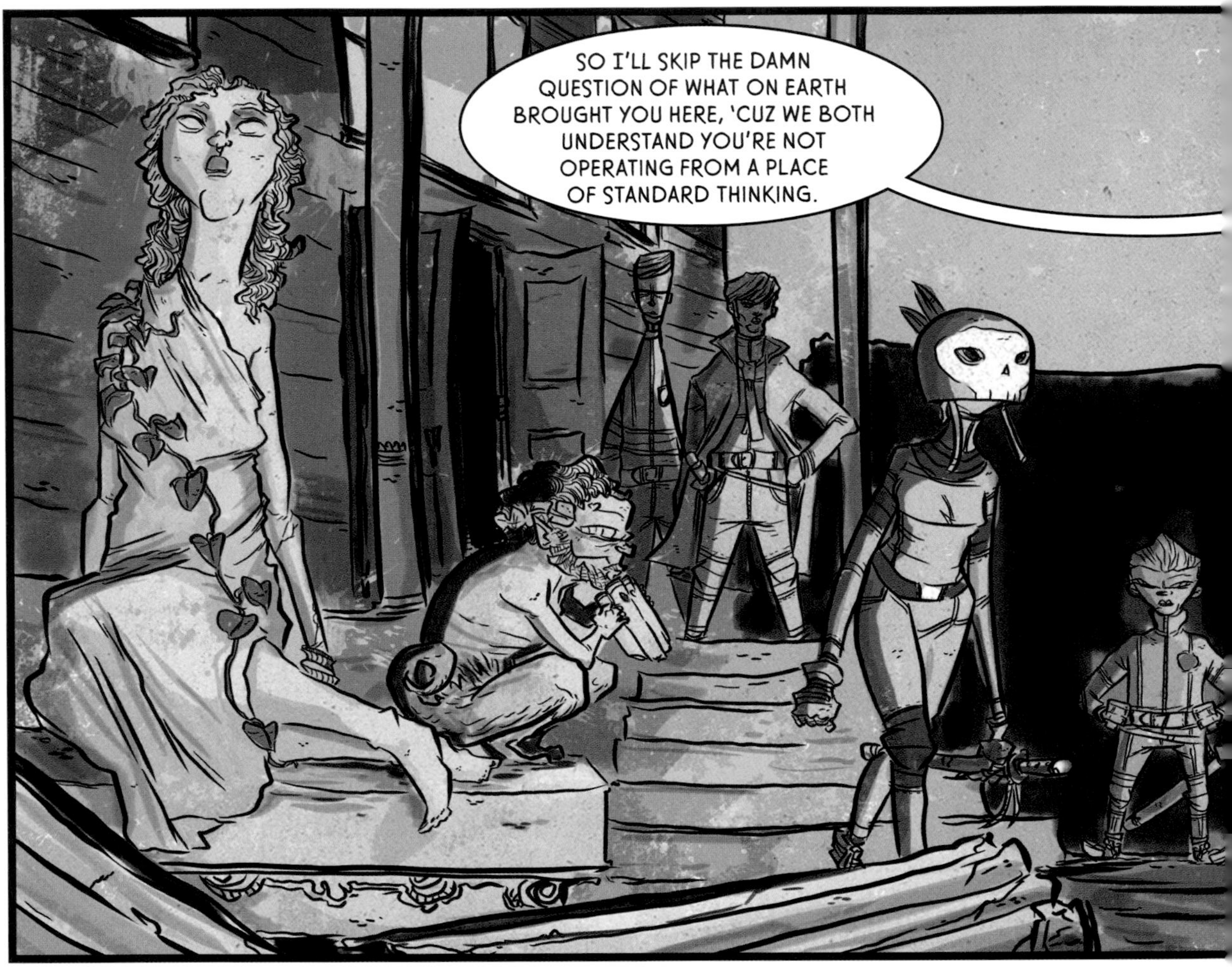
SO I'LL SKIP THE DAMN QUESTION OF WHAT ON EARTH BROUGHT YOU HERE, 'CUZ WE BOTH UNDERSTAND YOU'RE NOT OPERATING FROM A PLACE OF STANDARD THINKING.

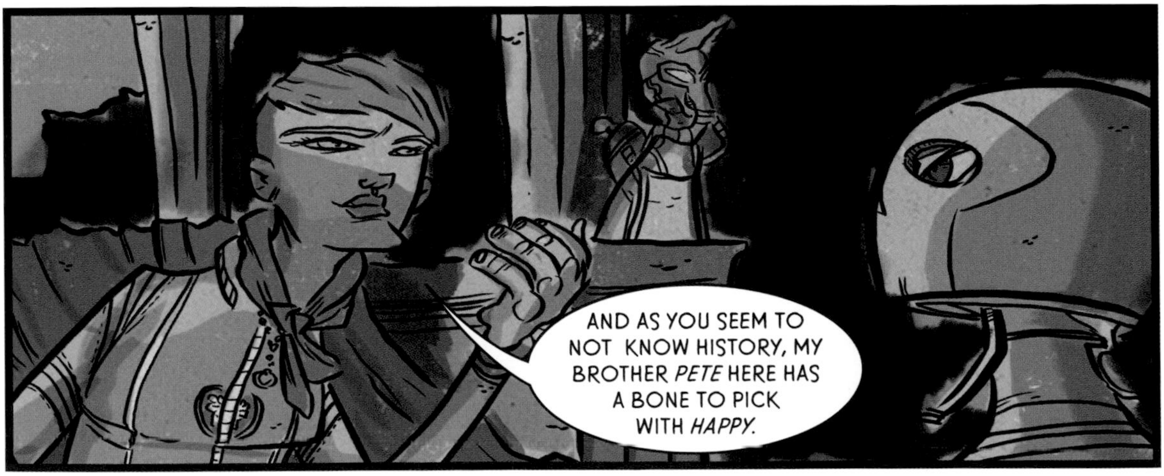
AND AS YOU SEEM TO NOT KNOW HISTORY, MY BROTHER *PETE* HERE HAS A BONE TO PICK WITH *HAPPY*.

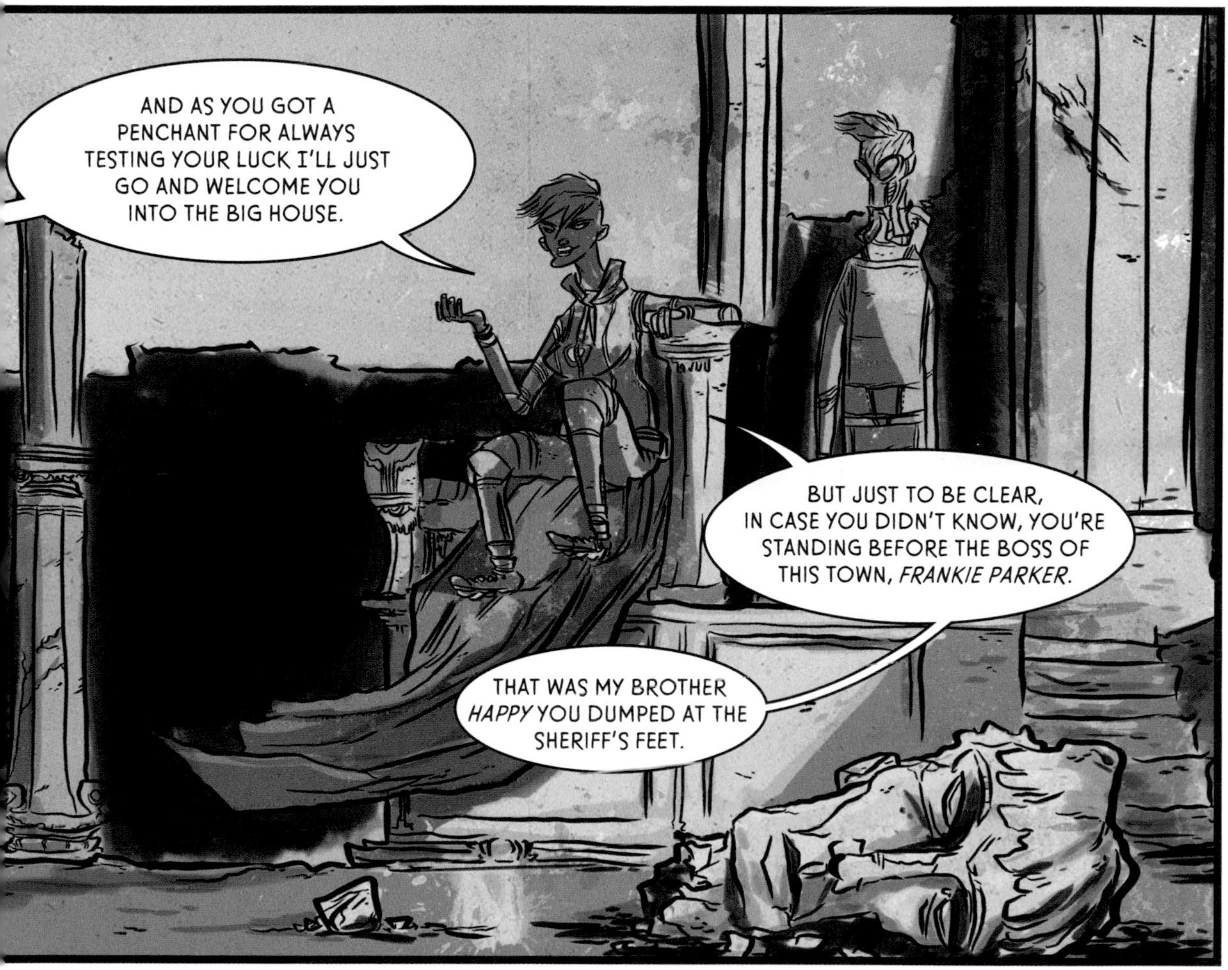
AND AS YOU GOT A PENCHANT FOR ALWAYS TESTING YOUR LUCK I'LL JUST GO AND WELCOME YOU INTO THE BIG HOUSE.
BUT JUST TO BE CLEAR, IN CASE YOU DIDN'T KNOW, YOU'RE STANDING BEFORE THE BOSS OF THIS TOWN, *FRANKIE PARKER.*
THAT WAS MY BROTHER *HAPPY* YOU DUMPED AT THE SHERIFF'S FEET.

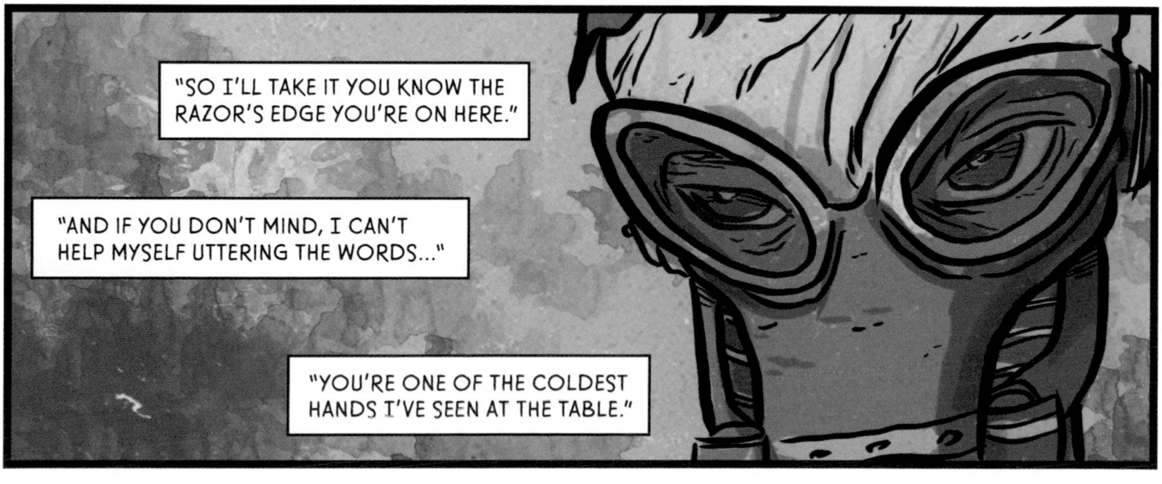
"SO I'LL TAKE IT YOU KNOW THE RAZOR'S EDGE YOU'RE ON HERE."
"AND IF YOU DON'T MIND, I CAN'T HELP MYSELF UTTERING THE WORDS..."
"YOU'RE ONE OF THE COLDEST HANDS I'VE SEEN AT THE TABLE."

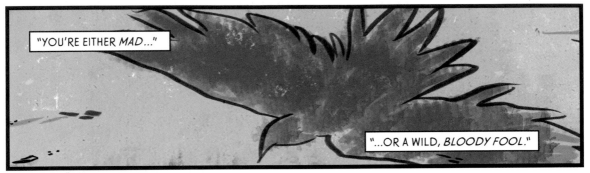

"YOU'RE EITHER *MAD*..."

"...OR A WILD, *BLOODY FOOL*."

"BUT FOOLS AND MADMEN ARE ALL WE GOT IN THE RANKS HERE."

"SO EITHER WAY, THIS IS SURE ENOUGH THE PLACE FOR YOU."

CONSIDERING HAPPY IS WANTED FOR KILLING YOUR LATE HUSBAND I'D FIGURE YOU'D HAVE A BEEF...

UM?

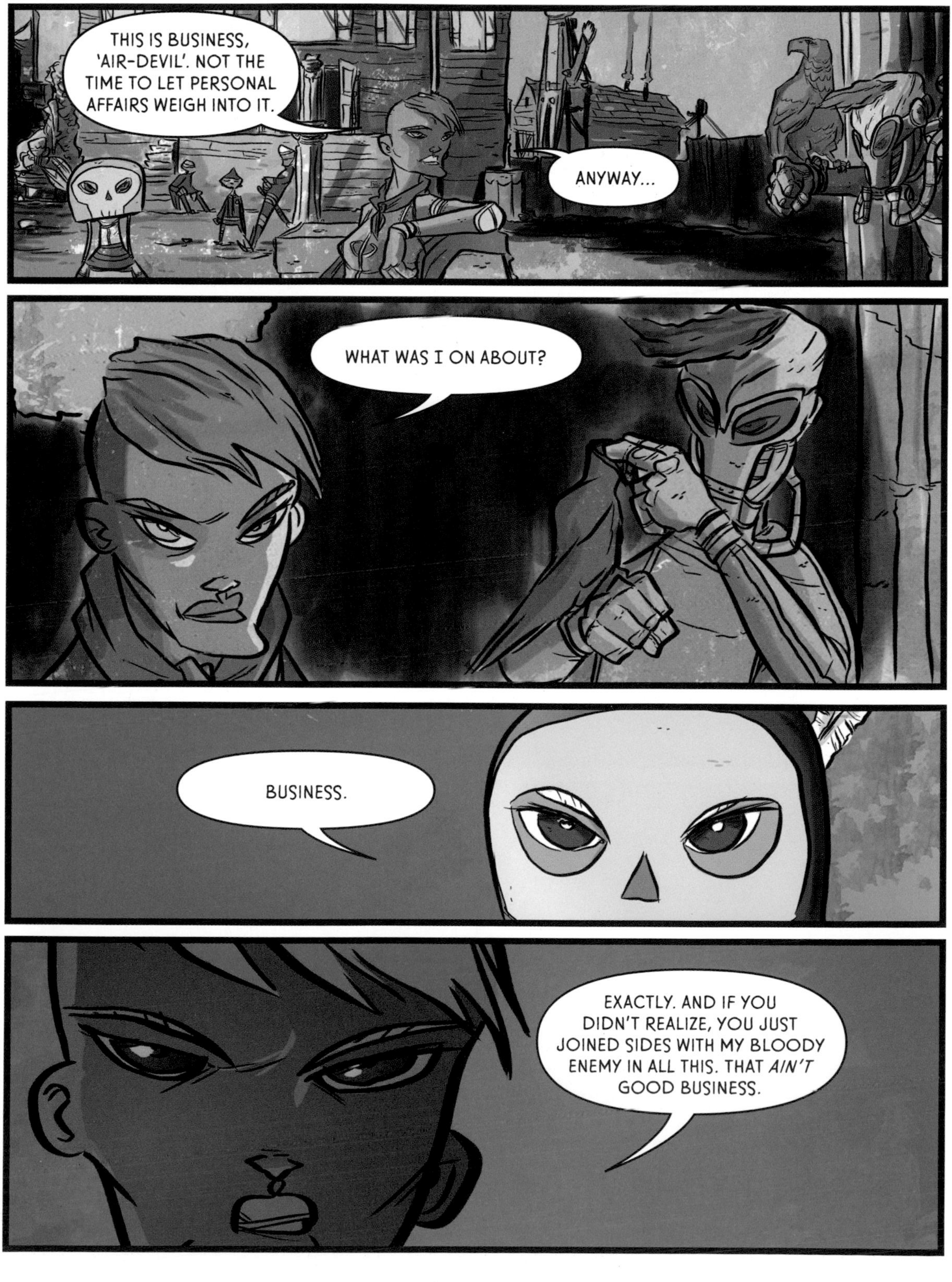
THIS IS BUSINESS, 'AIR-DEVIL'. NOT THE TIME TO LET PERSONAL AFFAIRS WEIGH INTO IT.
ANYWAY...
WHAT WAS I ON ABOUT?
BUSINESS.
EXACTLY. AND IF YOU DIDN'T REALIZE, YOU JUST JOINED SIDES WITH MY BLOODY ENEMY IN ALL THIS. THAT *AIN'T* GOOD BUSINESS.

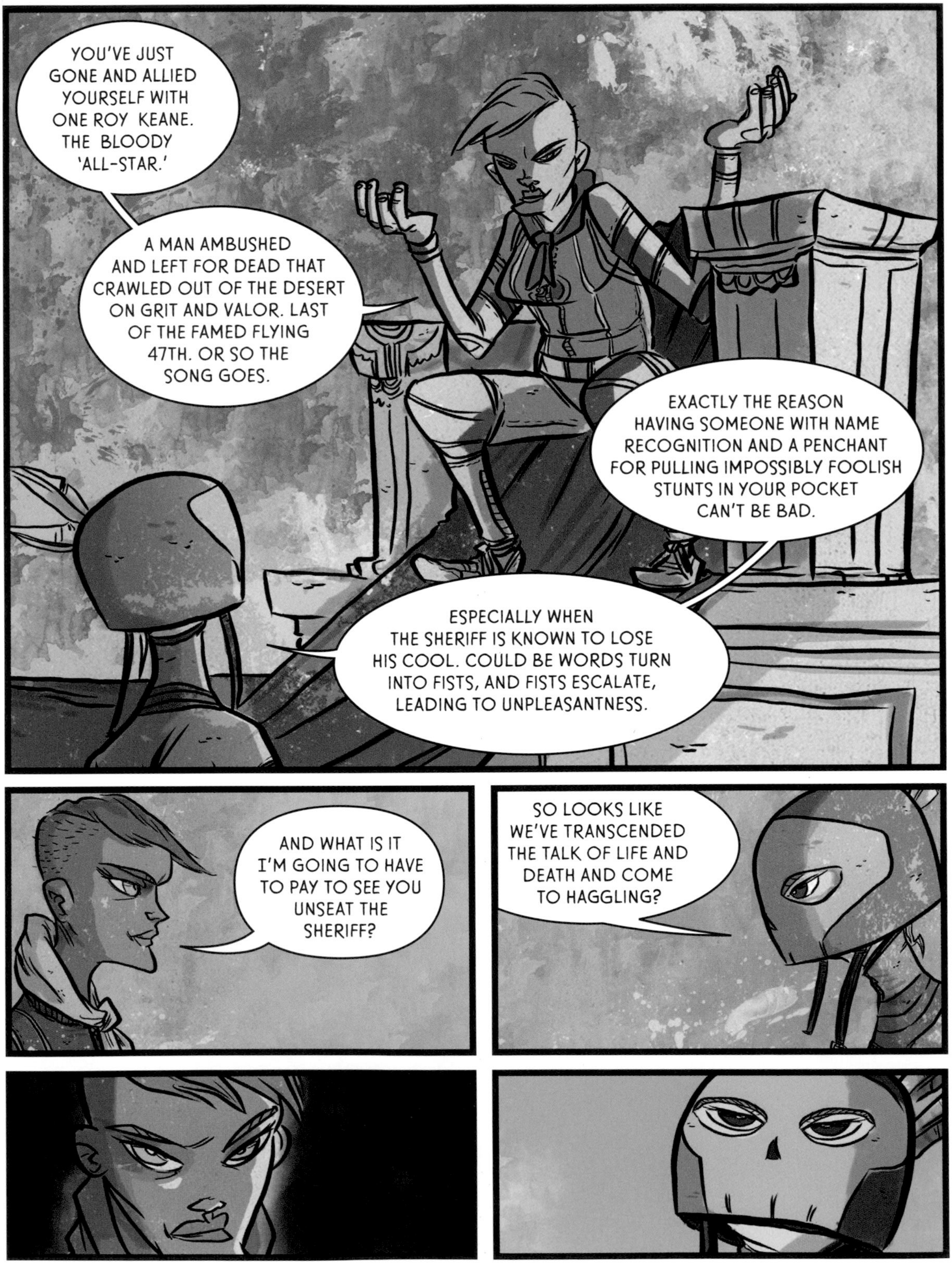

YOU'VE JUST GONE AND ALLIED YOURSELF WITH ONE ROY KEANE. THE BLOODY 'ALL-STAR.'
A MAN AMBUSHED AND LEFT FOR DEAD THAT CRAWLED OUT OF THE DESERT ON GRIT AND VALOR. LAST OF THE FAMED FLYING 47TH. OR SO THE SONG GOES.
EXACTLY THE REASON HAVING SOMEONE WITH NAME RECOGNITION AND A PENCHANT FOR PULLING IMPOSSIBLY FOOLISH STUNTS IN YOUR POCKET CAN'T BE BAD.
ESPECIALLY WHEN THE SHERIFF IS KNOWN TO LOSE HIS COOL. COULD BE WORDS TURN INTO FISTS, AND FISTS ESCALATE, LEADING TO UNPLEASANTNESS.
AND WHAT IS IT I'M GOING TO HAVE TO PAY TO SEE YOU UNSEAT THE SHERIFF?
SO LOOKS LIKE WE'VE TRANSCENDED THE TALK OF LIFE AND DEATH AND COME TO HAGGLING?

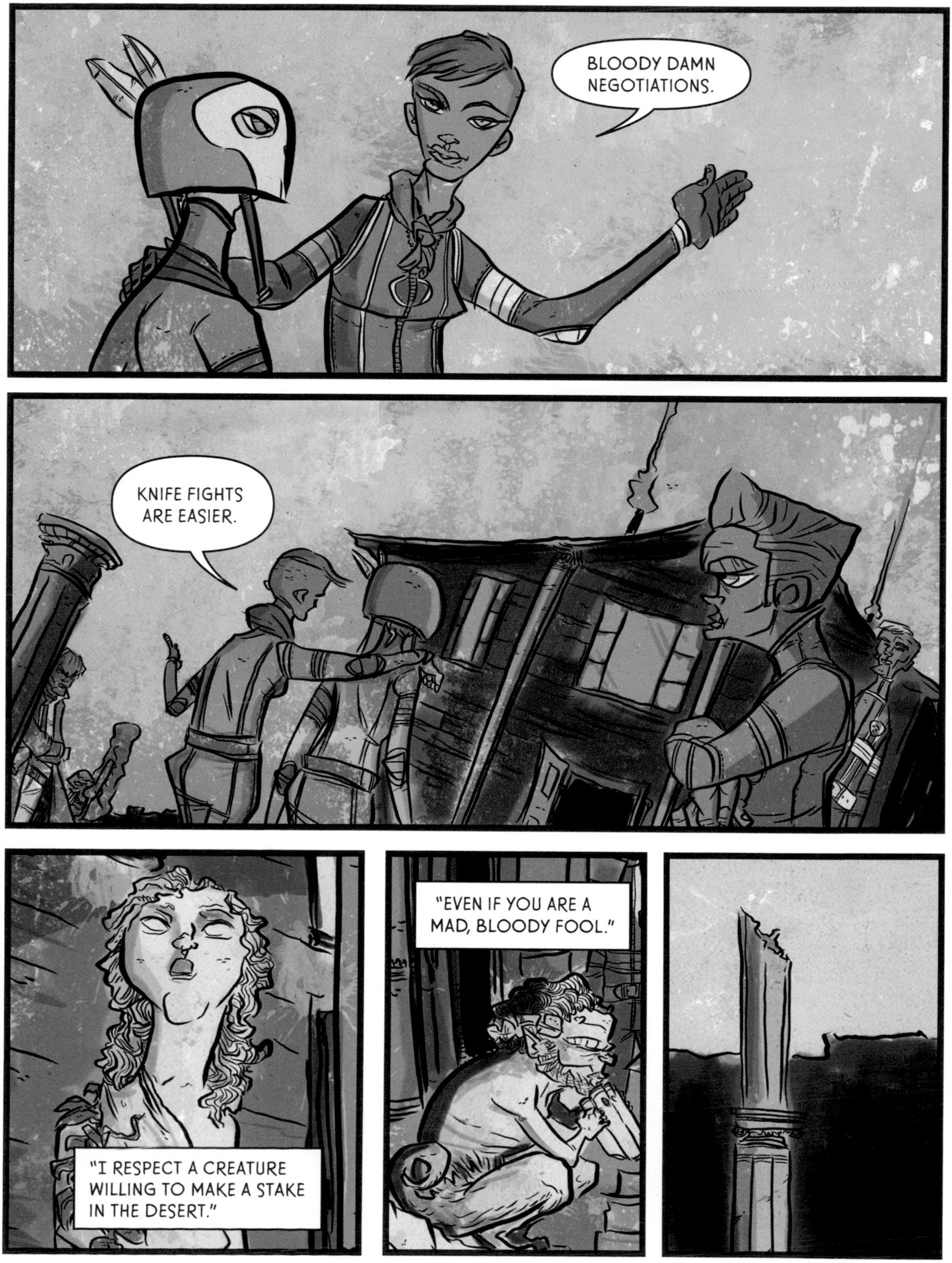
BLOODY DAMN NEGOTIATIONS.
KNIFE FIGHTS ARE EASIER.
"I RESPECT A CREATURE WILLING TO MAKE A STAKE IN THE DESERT."
"EVEN IF YOU ARE A MAD, BLOODY FOOL."

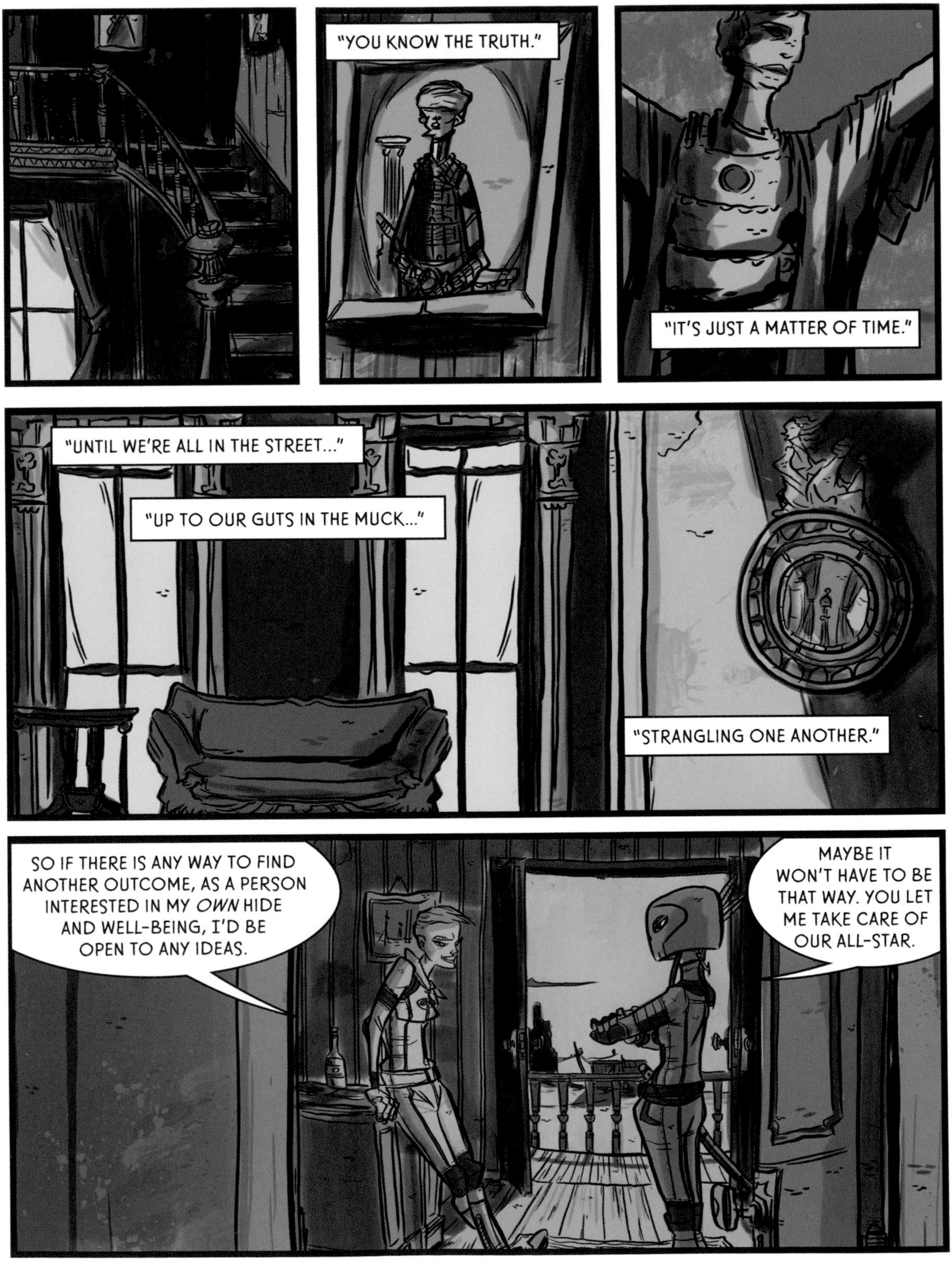
"YOU KNOW THE TRUTH."
"IT'S JUST A MATTER OF TIME."
"UNTIL WE'RE ALL IN THE STREET..."
"UP TO OUR GUTS IN THE MUCK..."
"STRANGLING ONE ANOTHER."
SO IF THERE IS ANY WAY TO FIND ANOTHER OUTCOME, AS A PERSON INTERESTED IN MY *OWN* HIDE AND WELL-BEING, I'D BE OPEN TO ANY IDEAS.
MAYBE IT WON'T HAVE TO BE THAT WAY. YOU LET ME TAKE CARE OF OUR ALL-STAR.

YOU MENTIONED HISTORY. I'VE GOT MY OWN SITUATION TO REMEDY.

YOU HEAR OF *THE HORNETS*?

THESE ARE THE BADLANDS, MY DEAR WHITE BOLT. EVERYONE KNOWS OF THE HORNETS.

WELL, I'M SEEKING ONE OF THEM BY NAME. *THE BUTCHER.*

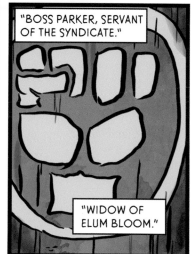

"BOSS PARKER, SERVANT OF THE SYNDICATE."

"WIDOW OF ELUM BLOOM."

"I OFFER YOU A PACT."

"I OFFER TO GIVE YOU THE ALL-STAR, ROY KEANE, LAST OF THE FLYING 47TH."

"YOU GIVE ME THE BUTCHER."

SO THE SHERIFF FOR THE BUTCHER.

ANYTHING ELSE?

ONE QUESTION.

"THAT THING STILL WORK?"

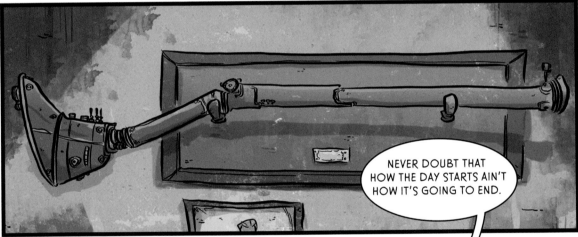

NEVER DOUBT THAT HOW THE DAY STARTS AIN'T HOW IT'S GOING TO END.

AND THANK YOUR LUCKY STARS FOR FORTUITOUS TURNS OF BLOODY EVENTS.

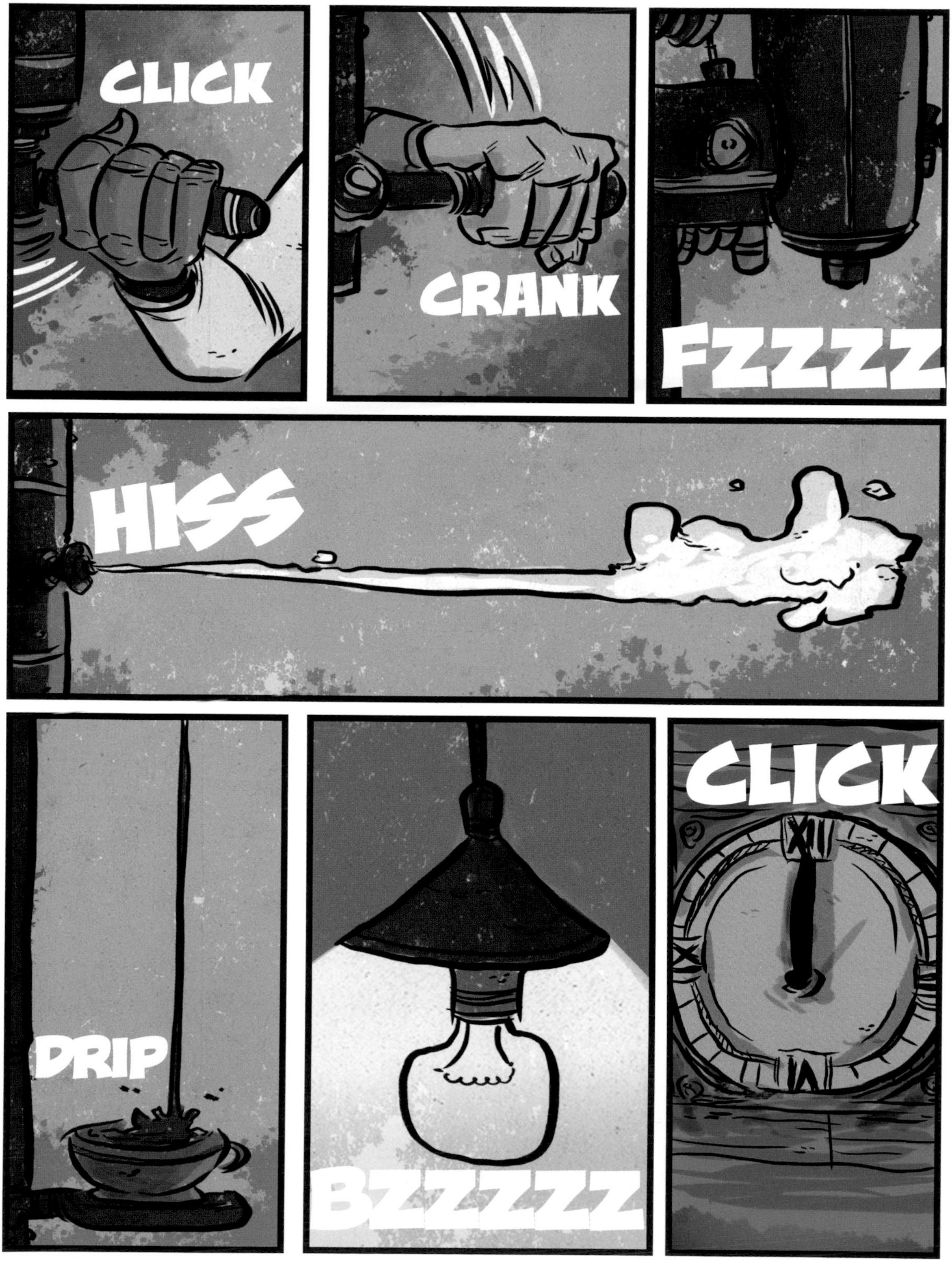
CLICK
CRANK
FZZZZ
HISS
DRIP
BZZZZZ
CLICK

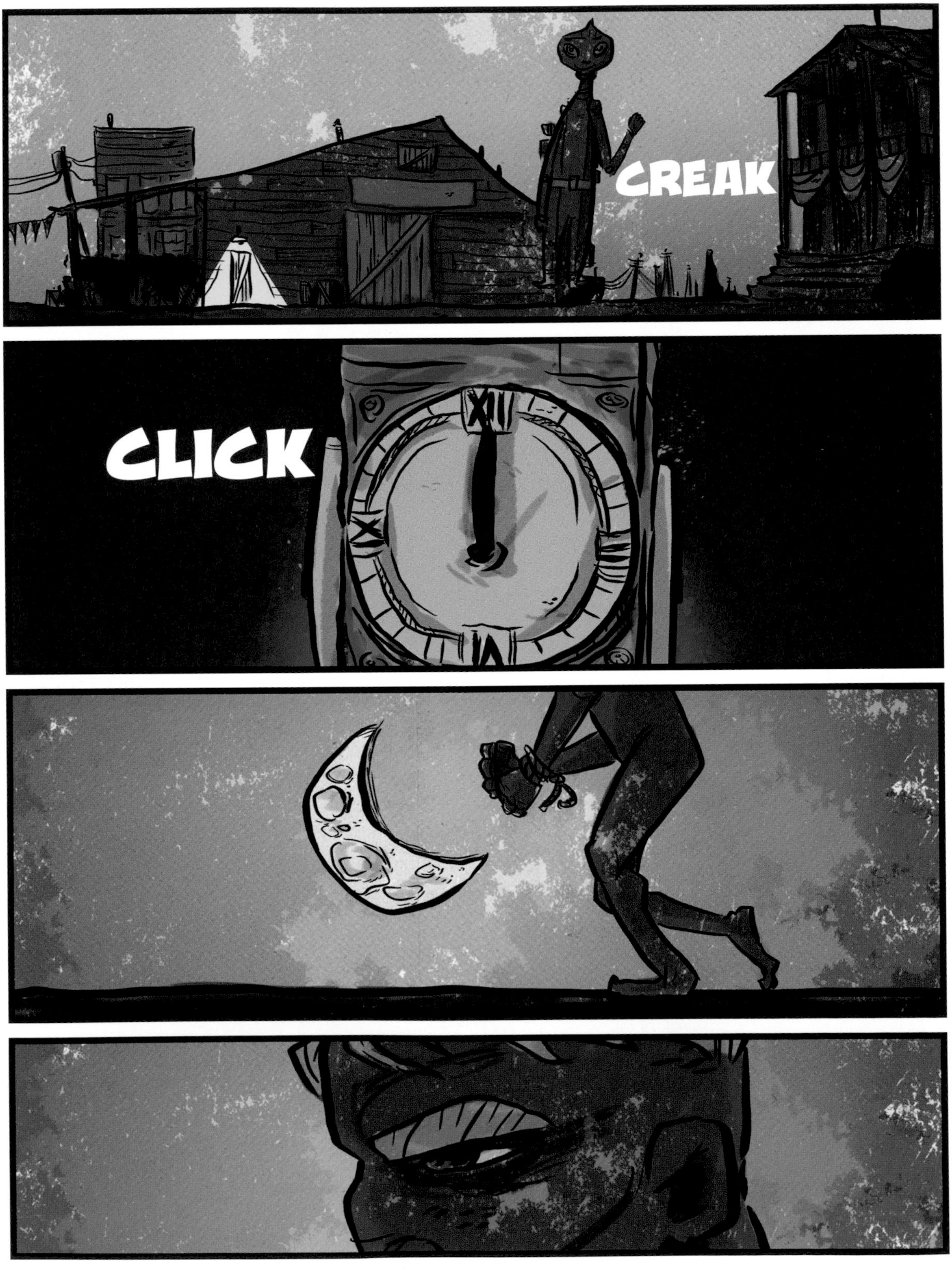
CREAK
CLICK

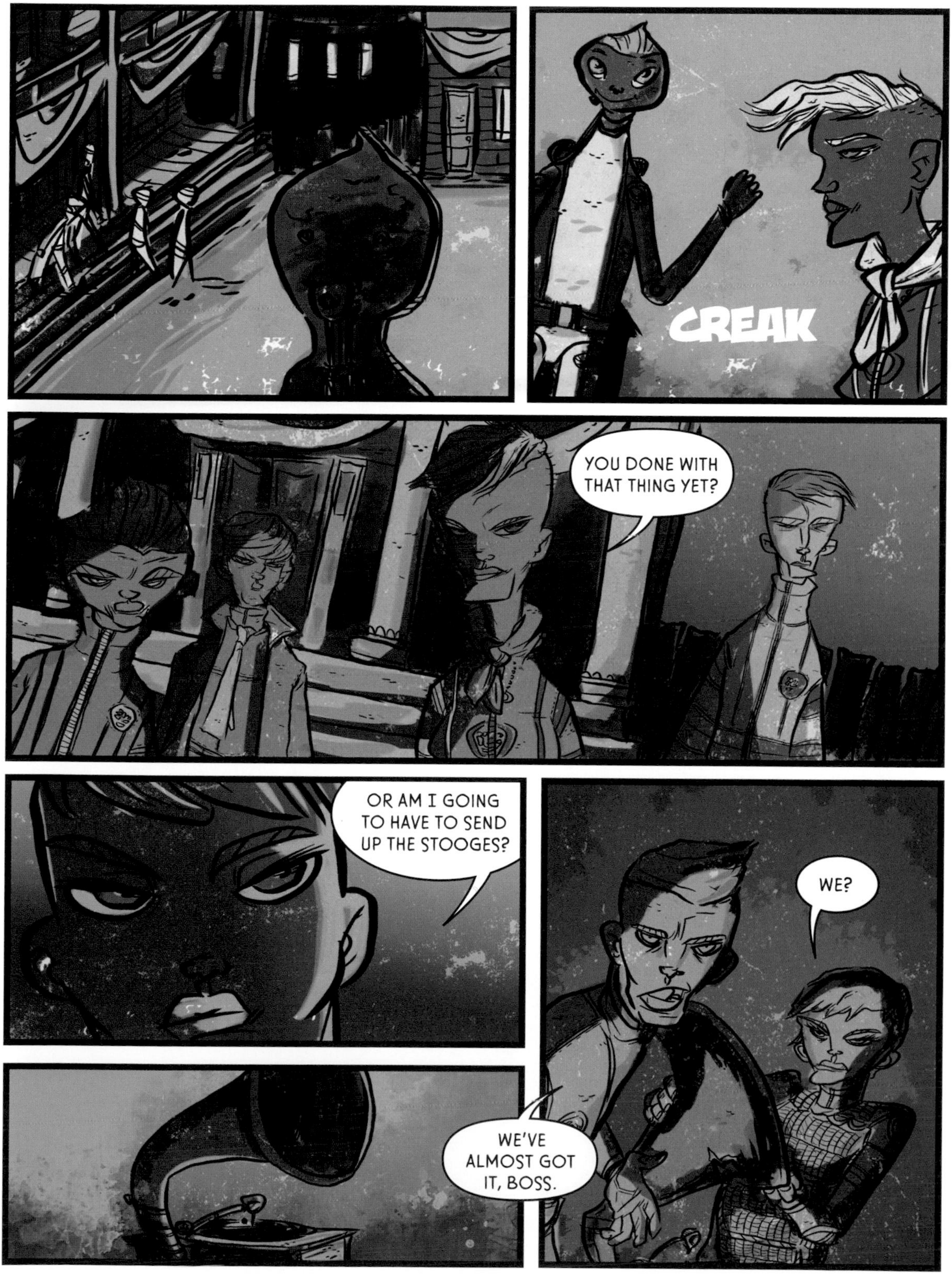
CREAK
YOU DONE WITH THAT THING YET?
OR AM I GOING TO HAVE TO SEND UP THE STOOGES?
WE?
WE'VE ALMOST GOT IT, BOSS.

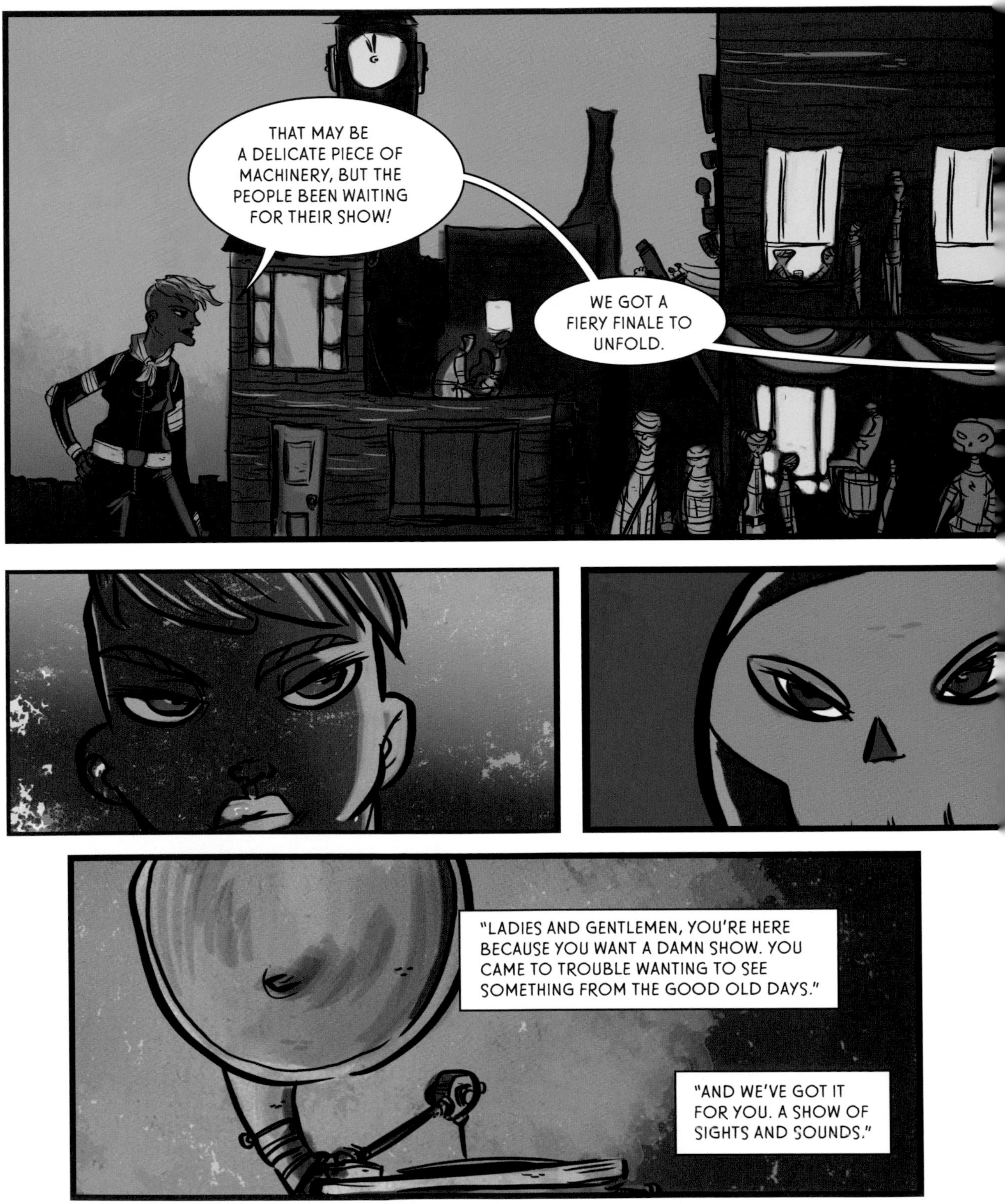
THAT MAY BE A DELICATE PIECE OF MACHINERY, BUT THE PEOPLE BEEN WAITING FOR THEIR SHOW!
WE GOT A FIERY FINALE TO UNFOLD.
"LADIES AND GENTLEMEN, YOU'RE HERE BECAUSE YOU WANT A DAMN SHOW. YOU CAME TO TROUBLE WANTING TO SEE SOMETHING FROM THE GOOD OLD DAYS."
"AND WE'VE GOT IT FOR YOU. A SHOW OF SIGHTS AND SOUNDS."

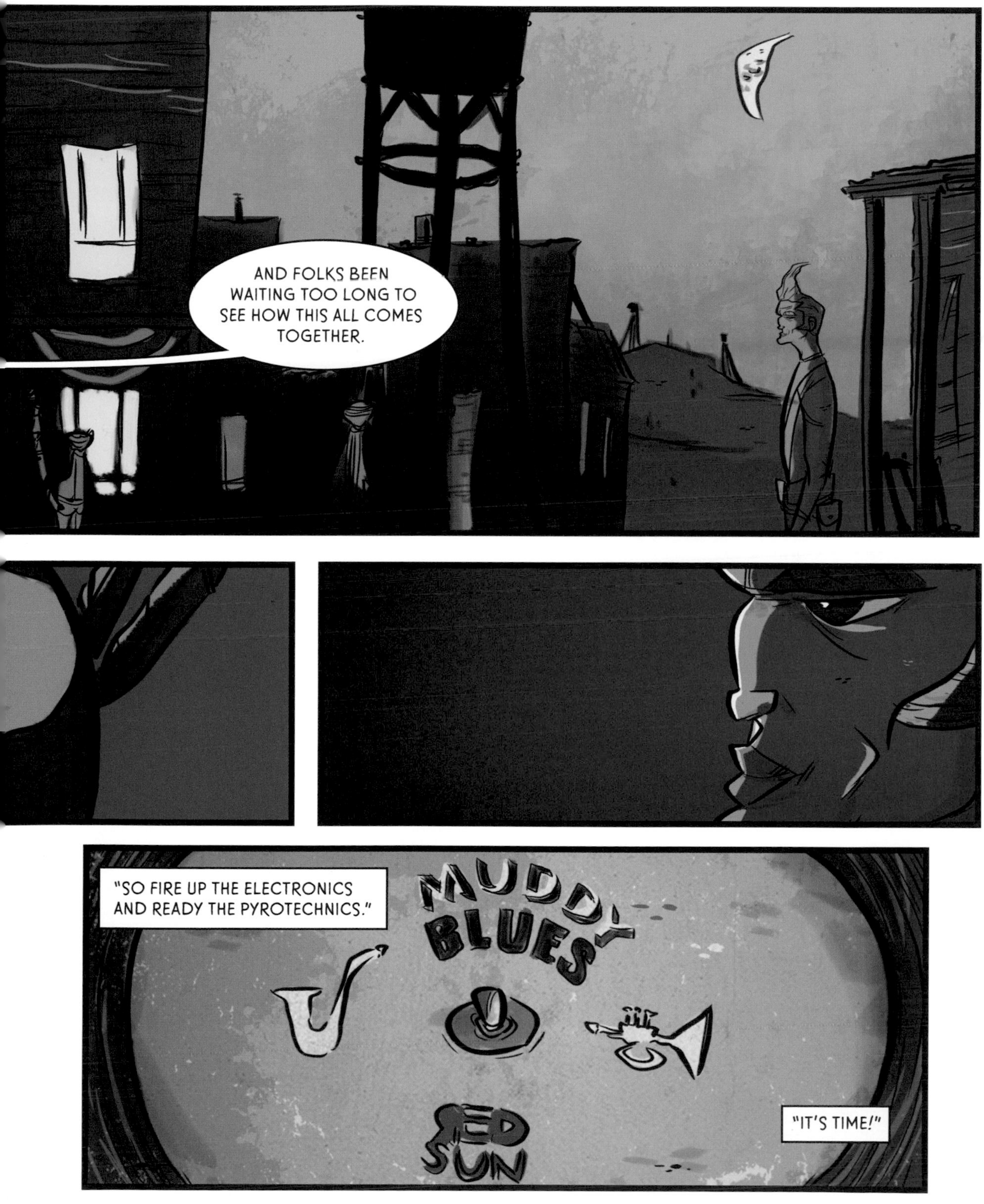
AND FOLKS BEEN WAITING TOO LONG TO SEE HOW THIS ALL COMES TOGETHER.
"SO FIRE UP THE ELECTRONICS AND READY THE PYROTECHNICS."
MUDDY BLUES
RED SUN
"IT'S TIME!"

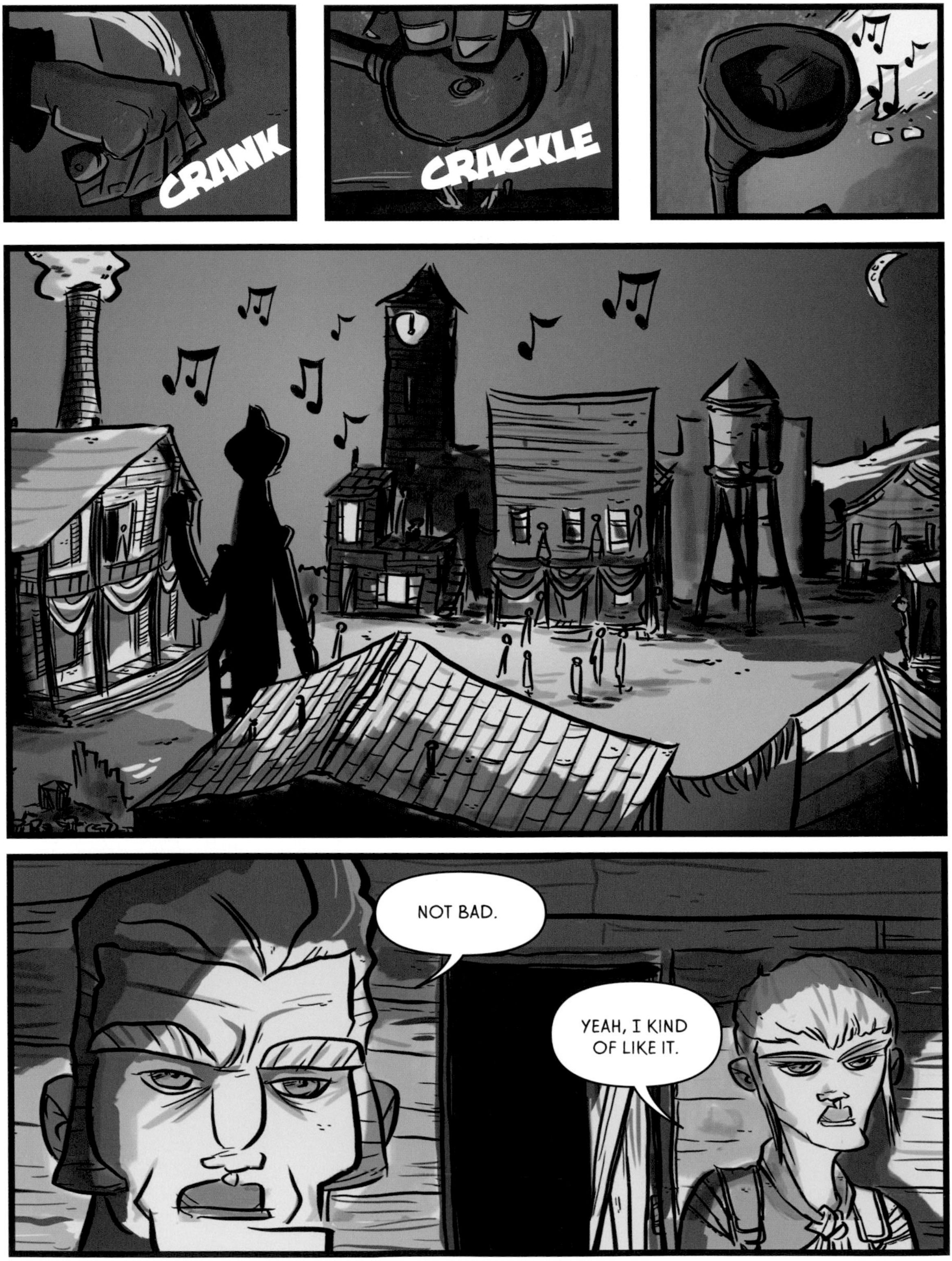
CRANK
CRACKLE
NOT BAD.
YEAH, I KIND OF LIKE IT.

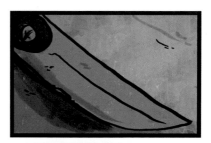

IT'S TIME, CHARLIE.

"TIME FOR A CHANGE."

"TIME TO SEE IT THROUGH."

"TIME TO START ANEW."

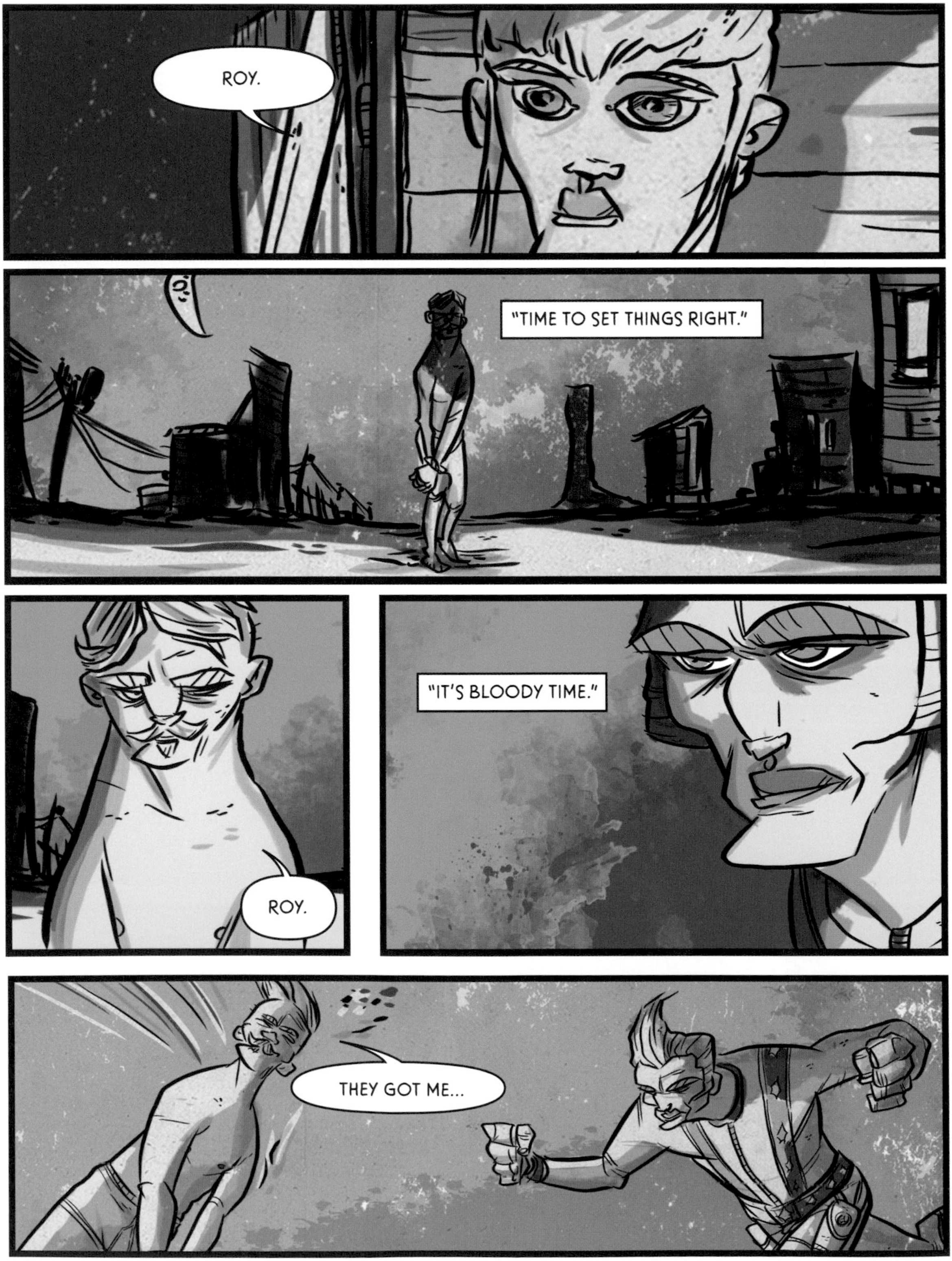
ROY.
"TIME TO SET THINGS RIGHT."
ROY.
"IT'S BLOODY TIME."
THEY GOT ME...

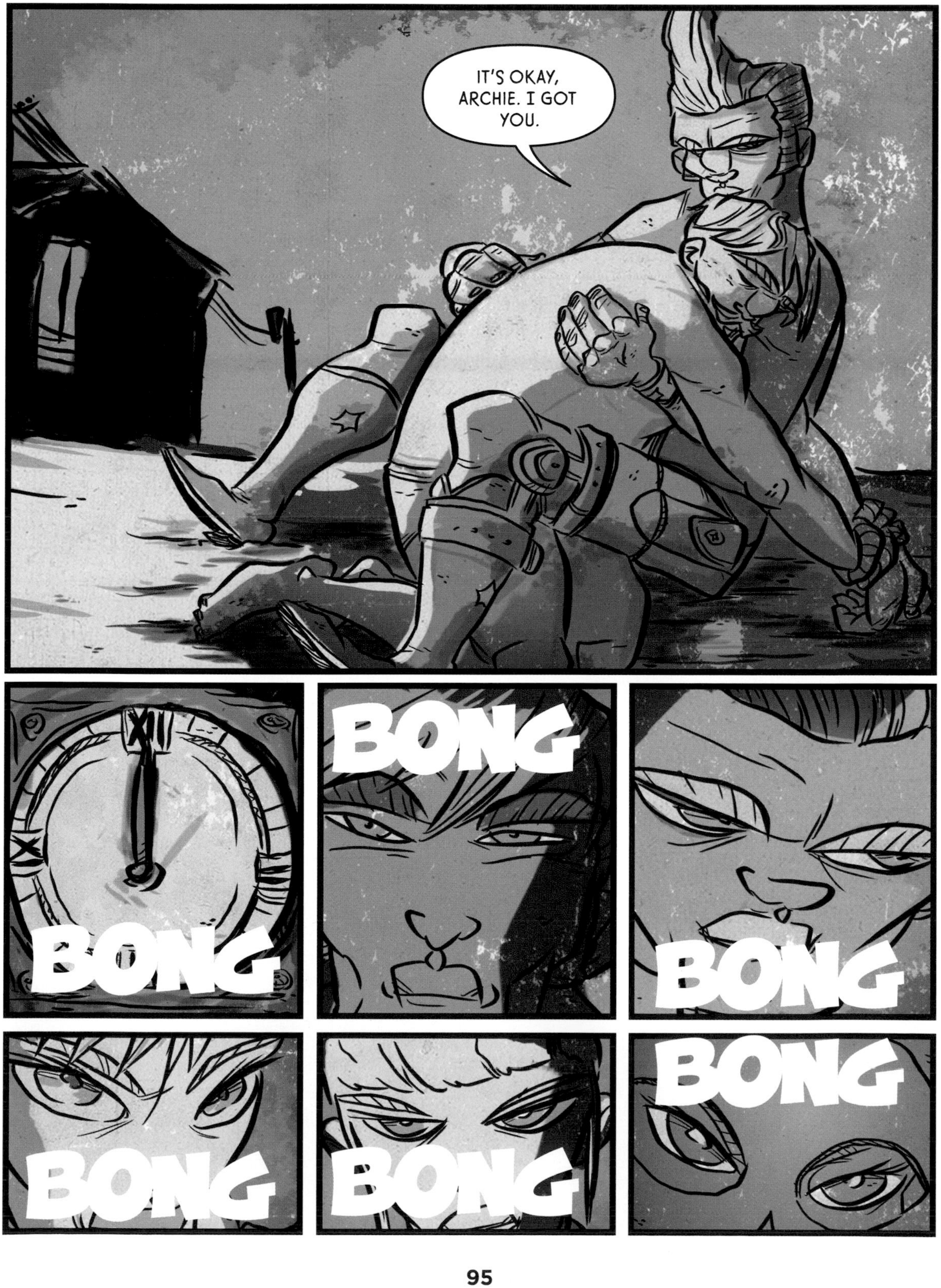

IT'S OKAY, ARCHIE. I GOT YOU.
BONG
BONG
BONG
BONG
BONG
BONG

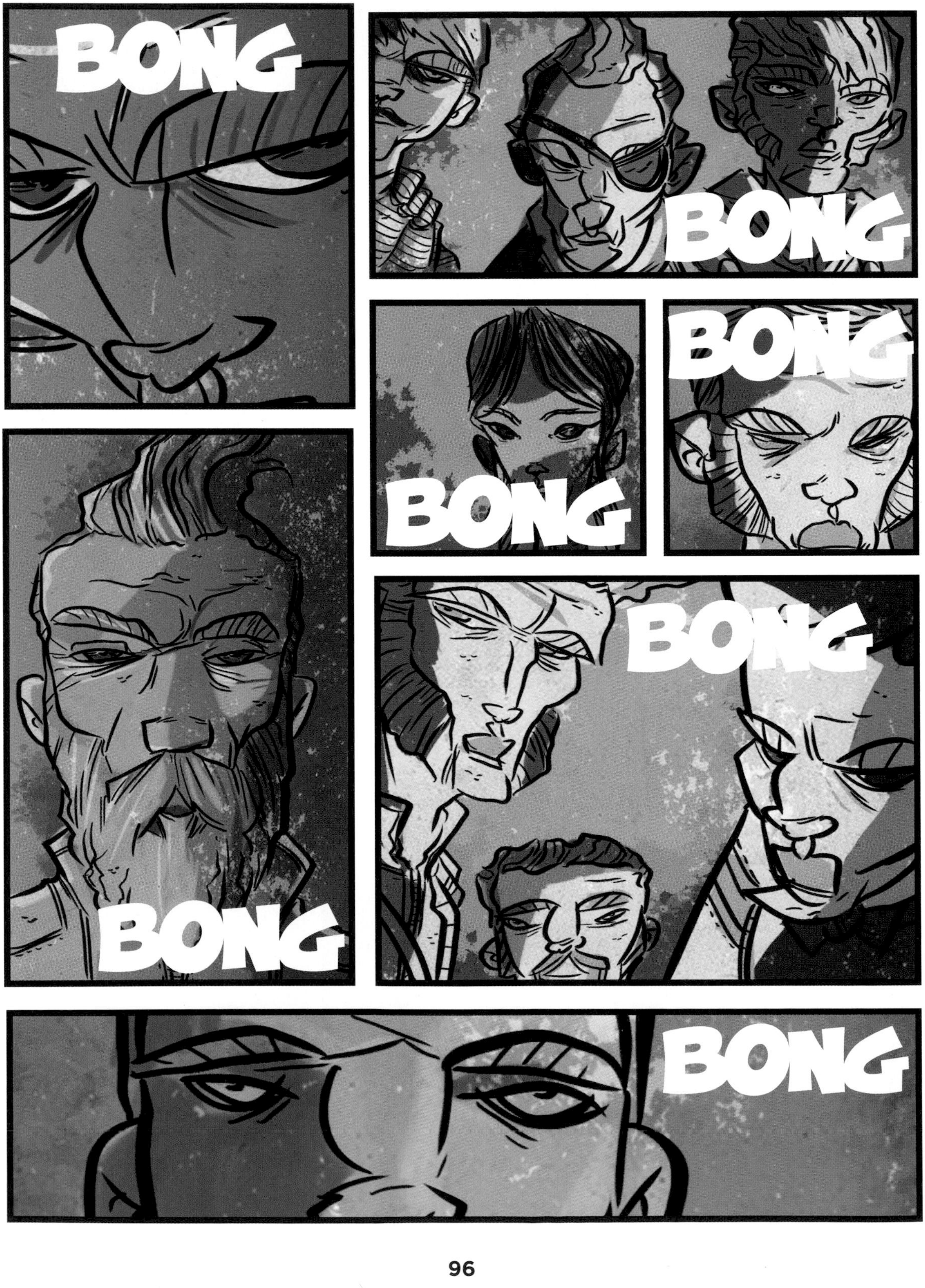
BONG
BONG
BONG
BONG
BONG
BONG
BONG

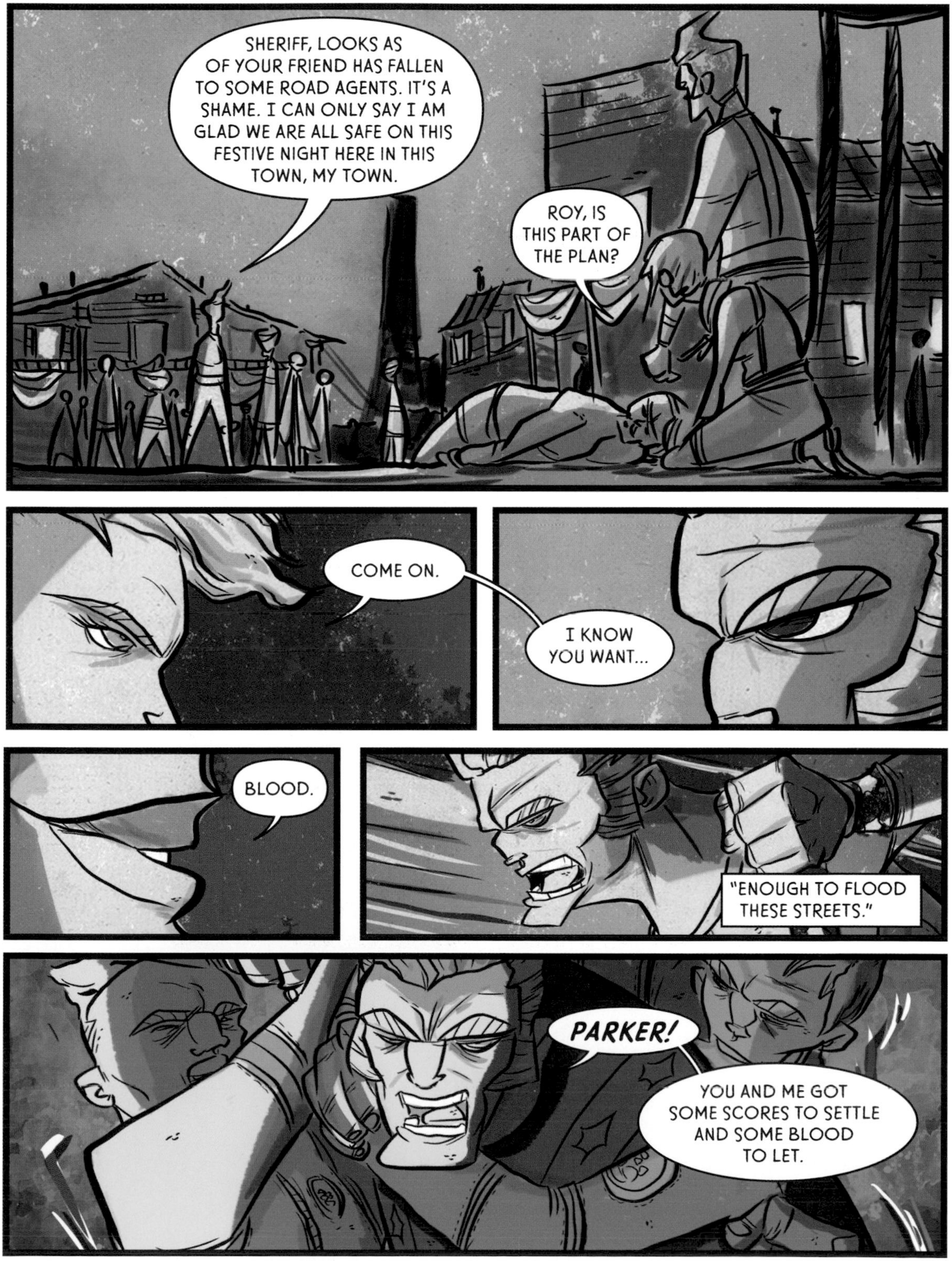
SHERIFF, LOOKS AS OF YOUR FRIEND HAS FALLEN TO SOME ROAD AGENTS. IT'S A SHAME. I CAN ONLY SAY I AM GLAD WE ARE ALL SAFE ON THIS FESTIVE NIGHT HERE IN THIS TOWN, MY TOWN.
ROY, IS THIS PART OF THE PLAN?
COME ON.
I KNOW YOU WANT...
BLOOD.
"ENOUGH TO FLOOD THESE STREETS."
PARKER!
YOU AND ME GOT SOME SCORES TO SETTLE AND SOME BLOOD TO LET.

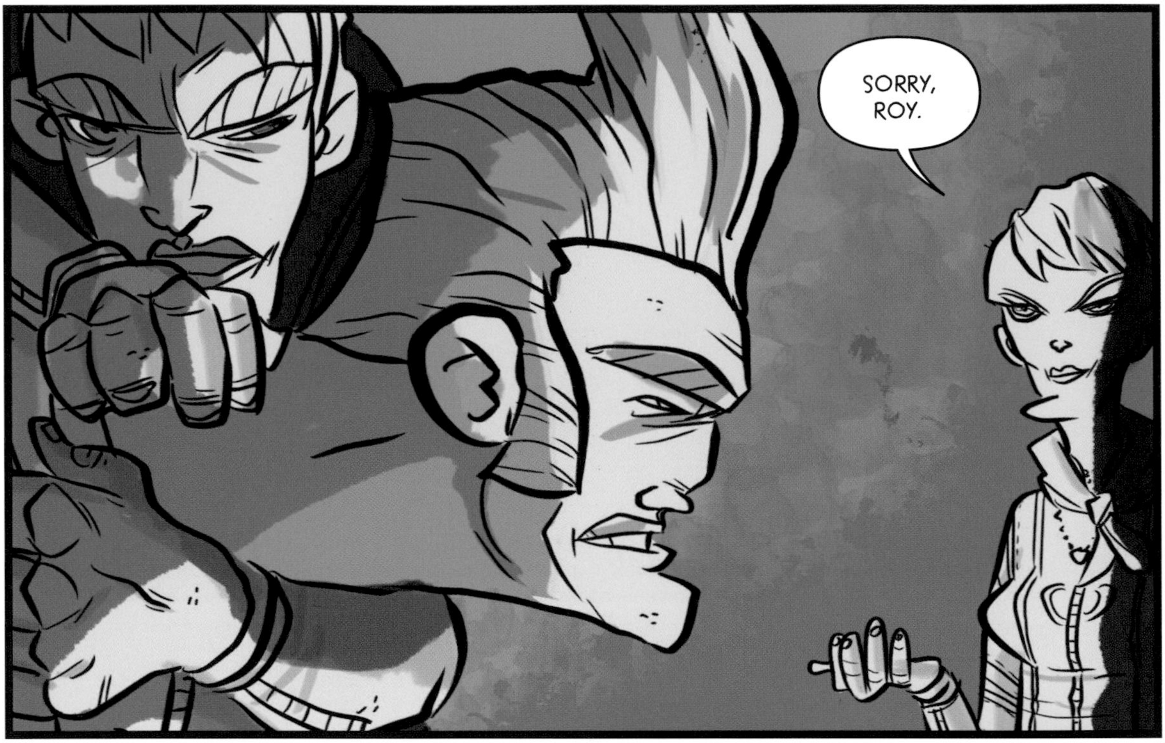
SORRY, ROY.

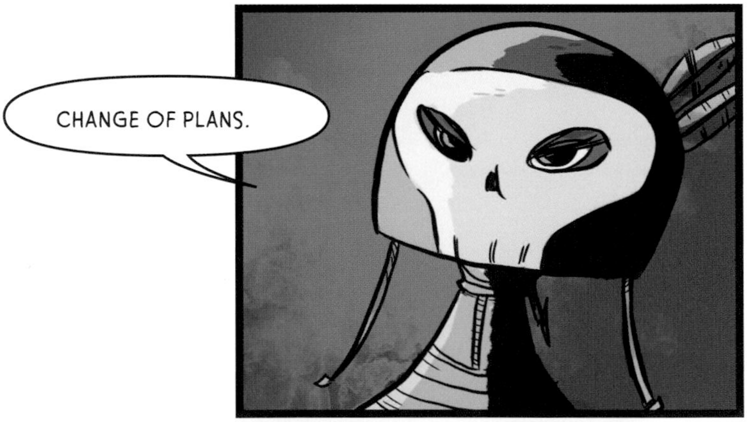
CHANGE OF PLANS.

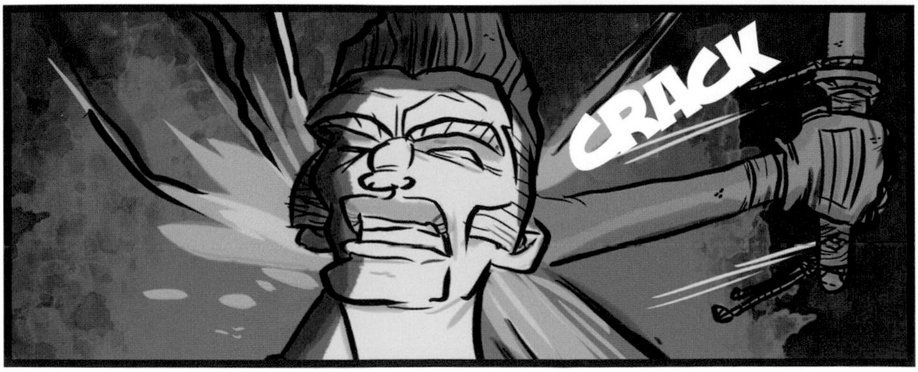
CRACK

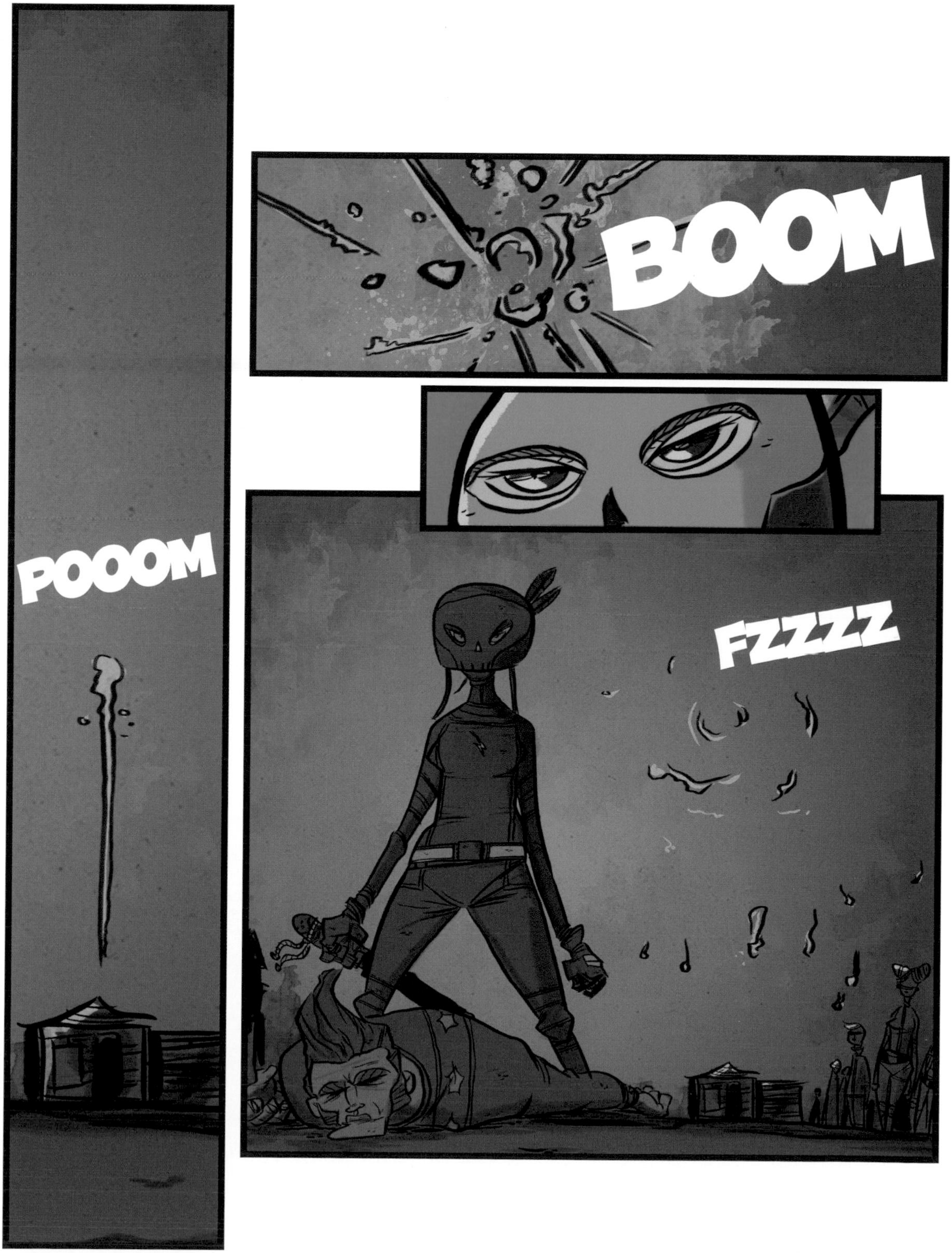
POOOM
BOOM
FZZZZ

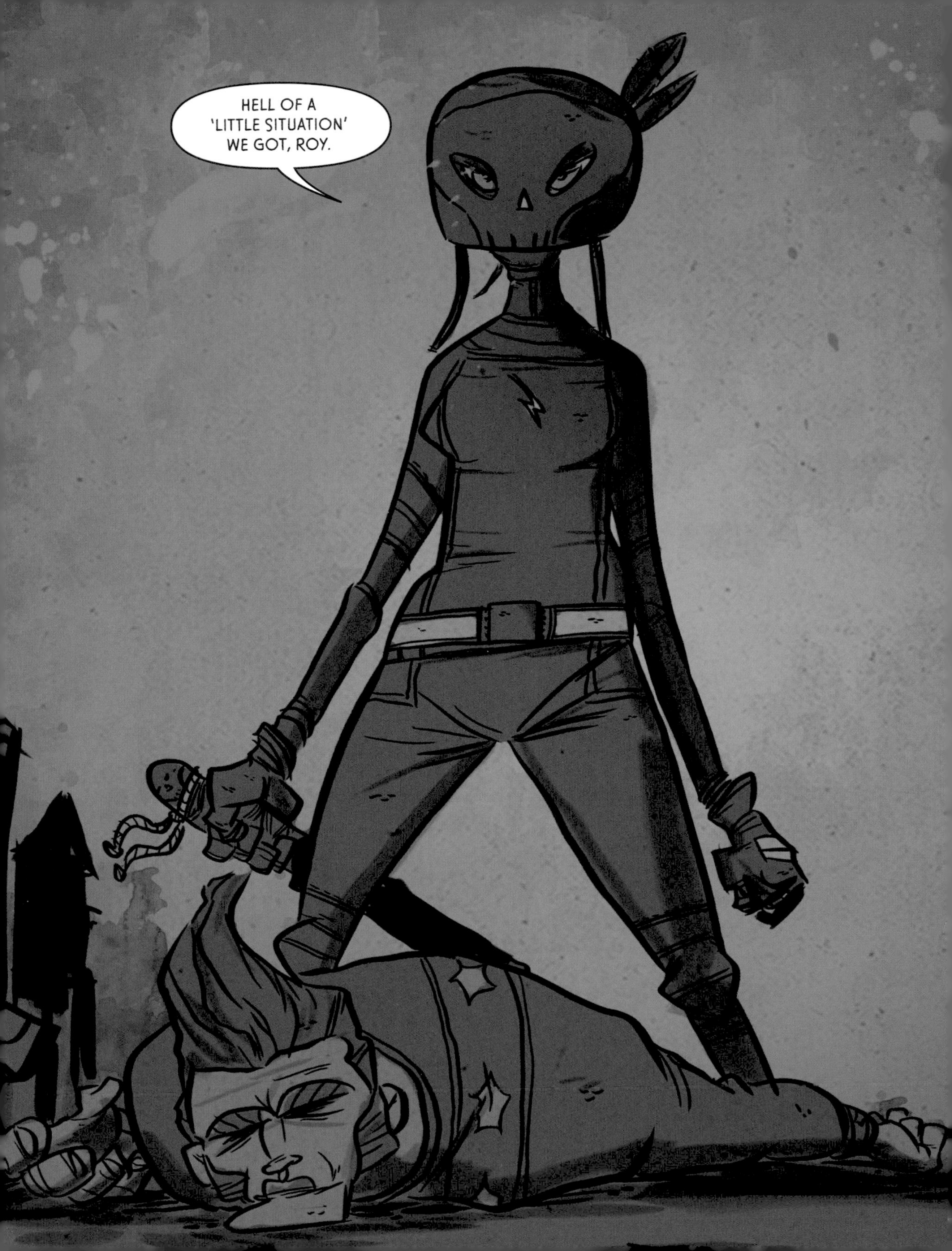
HELL OF A 'LITTLE SITUATION' WE GOT, ROY.

SHADOWS
and
RUST

CHAPTER FOUR

MOTORCYCLE SAMURAI

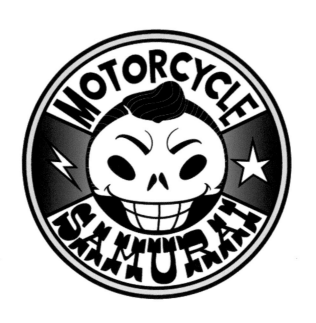

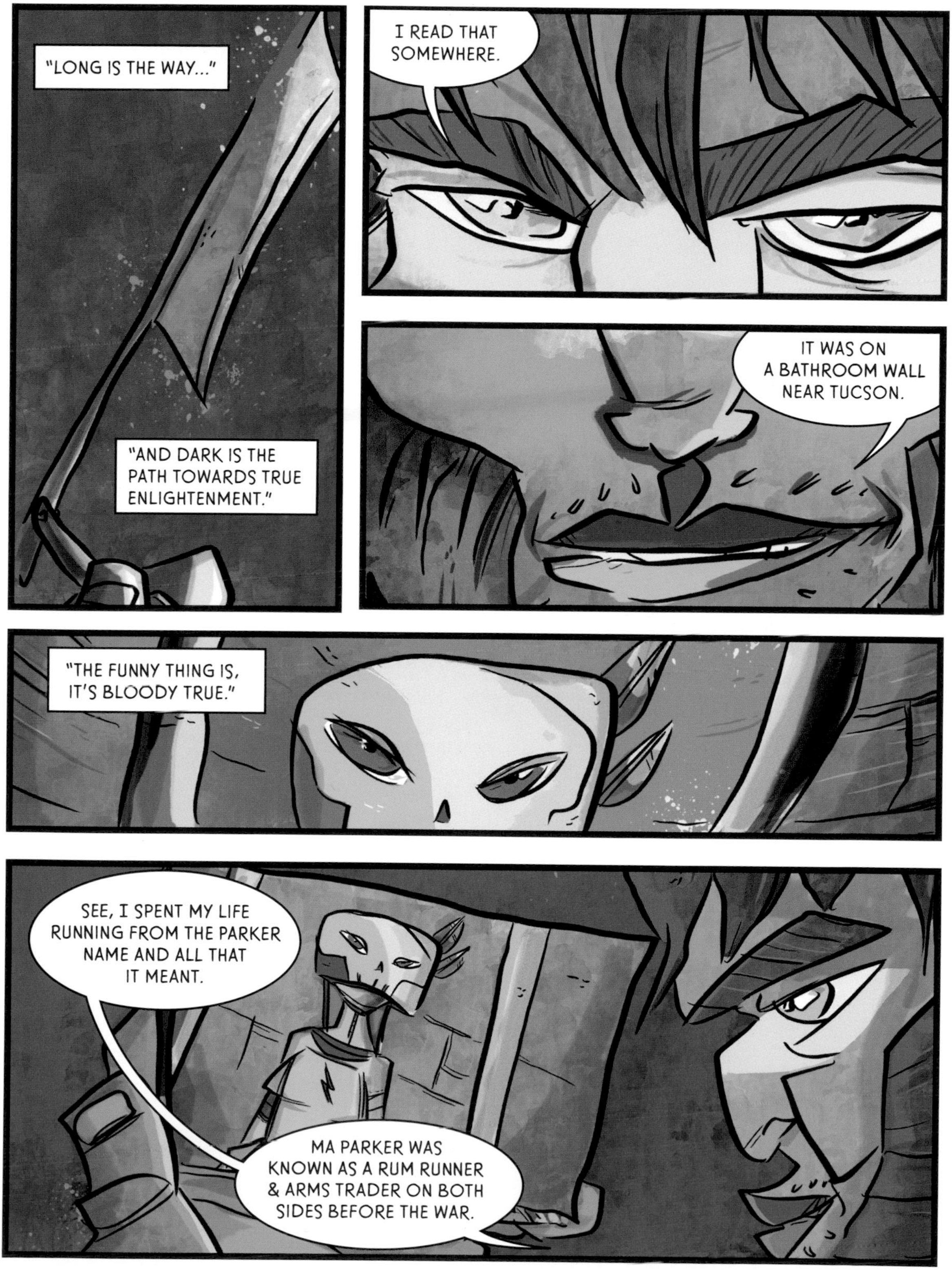
"LONG IS THE WAY..."
I READ THAT SOMEWHERE.
IT WAS ON A BATHROOM WALL NEAR TUCSON.
"AND DARK IS THE PATH TOWARDS TRUE ENLIGHTENMENT."
"THE FUNNY THING IS, IT'S BLOODY TRUE."
SEE, I SPENT MY LIFE RUNNING FROM THE PARKER NAME AND ALL THAT IT MEANT.
MA PARKER WAS KNOWN AS A RUM RUNNER & ARMS TRADER ON BOTH SIDES BEFORE THE WAR.

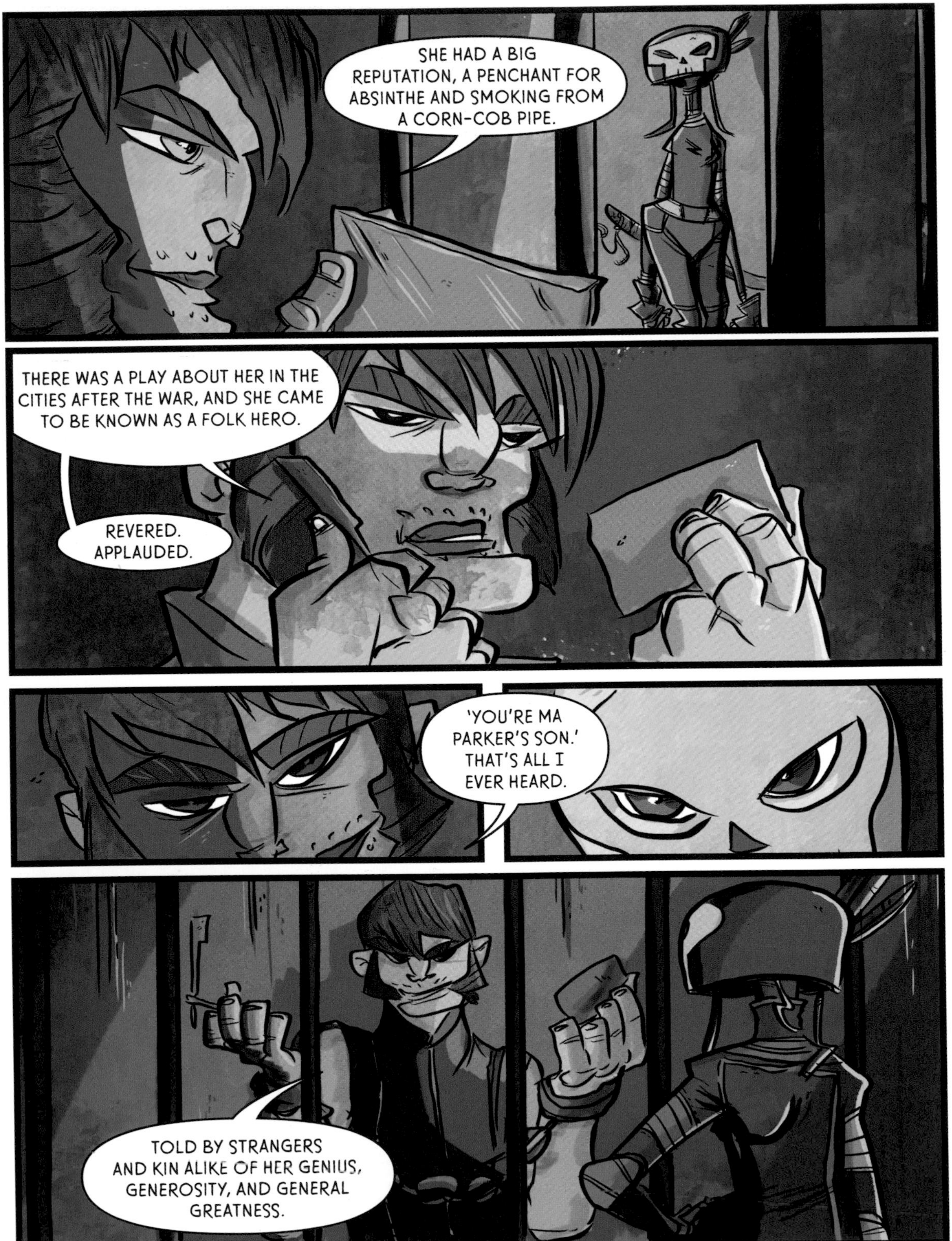
SHE HAD A BIG REPUTATION, A PENCHANT FOR ABSINTHE AND SMOKING FROM A CORN-COB PIPE.
THERE WAS A PLAY ABOUT HER IN THE CITIES AFTER THE WAR, AND SHE CAME TO BE KNOWN AS A FOLK HERO.
REVERED. APPLAUDED.
'YOU'RE MA PARKER'S SON.' THAT'S ALL I EVER HEARD.
TOLD BY STRANGERS AND KIN ALIKE OF HER GENIUS, GENEROSITY, AND GENERAL GREATNESS.

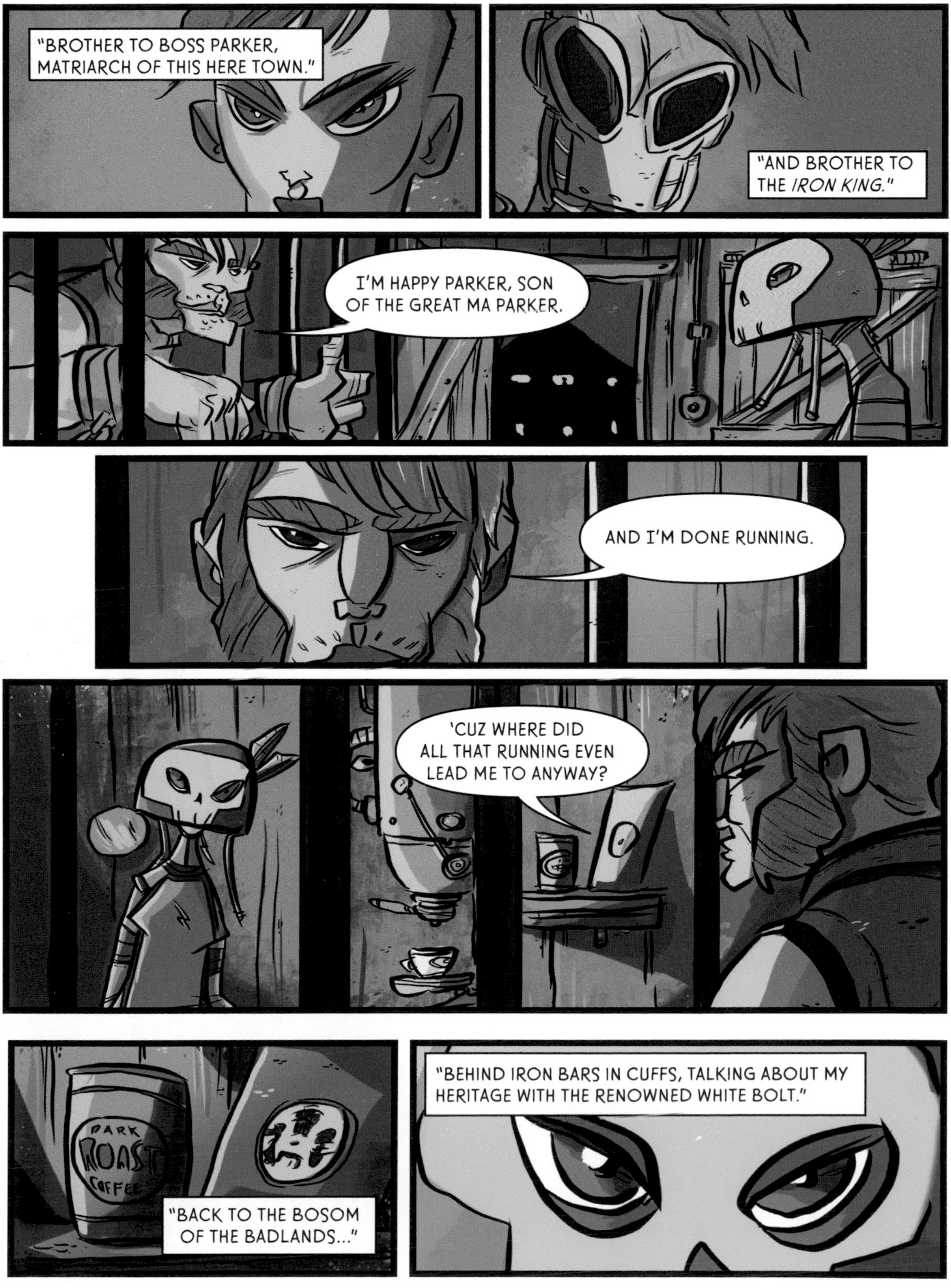
"BROTHER TO BOSS PARKER, MATRIARCH OF THIS HERE TOWN."
"AND BROTHER TO THE *IRON KING.*"
I'M HAPPY PARKER, SON OF THE GREAT MA PARKER.
AND I'M DONE RUNNING.
'CUZ WHERE DID ALL THAT RUNNING EVEN LEAD ME TO ANYWAY?
DARK ROAST COFFEE
"BACK TO THE BOSOM OF THE BADLANDS..."
"BEHIND IRON BARS IN CUFFS, TALKING ABOUT MY HERITAGE WITH THE RENOWNED WHITE BOLT."

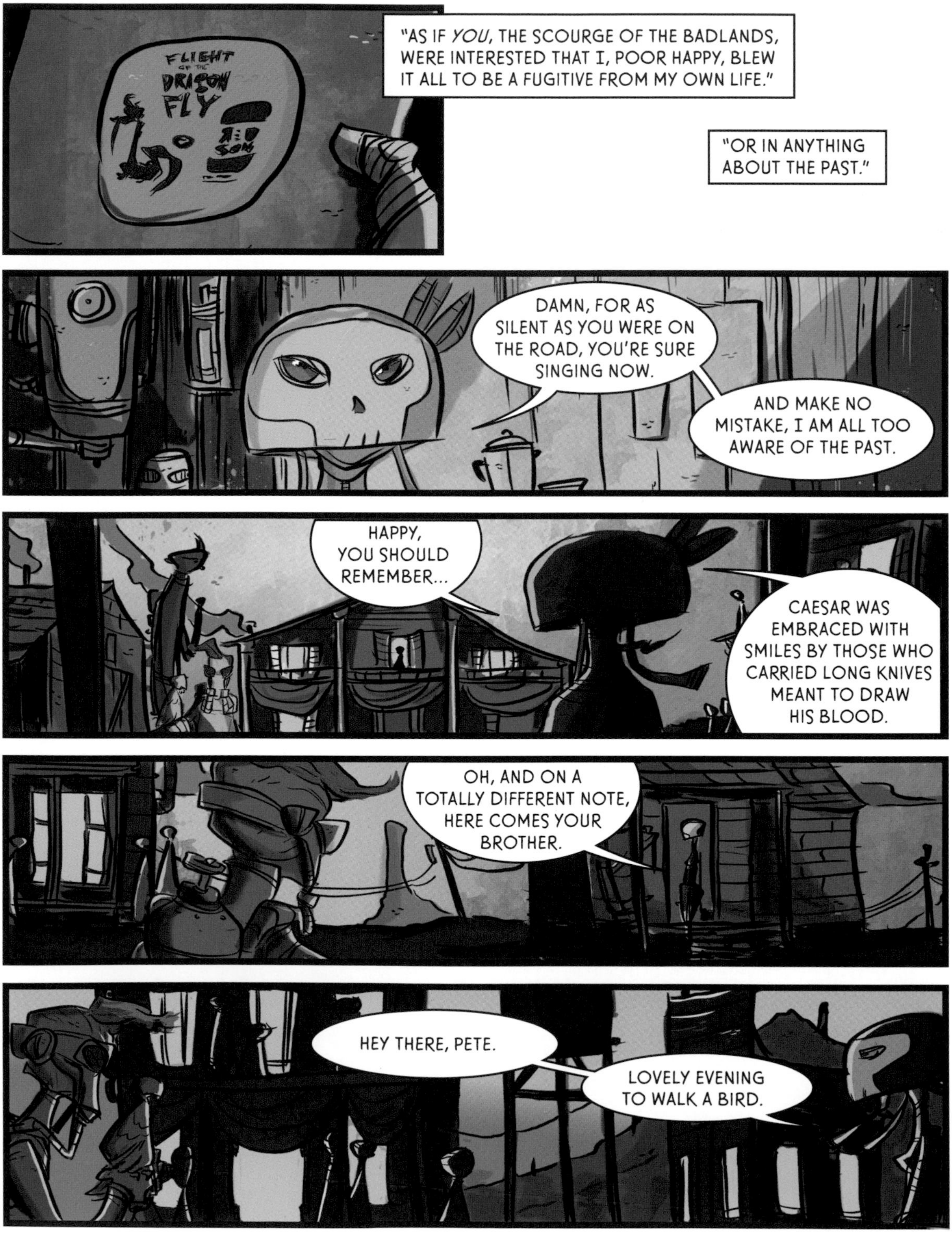
FLIGHT OF THE DRAGON FLY
"AS IF *YOU*, THE SCOURGE OF THE BADLANDS, WERE INTERESTED THAT I, POOR HAPPY, BLEW IT ALL TO BE A FUGITIVE FROM MY OWN LIFE."
"OR IN ANYTHING ABOUT THE PAST."
DAMN, FOR AS SILENT AS YOU WERE ON THE ROAD, YOU'RE SURE SINGING NOW.
AND MAKE NO MISTAKE, I AM ALL TOO AWARE OF THE PAST.
HAPPY, YOU SHOULD REMEMBER...
CAESAR WAS EMBRACED WITH SMILES BY THOSE WHO CARRIED LONG KNIVES MEANT TO DRAW HIS BLOOD.
OH, AND ON A TOTALLY DIFFERENT NOTE, HERE COMES YOUR BROTHER.
HEY THERE, PETE.
LOVELY EVENING TO WALK A BIRD.

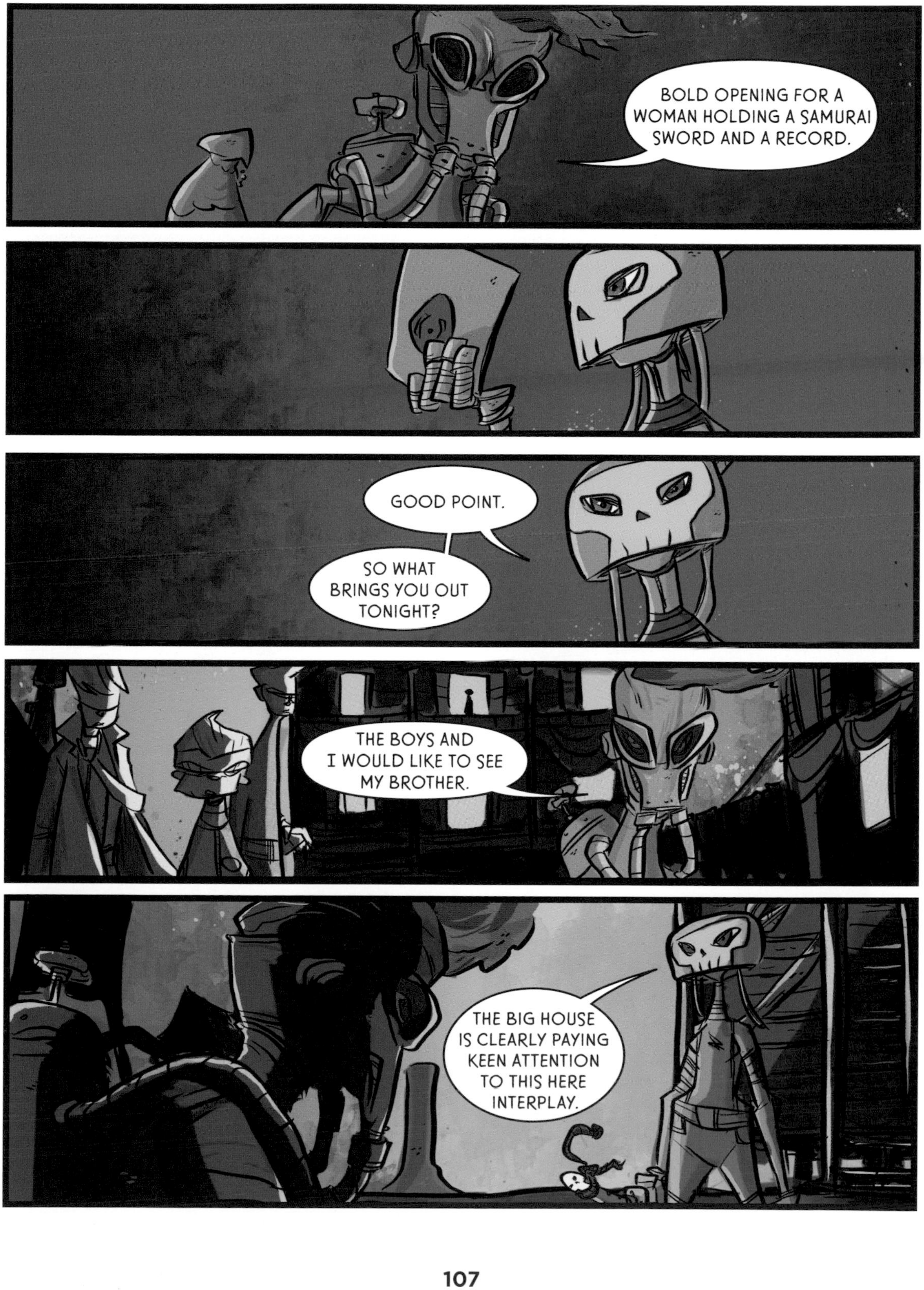
BOLD OPENING FOR A WOMAN HOLDING A SAMURAI SWORD AND A RECORD.
GOOD POINT.
SO WHAT BRINGS YOU OUT TONIGHT?
THE BOYS AND I WOULD LIKE TO SEE MY BROTHER.
THE BIG HOUSE IS CLEARLY PAYING KEEN ATTENTION TO THIS HERE INTERPLAY.

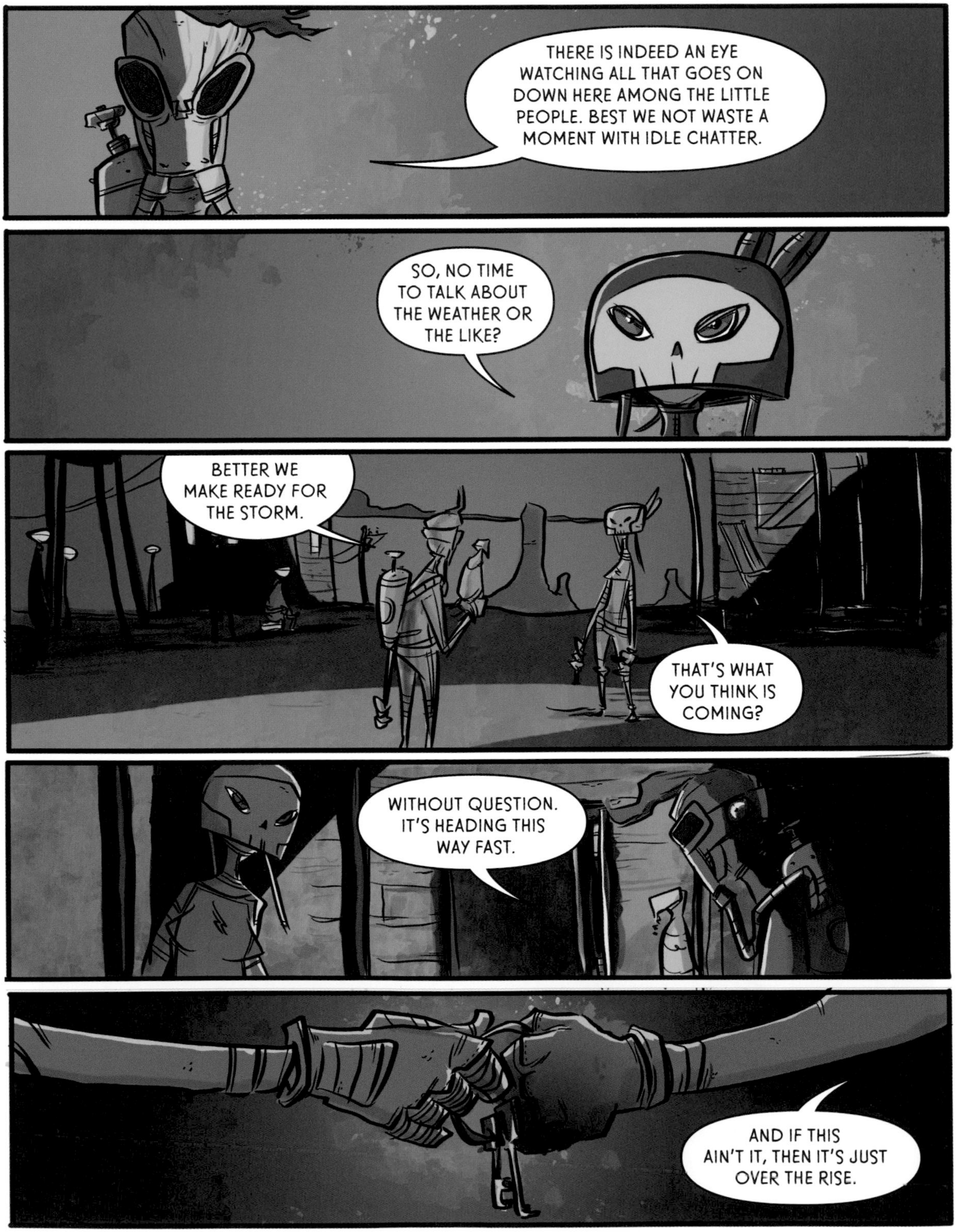
THERE IS INDEED AN EYE WATCHING ALL THAT GOES ON DOWN HERE AMONG THE LITTLE PEOPLE. BEST WE NOT WASTE A MOMENT WITH IDLE CHATTER.
SO, NO TIME TO TALK ABOUT THE WEATHER OR THE LIKE?
BETTER WE MAKE READY FOR THE STORM.
THAT'S WHAT YOU THINK IS COMING?
WITHOUT QUESTION. IT'S HEADING THIS WAY FAST.
AND IF THIS AIN'T IT, THEN IT'S JUST OVER THE RISE.

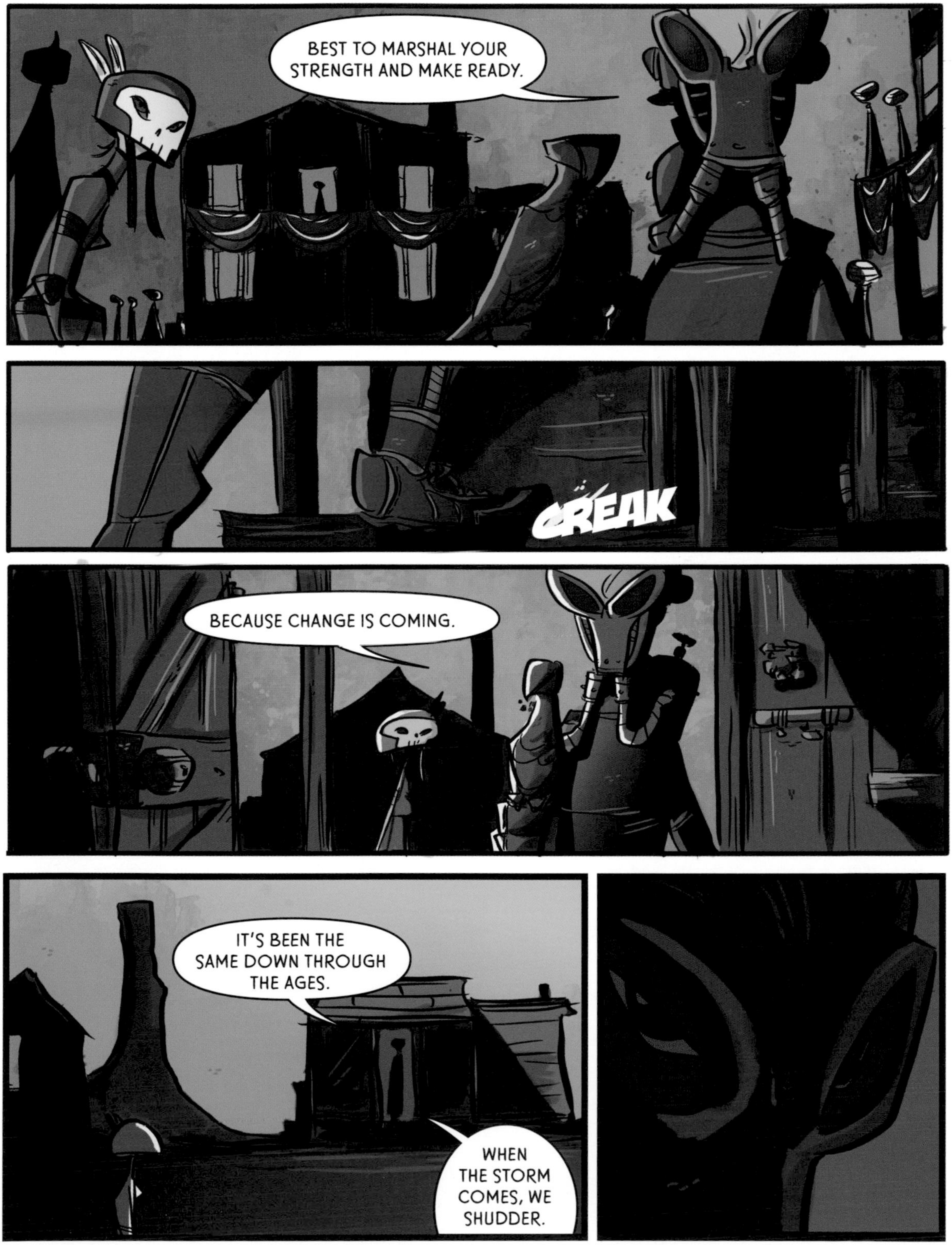
BEST TO MARSHAL YOUR STRENGTH AND MAKE READY.
CREAK
BECAUSE CHANGE IS COMING.
IT'S BEEN THE SAME DOWN THROUGH THE AGES.
WHEN THE STORM COMES, WE SHUDDER.

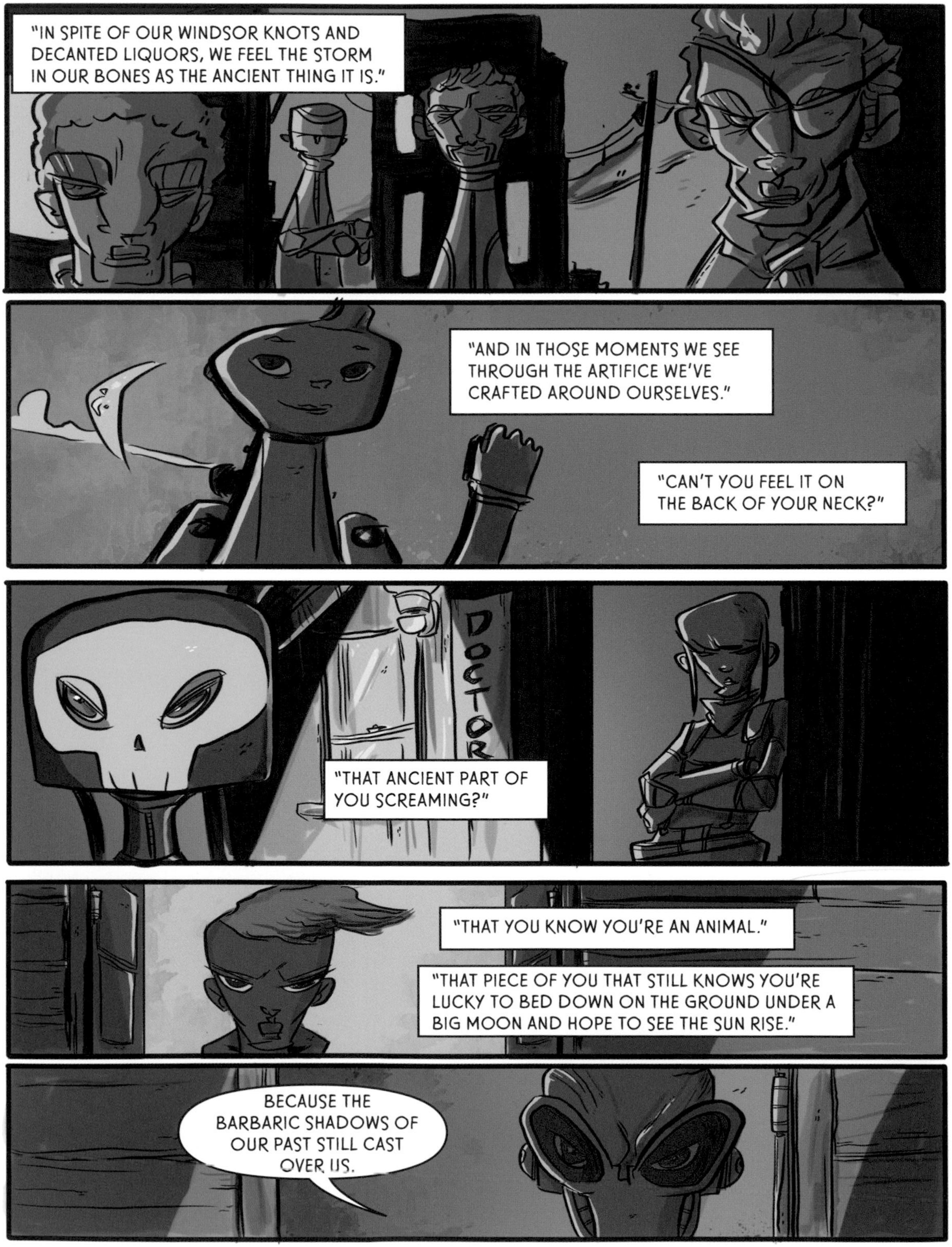
"IN SPITE OF OUR WINDSOR KNOTS AND DECANTED LIQUORS, WE FEEL THE STORM IN OUR BONES AS THE ANCIENT THING IT IS."
"AND IN THOSE MOMENTS WE SEE THROUGH THE ARTIFICE WE'VE CRAFTED AROUND OURSELVES."
"CAN'T YOU FEEL IT ON THE BACK OF YOUR NECK?"
DOCTOR
"THAT ANCIENT PART OF YOU SCREAMING?"
"THAT YOU KNOW YOU'RE AN ANIMAL."
"THAT PIECE OF YOU THAT STILL KNOWS YOU'RE LUCKY TO BED DOWN ON THE GROUND UNDER A BIG MOON AND HOPE TO SEE THE SUN RISE."
BECAUSE THE BARBARIC SHADOWS OF OUR PAST STILL CAST OVER US.

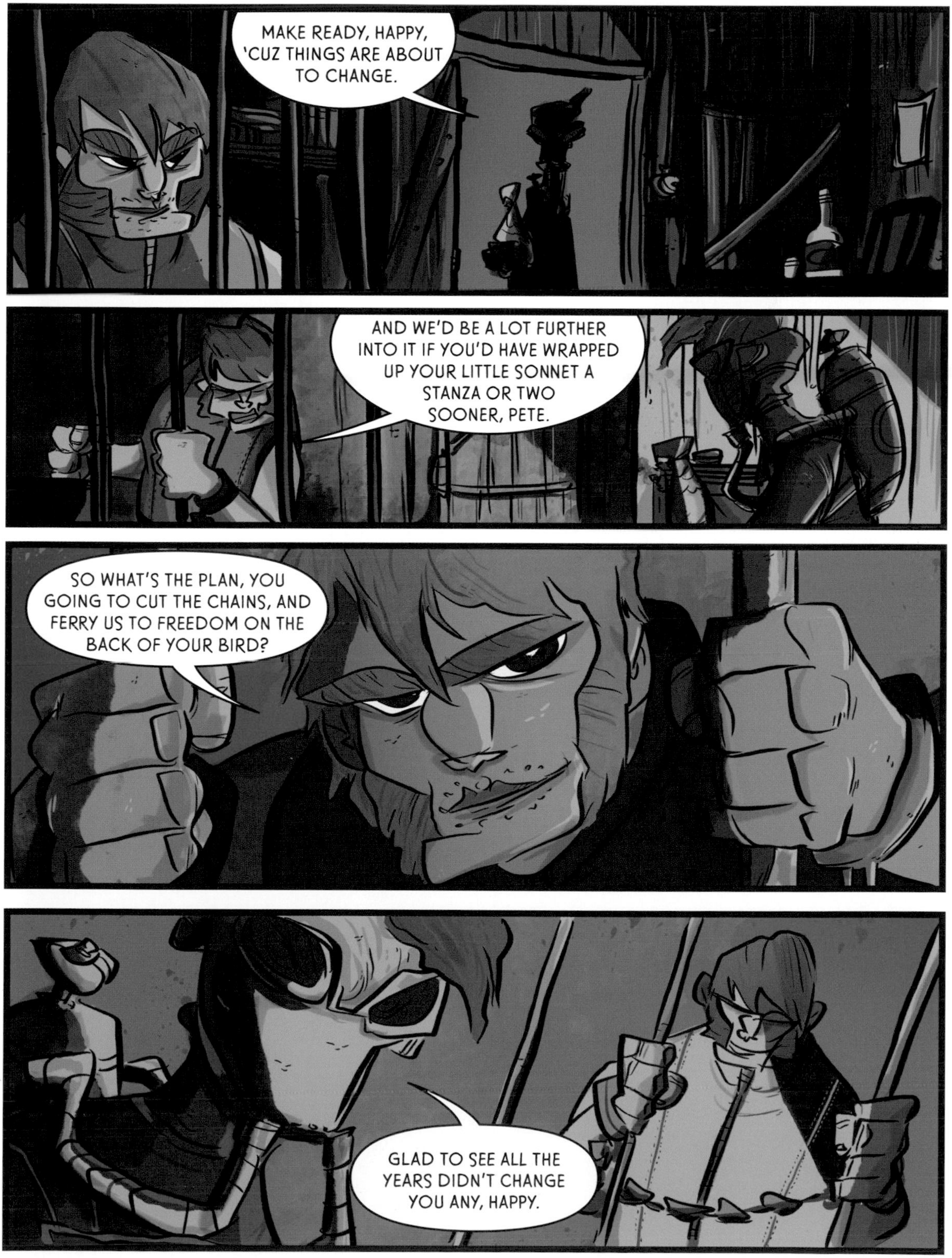
MAKE READY, HAPPY, 'CUZ THINGS ARE ABOUT TO CHANGE.
AND WE'D BE A LOT FURTHER INTO IT IF YOU'D HAVE WRAPPED UP YOUR LITTLE SONNET A STANZA OR TWO SOONER, PETE.
SO WHAT'S THE PLAN, YOU GOING TO CUT THE CHAINS, AND FERRY US TO FREEDOM ON THE BACK OF YOUR BIRD?
GLAD TO SEE ALL THE YEARS DIDN'T CHANGE YOU ANY, HAPPY.

YOU, TOO.

I AM HERE TO SET YOU FREE, HAPPY. COURTESY OF BOSS PARKER.

SHE'S WORRIED YOU'RE TIRED OF THE ROAD AND CAME BACK TO RAT HER OUT FOR THE MURDER SHE DID.

SHE REMEMBERS THE LESSON THE SYNDICATE HAD TO TEACH YOU FOR THAT SILVER TONGUE OF YOURS.

WHAT? YOU'RE GONNA SEW MY MOUTH SHUT AGAIN?

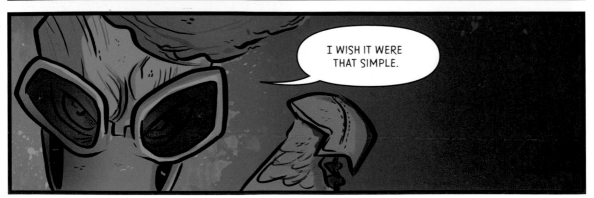

I WISH IT WERE THAT SIMPLE.

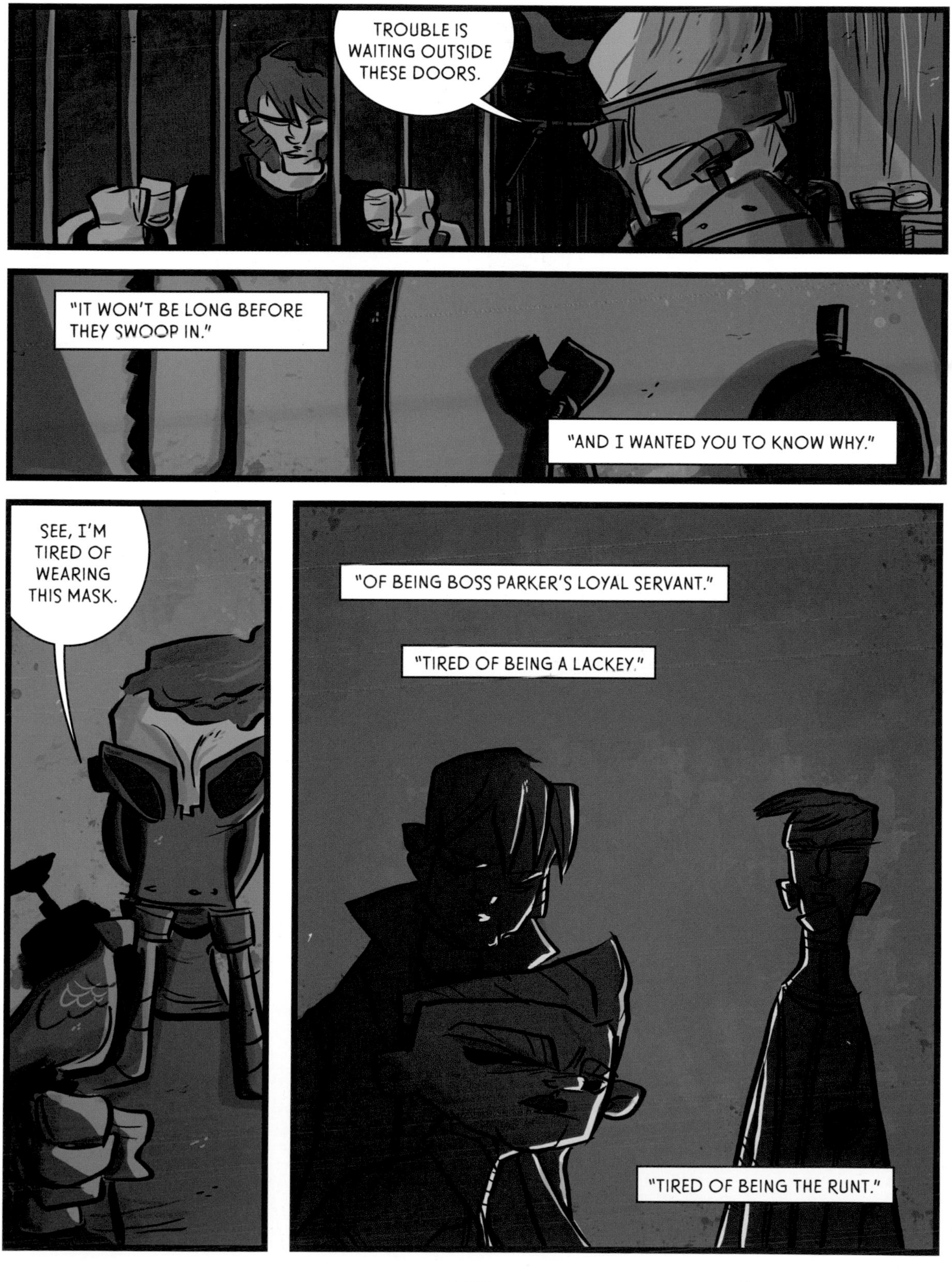
TROUBLE IS WAITING OUTSIDE THESE DOORS.
"IT WON'T BE LONG BEFORE THEY SWOOP IN."
"AND I WANTED YOU TO KNOW WHY."
SEE, I'M TIRED OF WEARING THIS MASK.
"OF BEING BOSS PARKER'S LOYAL SERVANT."
"TIRED OF BEING A LACKEY."
"TIRED OF BEING THE RUNT."

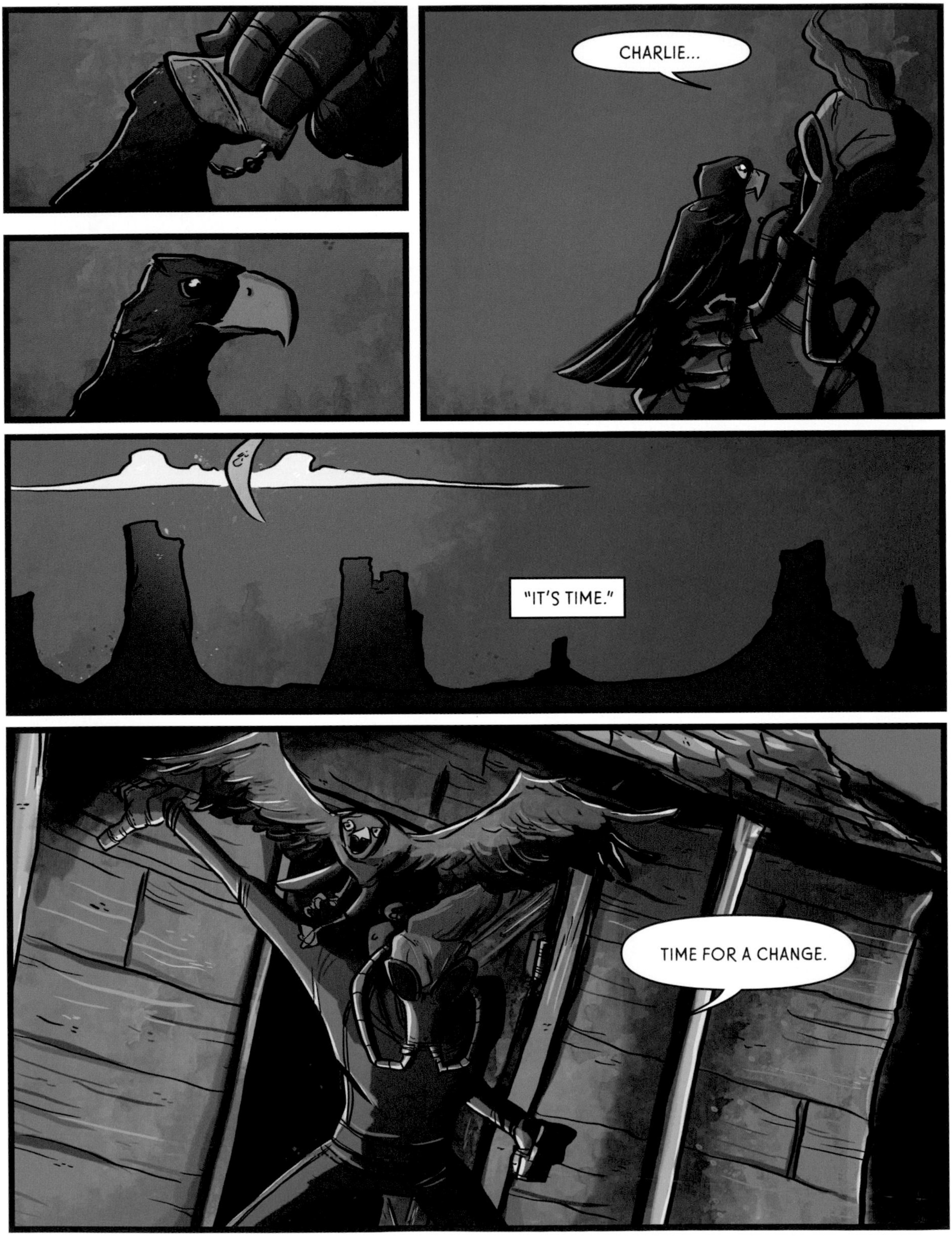
CHARLIE...
"IT'S TIME."
TIME FOR A CHANGE.

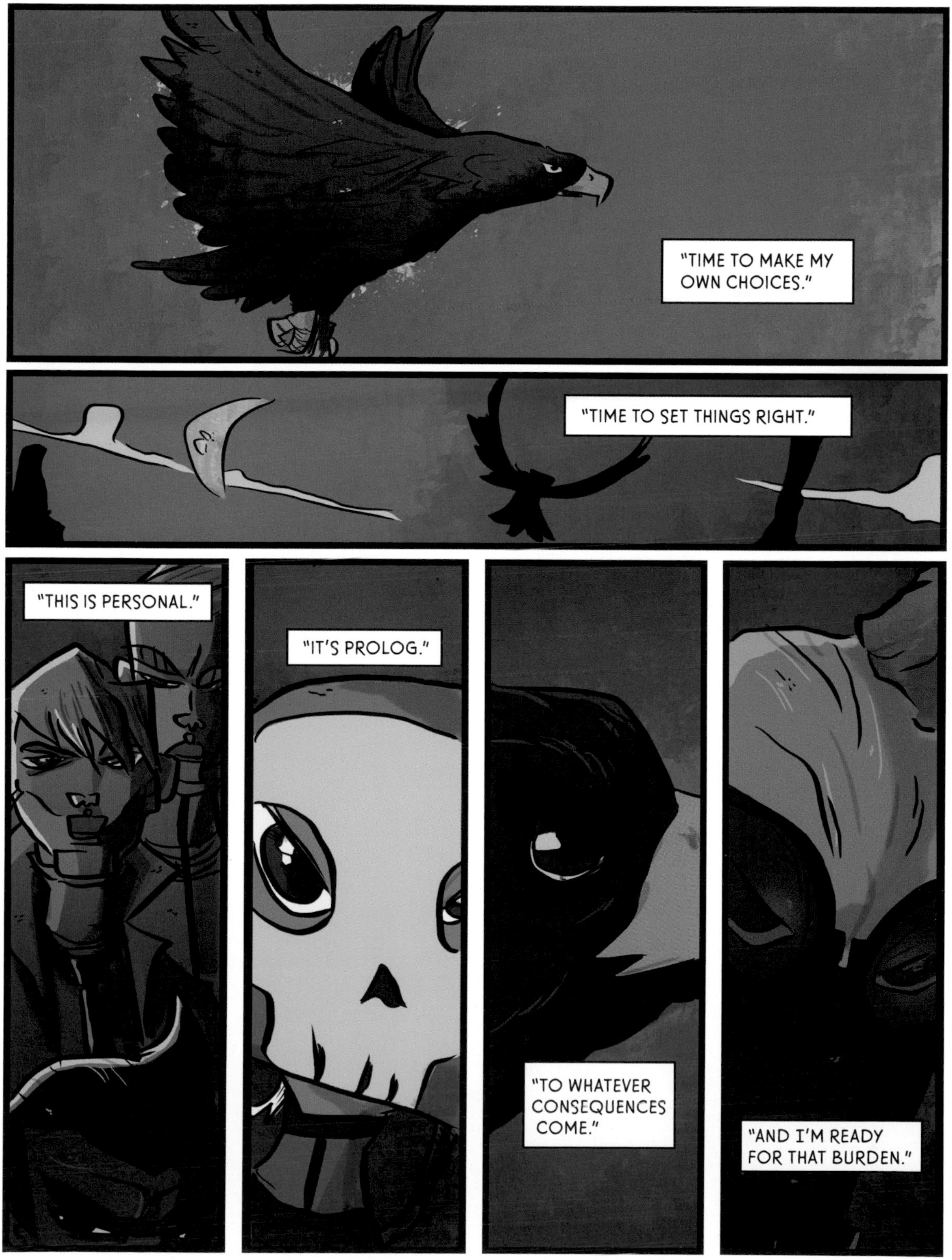
"TIME TO MAKE MY OWN CHOICES."
"TIME TO SET THINGS RIGHT."
"THIS IS PERSONAL."
"IT'S PROLOG."
"TO WHATEVER CONSEQUENCES COME."
"AND I'M READY FOR THAT BURDEN."

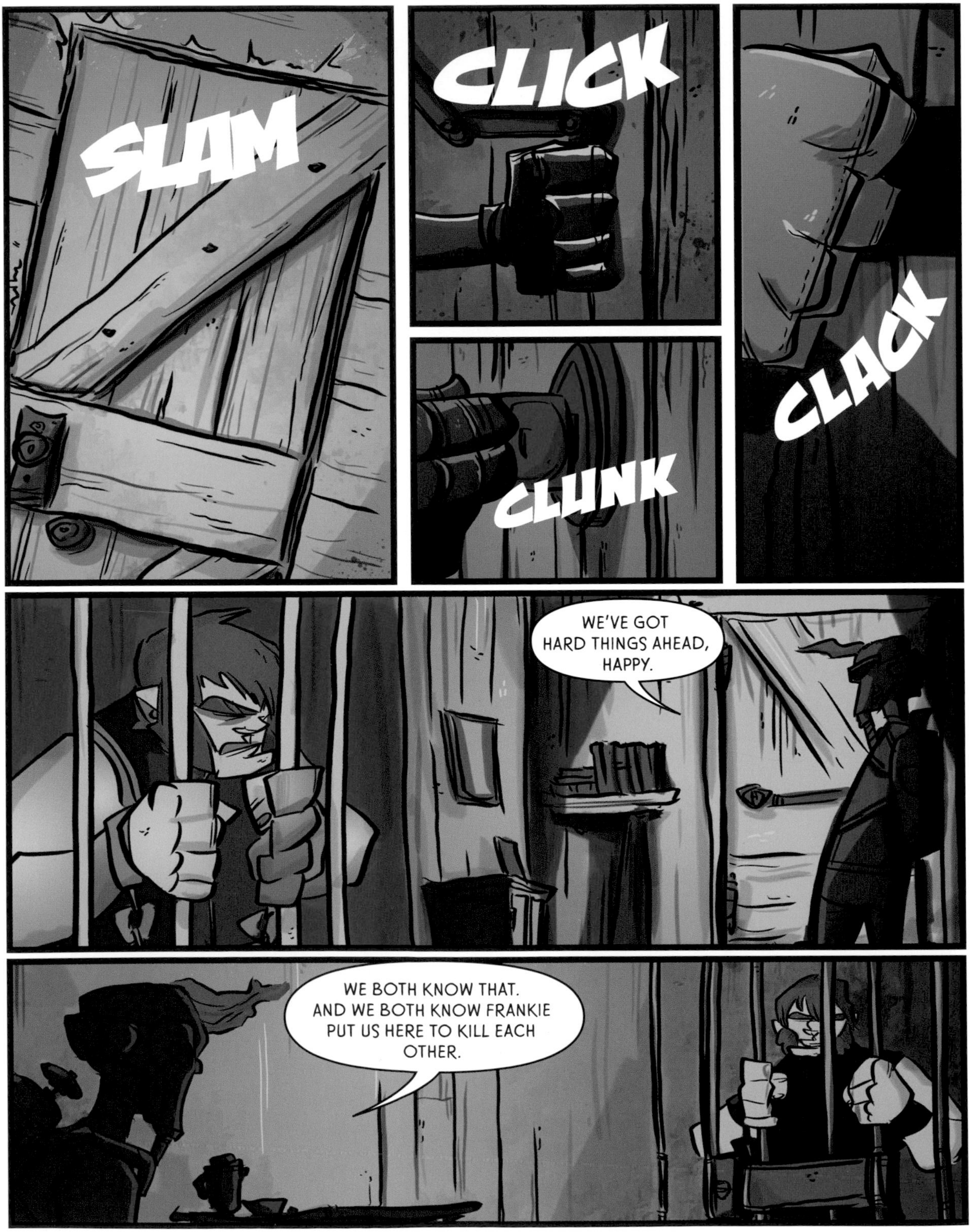
SLAM
CLICK
CLUNK
CLACK
WE'VE GOT HARD THINGS AHEAD, HAPPY.
WE BOTH KNOW THAT. AND WE BOTH KNOW FRANKIE PUT US HERE TO KILL EACH OTHER.

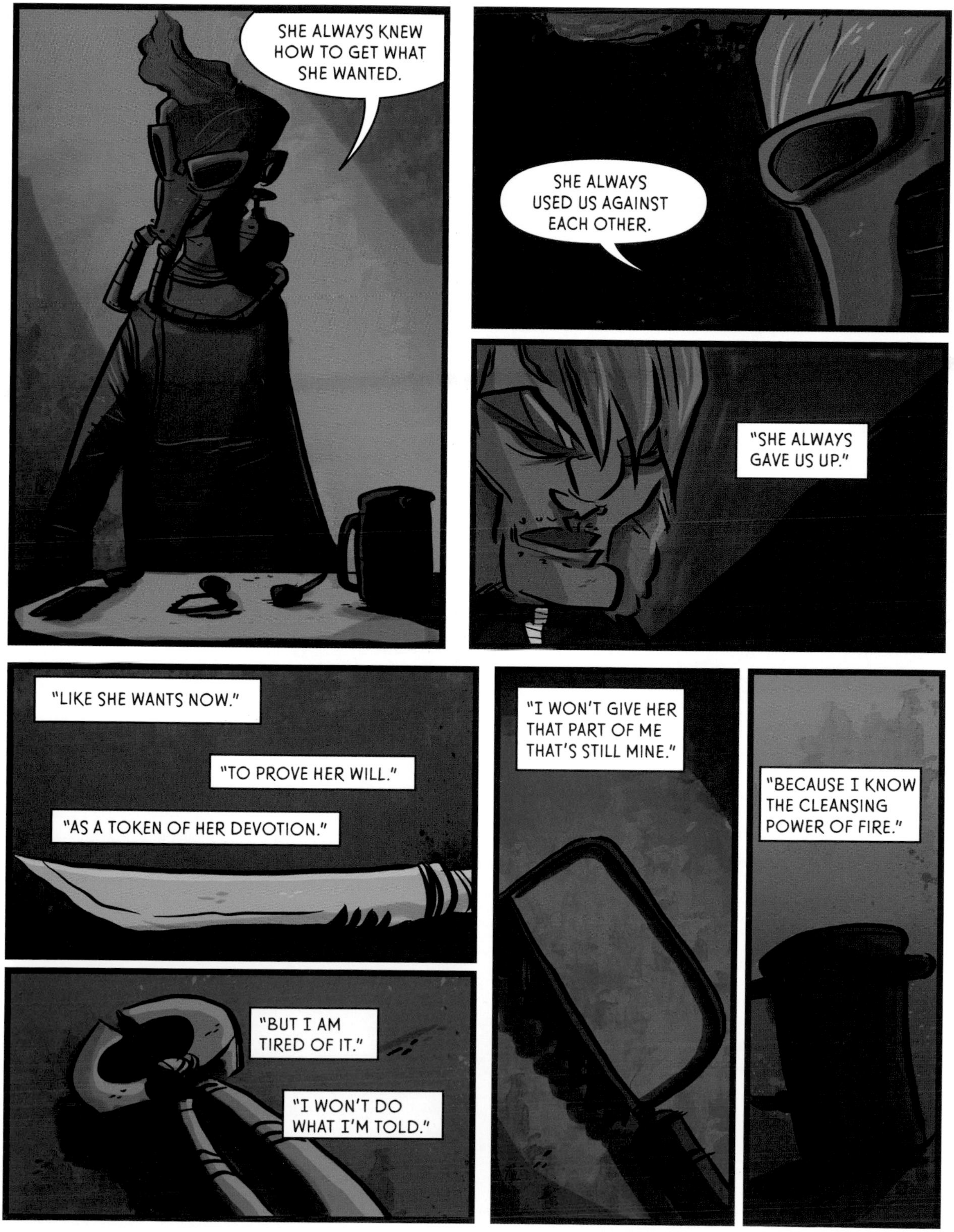
SHE ALWAYS KNEW HOW TO GET WHAT SHE WANTED.
SHE ALWAYS USED US AGAINST EACH OTHER.
"SHE ALWAYS GAVE US UP."
"LIKE SHE WANTS NOW."
"TO PROVE HER WILL."
"AS A TOKEN OF HER DEVOTION."
"BUT I AM TIRED OF IT."
"I WON'T DO WHAT I'M TOLD."
"I WON'T GIVE HER THAT PART OF ME THAT'S STILL MINE."
"BECAUSE I KNOW THE CLEANSING POWER OF FIRE."

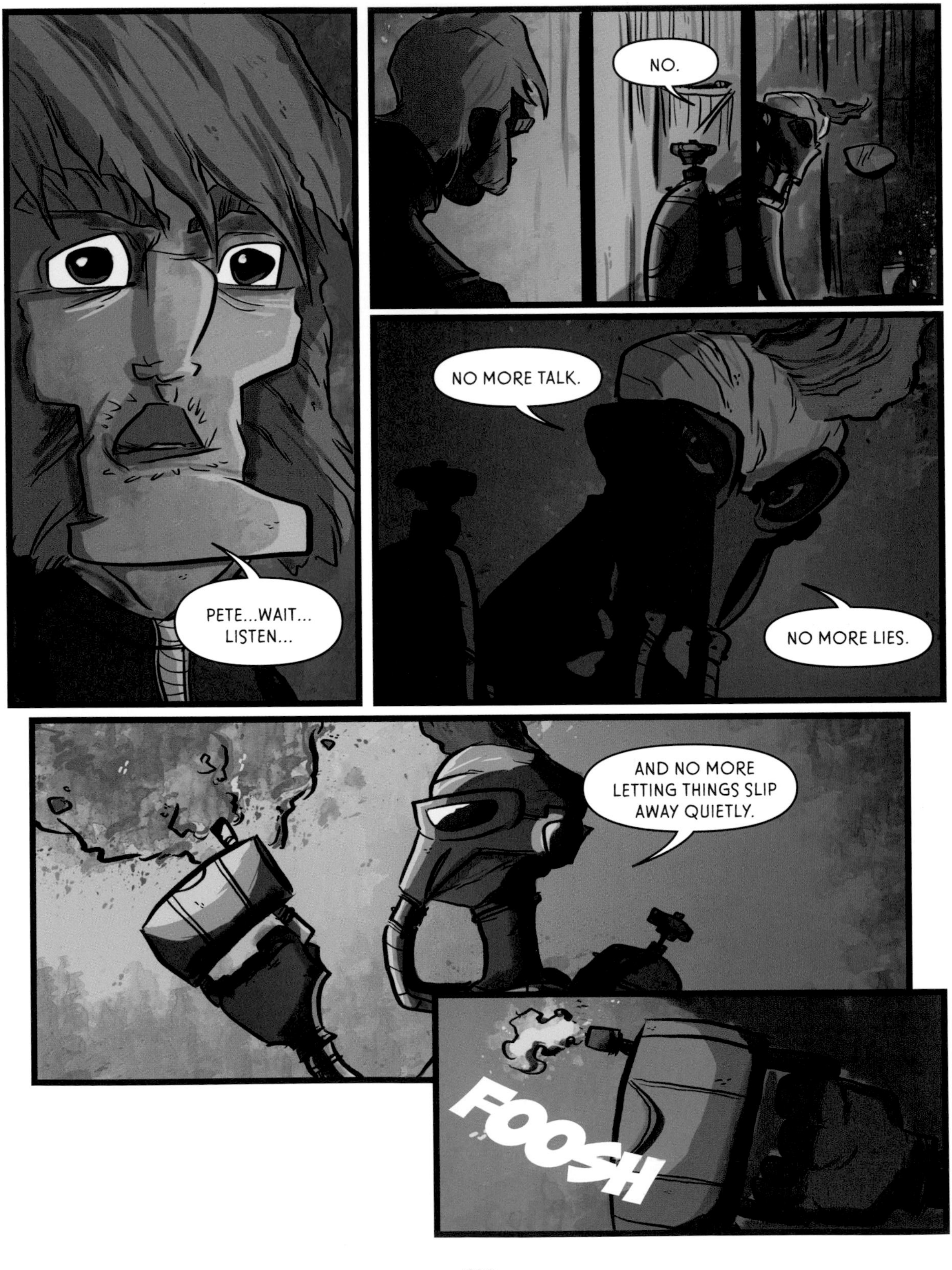
PETE...WAIT... LISTEN...
NO.
NO MORE TALK.
NO MORE LIES.
AND NO MORE LETTING THINGS SLIP AWAY QUIETLY.
FOOSH

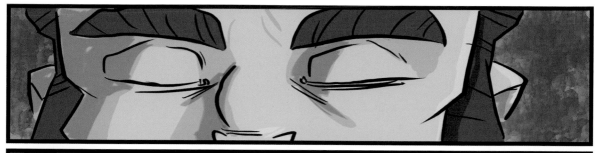

HMMM.

THIS ISN'T RIGHT.

"I SHOULD BE CROAKED."

"BURIED SIX FEET DEEP."

DOC, WHAT THE HELL?

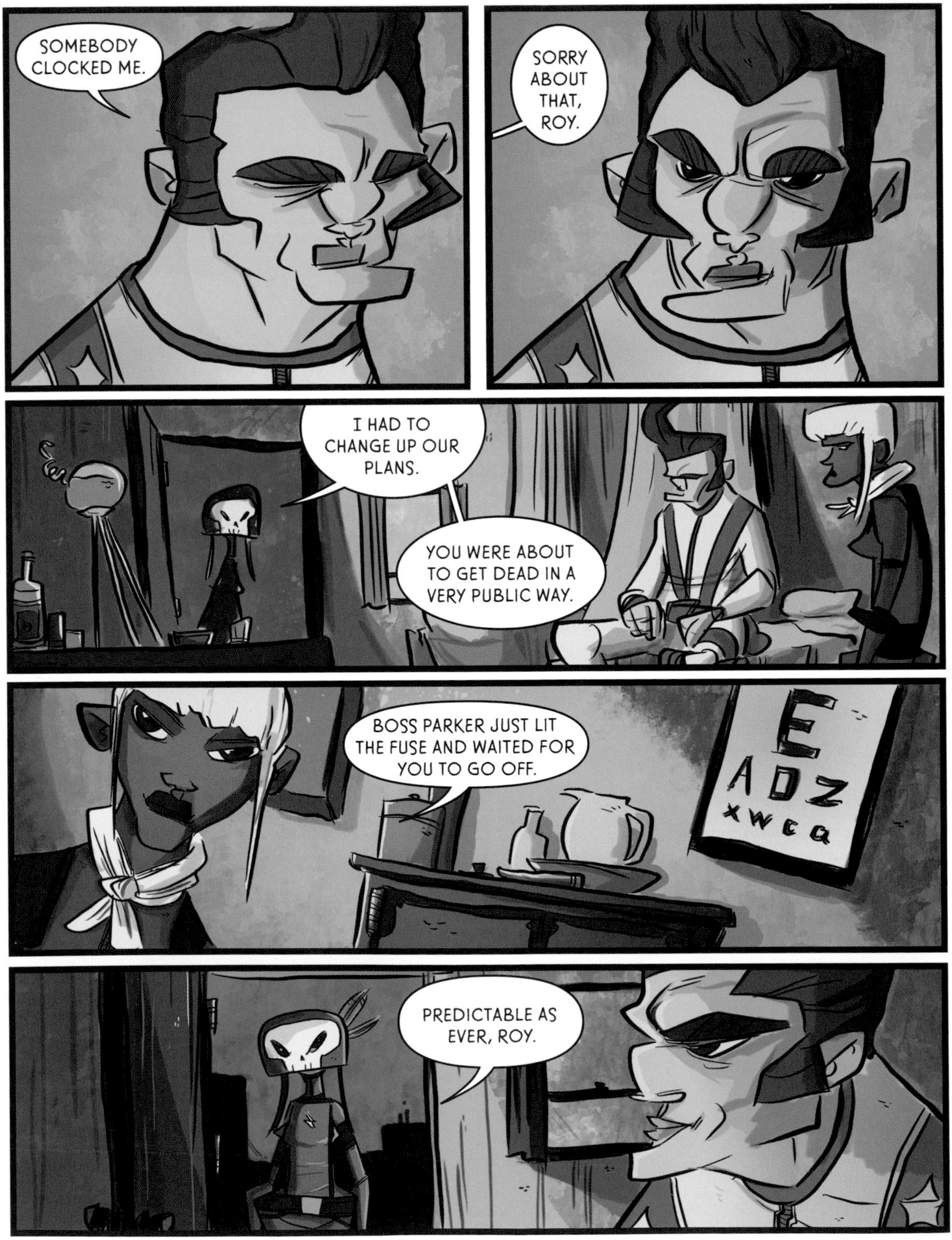
SOMEBODY CLOCKED ME.
SORRY ABOUT THAT, ROY.
I HAD TO CHANGE UP OUR PLANS.
YOU WERE ABOUT TO GET DEAD IN A VERY PUBLIC WAY.
BOSS PARKER JUST LIT THE FUSE AND WAITED FOR YOU TO GO OFF.
E
ADZ
XWCQ
PREDICTABLE AS EVER, ROY.

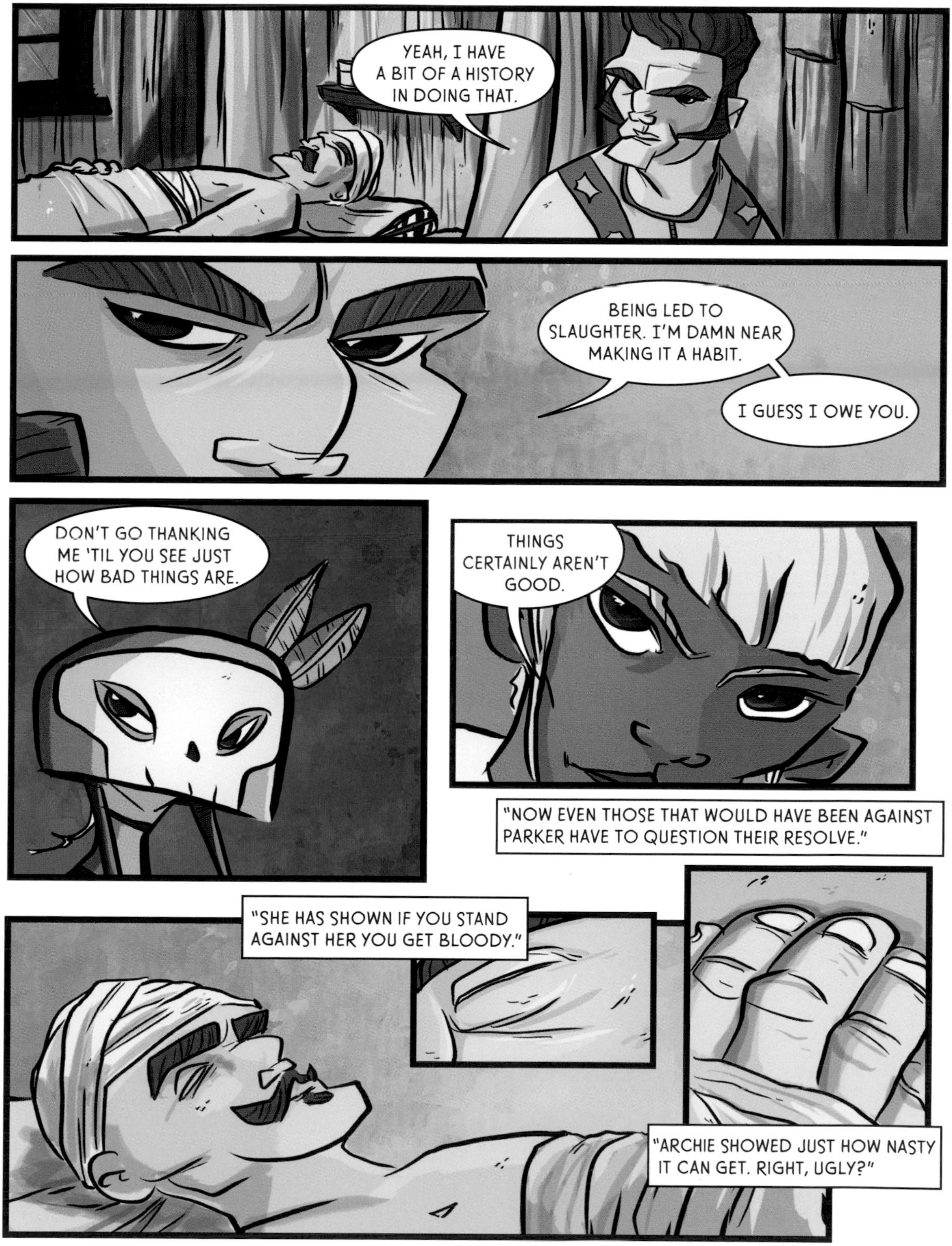
YEAH, I HAVE A BIT OF A HISTORY IN DOING THAT.
BEING LED TO SLAUGHTER. I'M DAMN NEAR MAKING IT A HABIT.
I GUESS I OWE YOU.
DON'T GO THANKING ME 'TIL YOU SEE JUST HOW BAD THINGS ARE.
THINGS CERTAINLY AREN'T GOOD.
"NOW EVEN THOSE THAT WOULD HAVE BEEN AGAINST PARKER HAVE TO QUESTION THEIR RESOLVE."
"SHE HAS SHOWN IF YOU STAND AGAINST HER YOU GET BLOODY."
"ARCHIE SHOWED JUST HOW NASTY IT CAN GET. RIGHT, UGLY?"

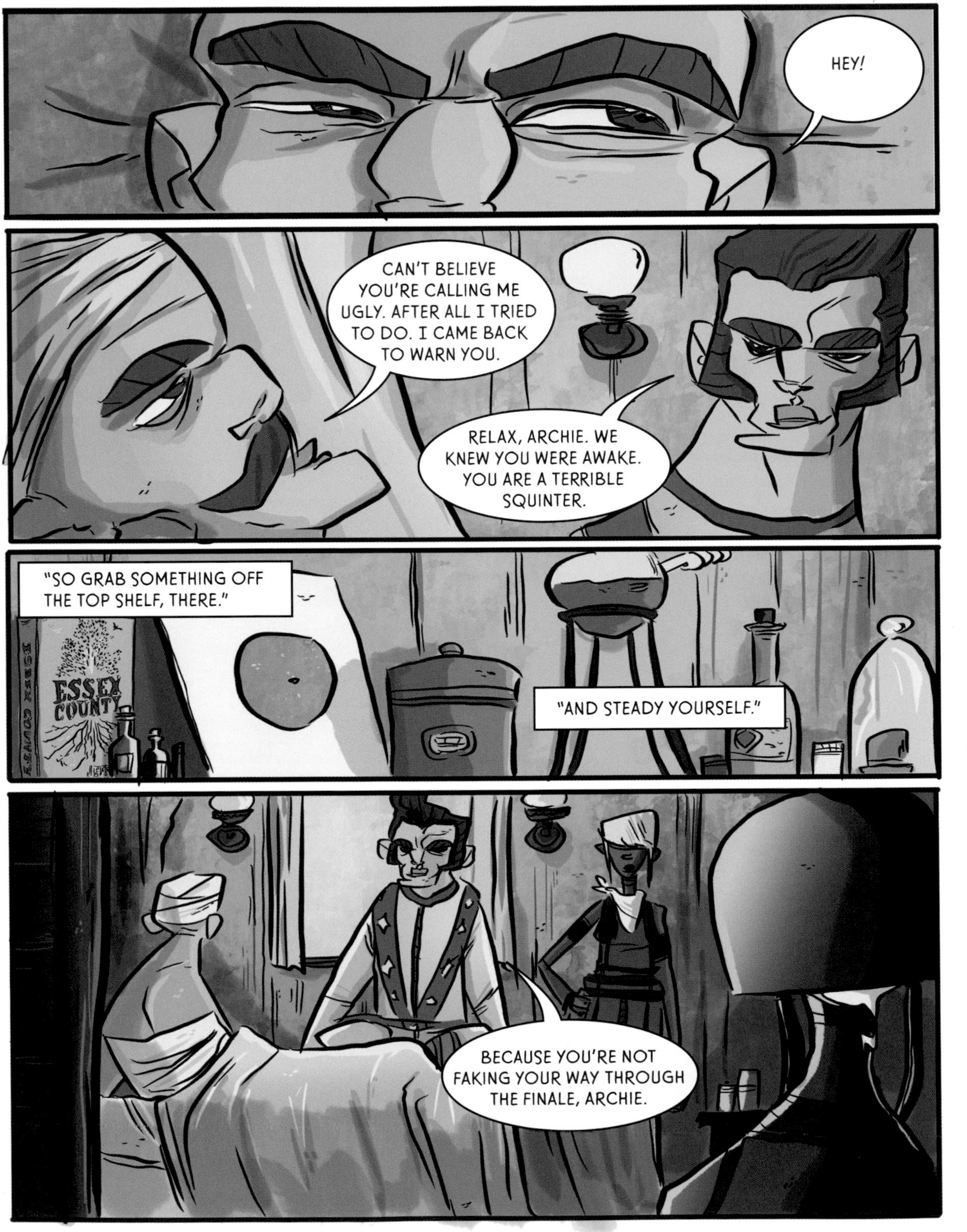
HEY!
CAN'T BELIEVE YOU'RE CALLING ME UGLY. AFTER ALL I TRIED TO DO. I CAME BACK TO WARN YOU.
RELAX, ARCHIE. WE KNEW YOU WERE AWAKE. YOU ARE A TERRIBLE SQUINTER.
"SO GRAB SOMETHING OFF THE TOP SHELF, THERE."
ESSEX COUNTY
"AND STEADY YOURSELF."
BECAUSE YOU'RE NOT FAKING YOUR WAY THROUGH THE FINALE, ARCHIE.

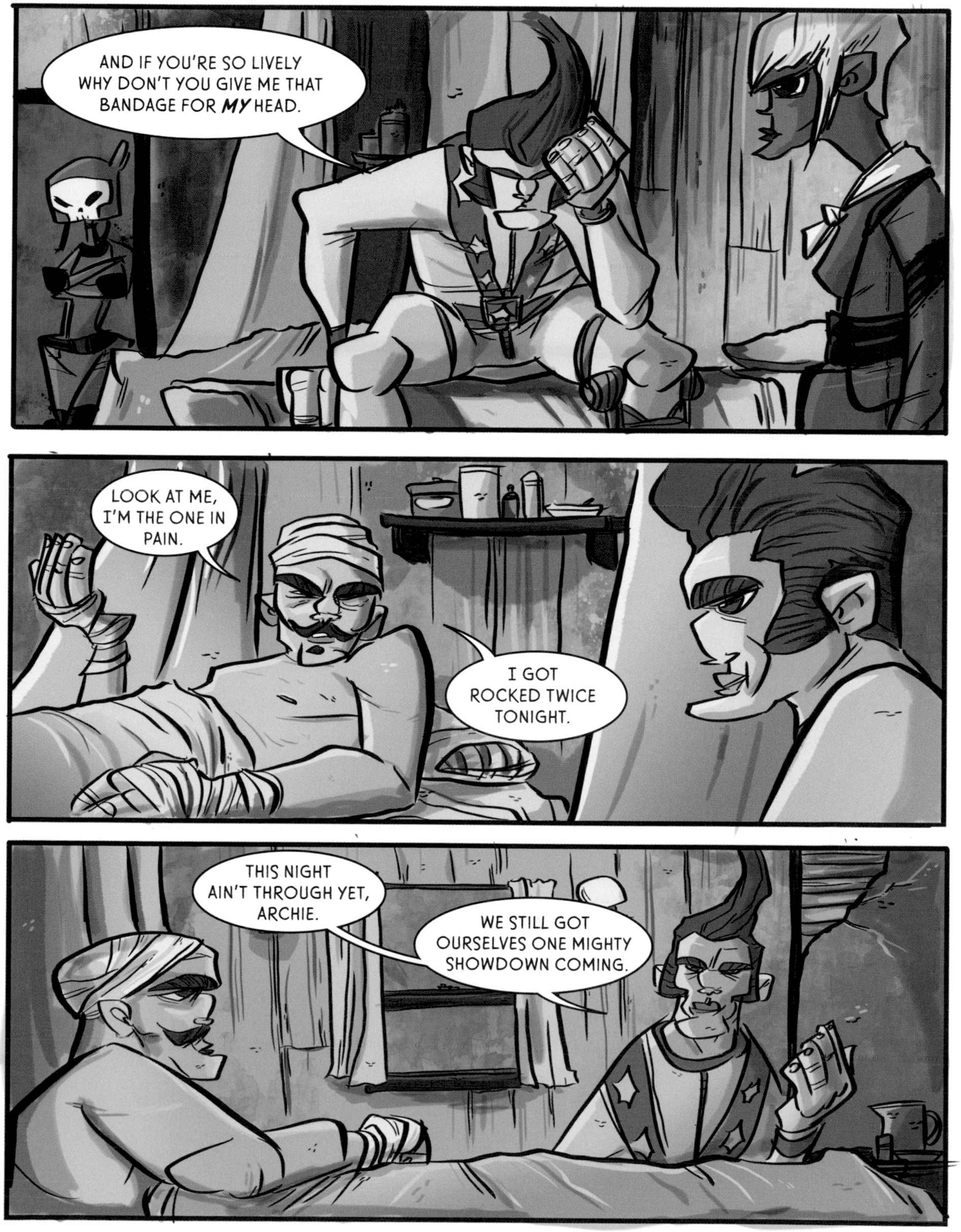
AND IF YOU'RE SO LIVELY WHY DON'T YOU GIVE ME THAT BANDAGE FOR *MY* HEAD.
LOOK AT ME, I'M THE ONE IN PAIN.
I GOT ROCKED TWICE TONIGHT.
THIS NIGHT AIN'T THROUGH YET, ARCHIE.
WE STILL GOT OURSELVES ONE MIGHTY SHOWDOWN COMING.

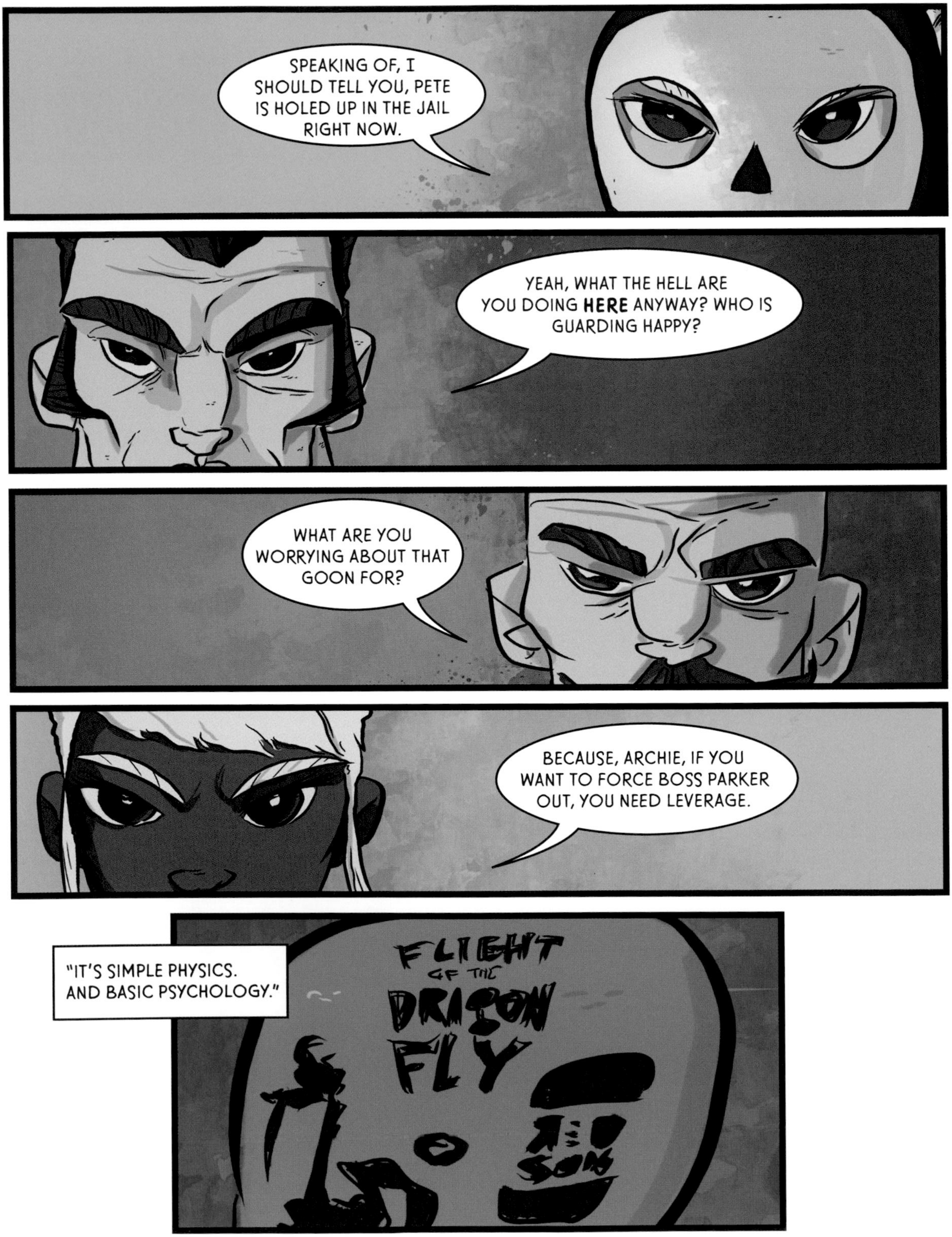
SPEAKING OF, I SHOULD TELL YOU, PETE IS HOLED UP IN THE JAIL RIGHT NOW.
YEAH, WHAT THE HELL ARE YOU DOING **HERE** ANYWAY? WHO IS GUARDING HAPPY?
WHAT ARE YOU WORRYING ABOUT THAT GOON FOR?
BECAUSE, ARCHIE, IF YOU WANT TO FORCE BOSS PARKER OUT, YOU NEED LEVERAGE.
"IT'S SIMPLE PHYSICS. AND BASIC PSYCHOLOGY."
FLIGHT OF THE DRAGON FLY

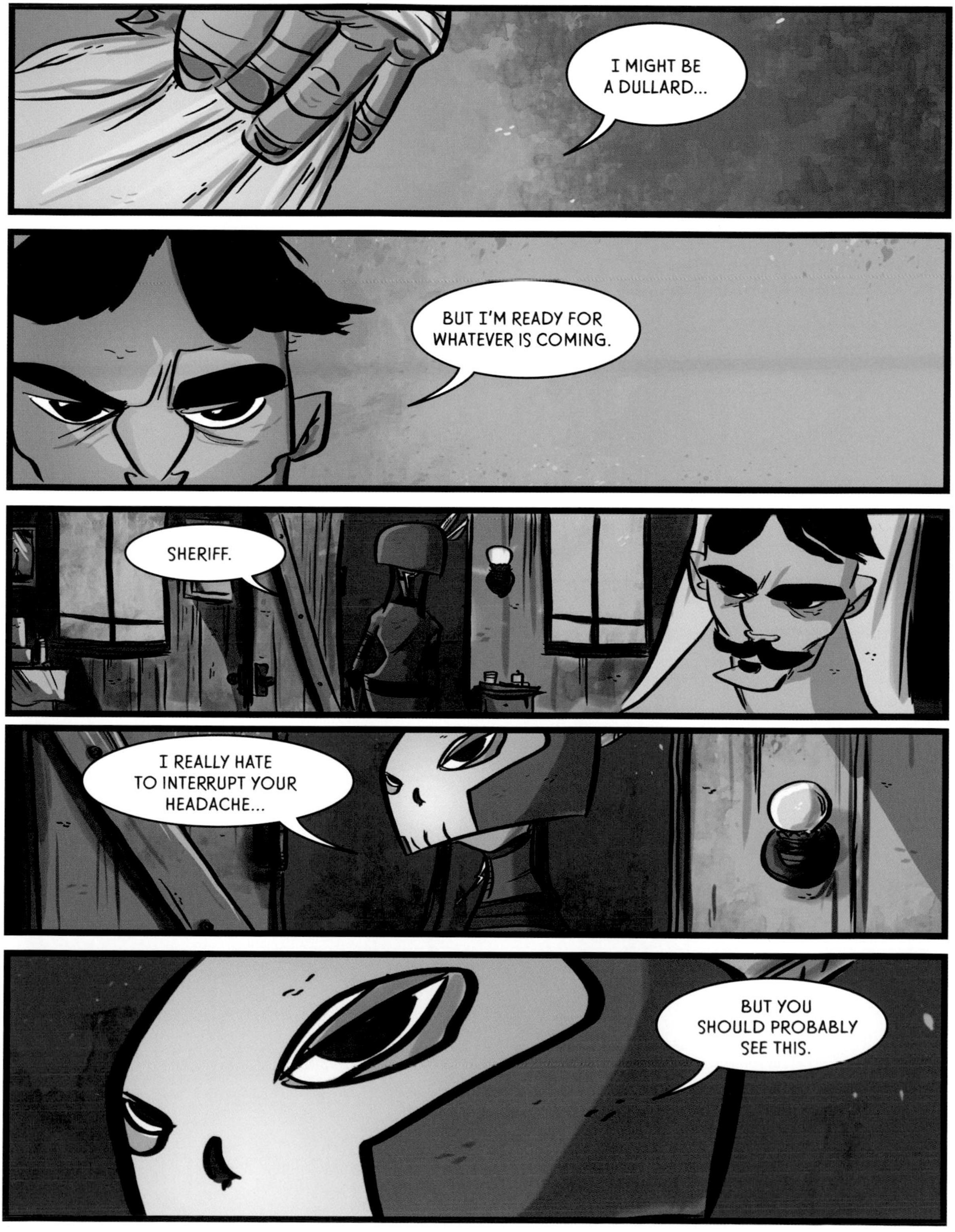
I MIGHT BE A DULLARD...
BUT I'M READY FOR WHATEVER IS COMING.
SHERIFF.
I REALLY HATE TO INTERRUPT YOUR HEADACHE...
BUT YOU SHOULD PROBABLY SEE THIS.

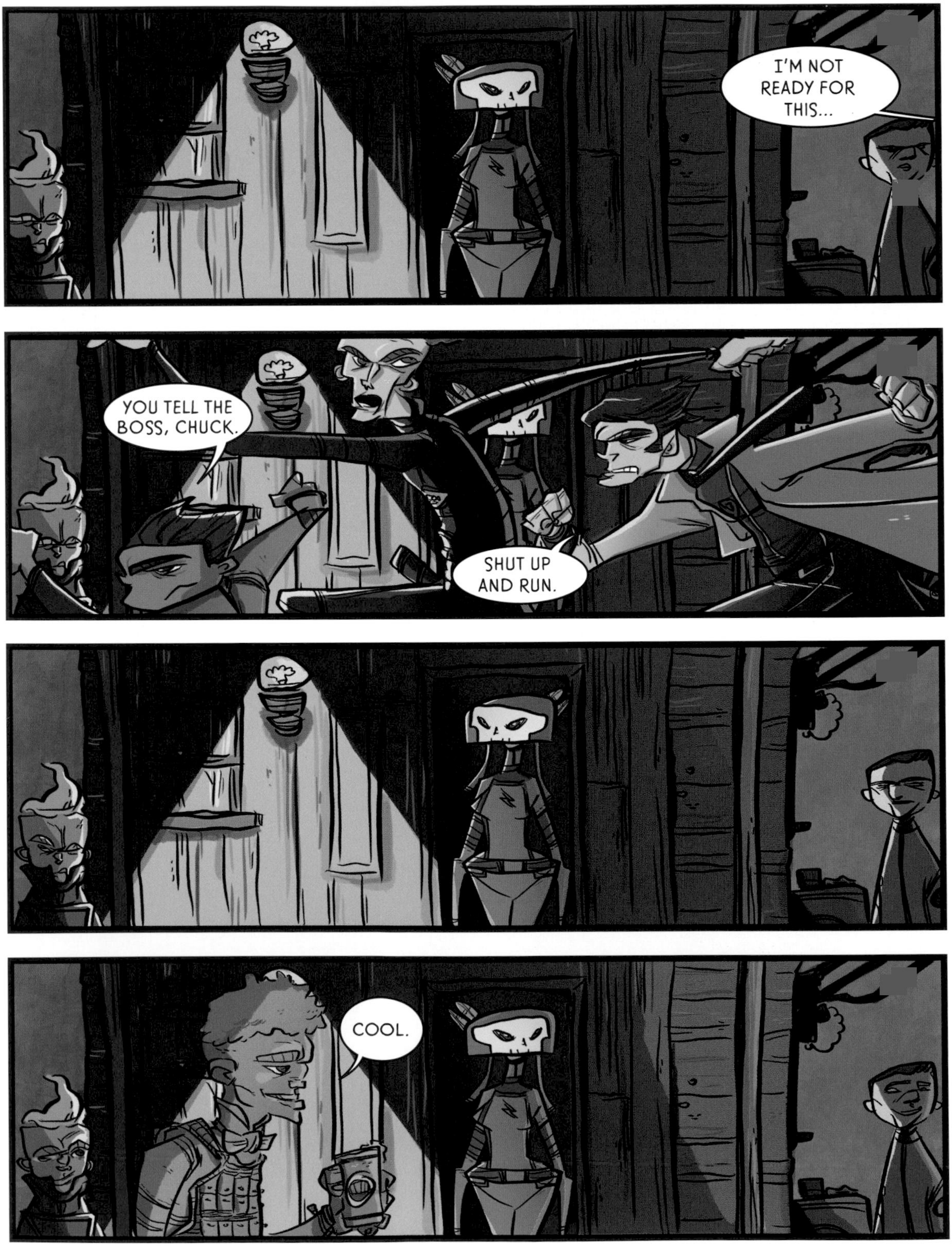
I'M NOT READY FOR THIS...
YOU TELL THE BOSS, CHUCK.
SHUT UP AND RUN.
COOL.

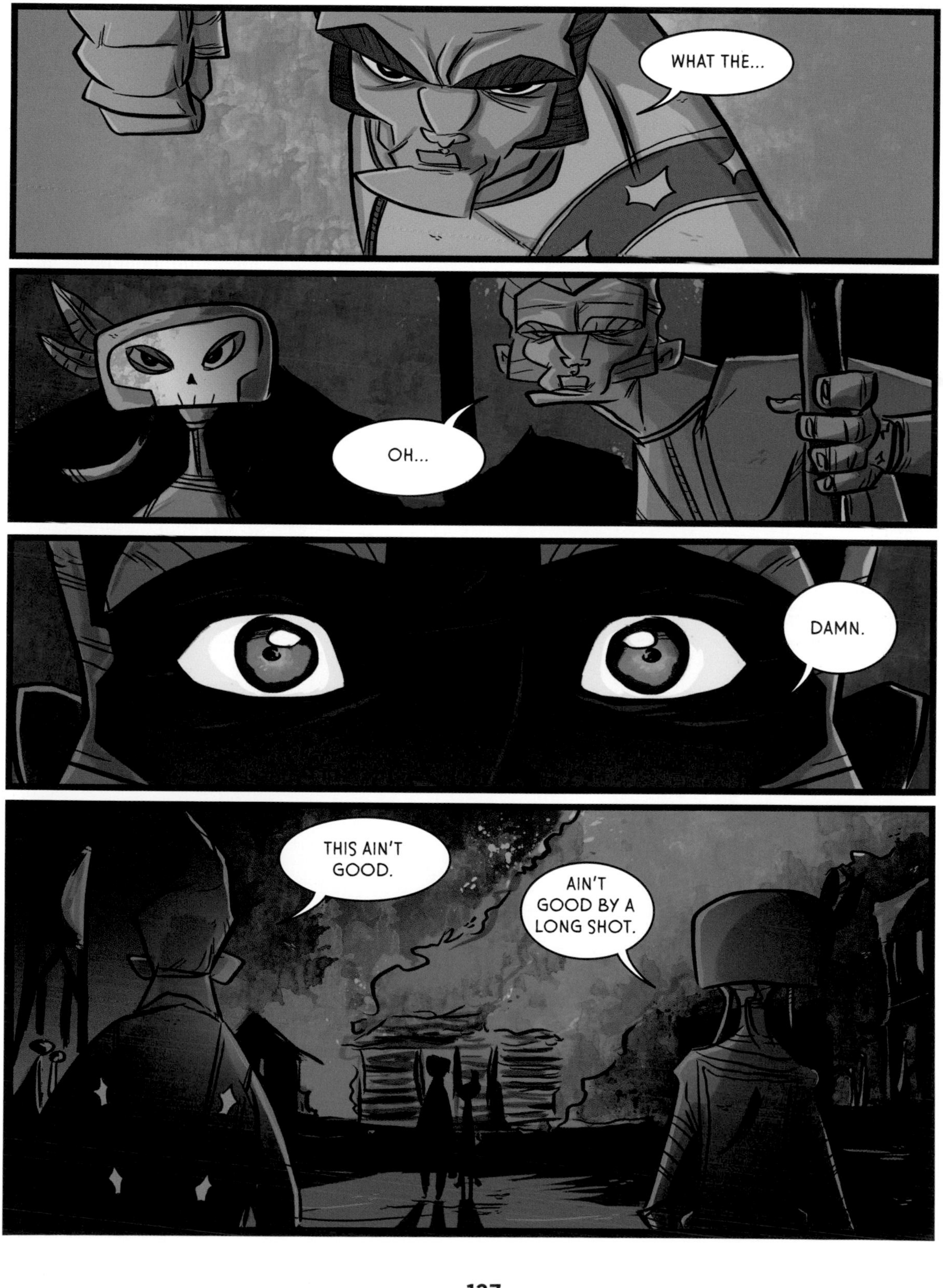
WHAT THE...
OH...
DAMN.
THIS AIN'T GOOD.
AIN'T GOOD BY A LONG SHOT.

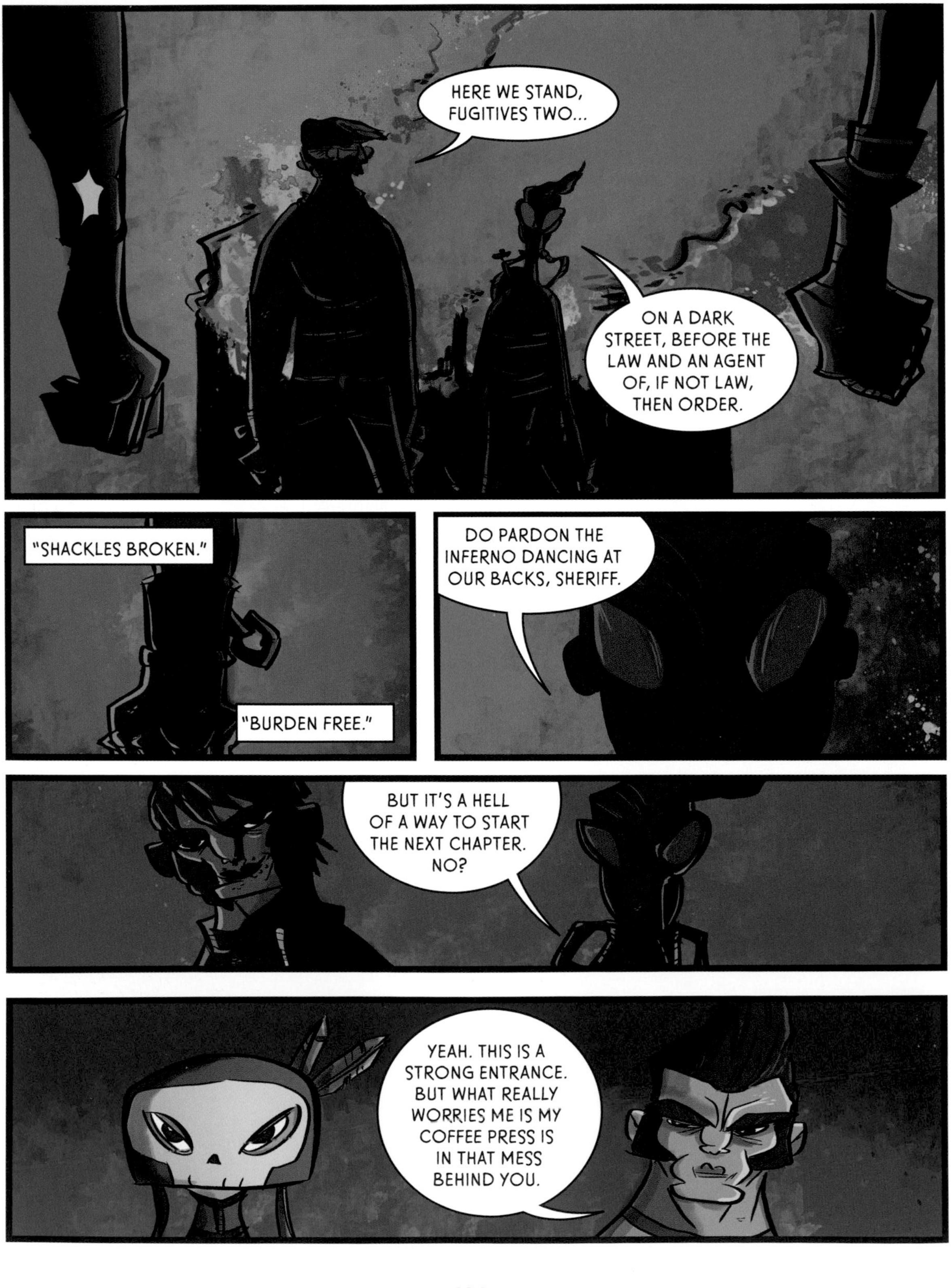
HERE WE STAND, FUGITIVES TWO...
ON A DARK STREET, BEFORE THE LAW AND AN AGENT OF, IF NOT LAW, THEN ORDER.
"SHACKLES BROKEN."
"BURDEN FREE."
DO PARDON THE INFERNO DANCING AT OUR BACKS, SHERIFF.
BUT IT'S A HELL OF A WAY TO START THE NEXT CHAPTER. NO?
YEAH. THIS IS A STRONG ENTRANCE. BUT WHAT REALLY WORRIES ME IS MY COFFEE PRESS IS IN THAT MESS BEHIND YOU.

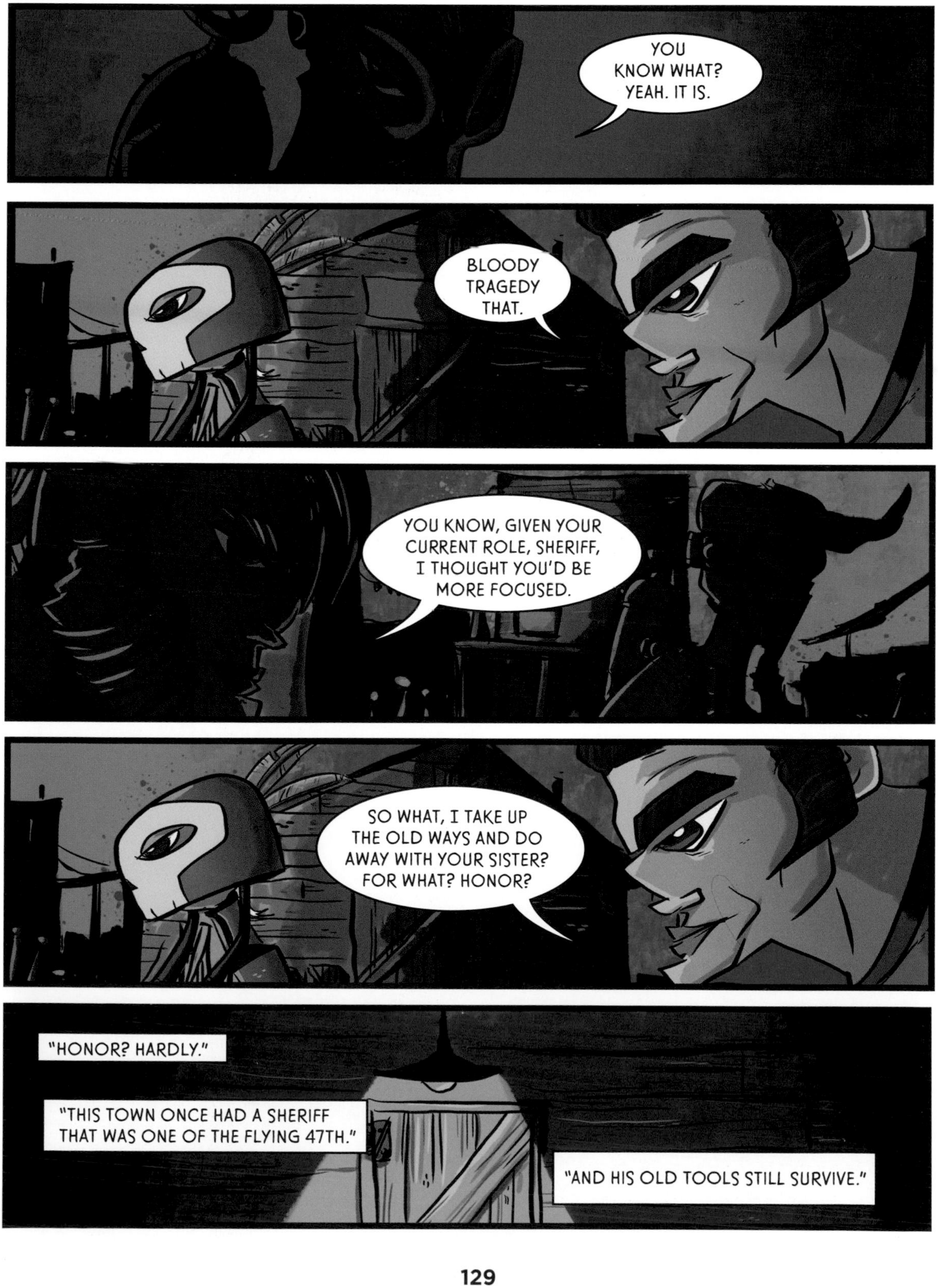
YOU KNOW WHAT? YEAH. IT IS.
BLOODY TRAGEDY THAT.
YOU KNOW, GIVEN YOUR CURRENT ROLE, SHERIFF, I THOUGHT YOU'D BE MORE FOCUSED.
SO WHAT, I TAKE UP THE OLD WAYS AND DO AWAY WITH YOUR SISTER? FOR WHAT? HONOR?
"HONOR? HARDLY."
"THIS TOWN ONCE HAD A SHERIFF THAT WAS ONE OF THE FLYING 47TH."
"AND HIS OLD TOOLS STILL SURVIVE."

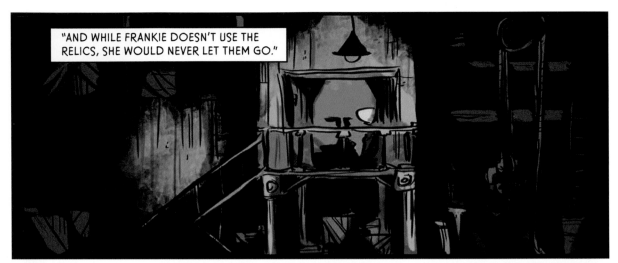

"AND WHILE FRANKIE DOESN'T USE THE RELICS, SHE WOULD NEVER LET THEM GO."

"SO THERE THEY SIT..."

"A LEGACY OF A BYGONE ERA."

"GATHERING RUST."

"FORGOTTEN."

"JUST WAITING TO BE RECLAIMED."

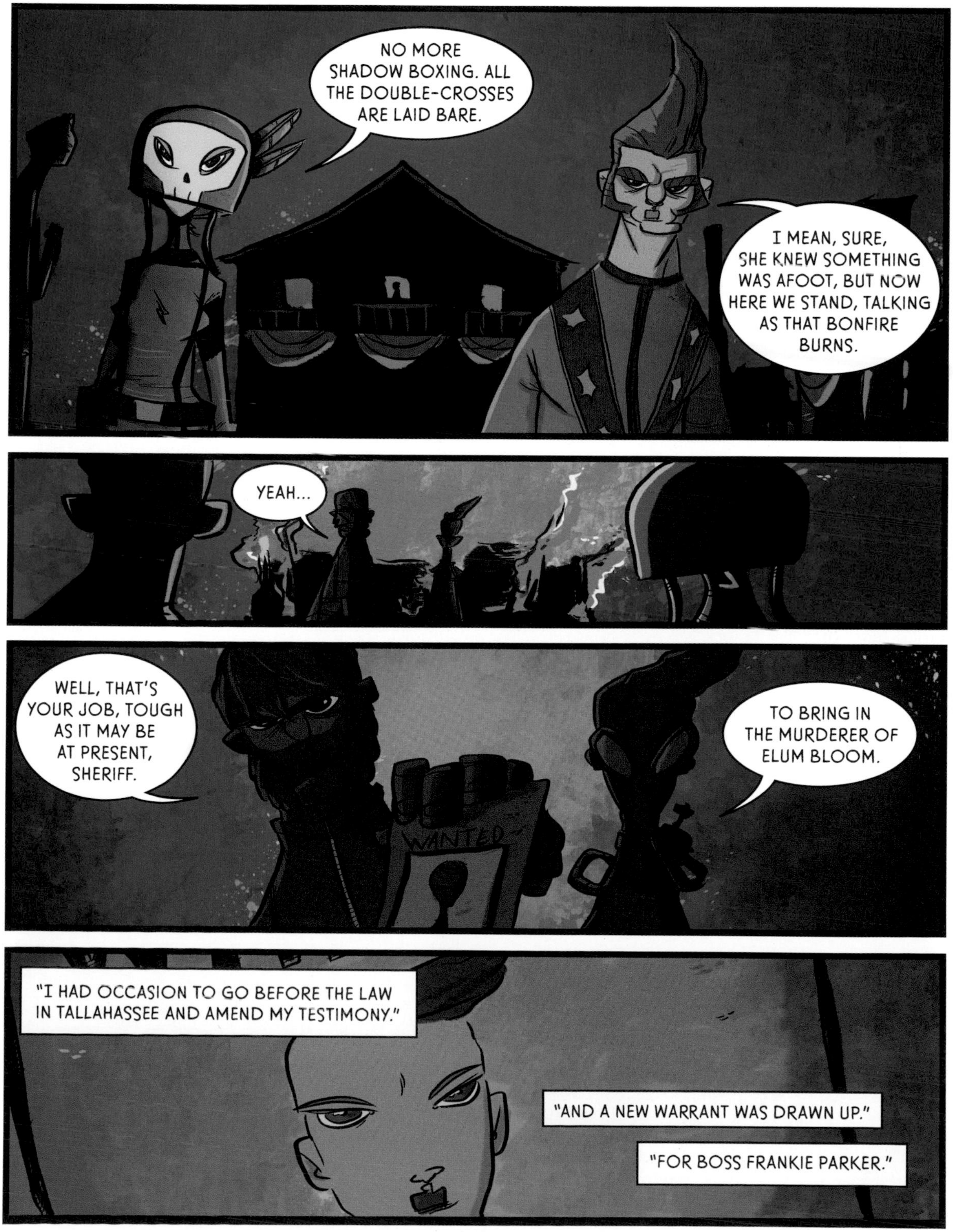
NO MORE SHADOW BOXING. ALL THE DOUBLE-CROSSES ARE LAID BARE.
I MEAN, SURE, SHE KNEW SOMETHING WAS AFOOT, BUT NOW HERE WE STAND, TALKING AS THAT BONFIRE BURNS.
YEAH...
WELL, THAT'S YOUR JOB, TOUGH AS IT MAY BE AT PRESENT, SHERIFF.
TO BRING IN THE MURDERER OF ELUM BLOOM.
WANTED
"I HAD OCCASION TO GO BEFORE THE LAW IN TALLAHASSEE AND AMEND MY TESTIMONY."
"AND A NEW WARRANT WAS DRAWN UP."
"FOR BOSS FRANKIE PARKER."

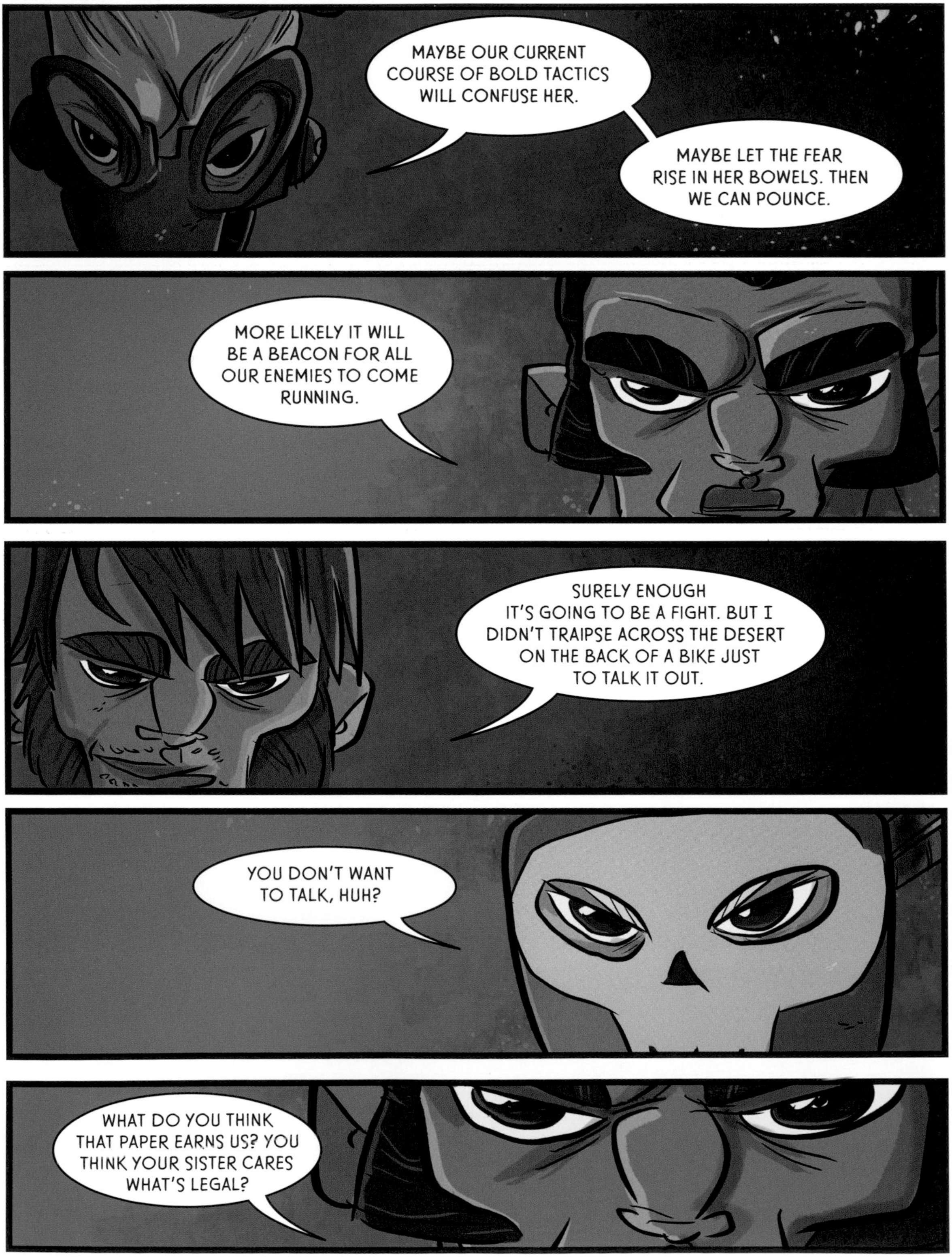
MAYBE OUR CURRENT COURSE OF BOLD TACTICS WILL CONFUSE HER.
MAYBE LET THE FEAR RISE IN HER BOWELS. THEN WE CAN POUNCE.
MORE LIKELY IT WILL BE A BEACON FOR ALL OUR ENEMIES TO COME RUNNING.
SURELY ENOUGH IT'S GOING TO BE A FIGHT. BUT I DIDN'T TRAIPSE ACROSS THE DESERT ON THE BACK OF A BIKE JUST TO TALK IT OUT.
YOU DON'T WANT TO TALK, HUH?
WHAT DO YOU THINK THAT PAPER EARNS US? YOU THINK YOUR SISTER CARES WHAT'S LEGAL?

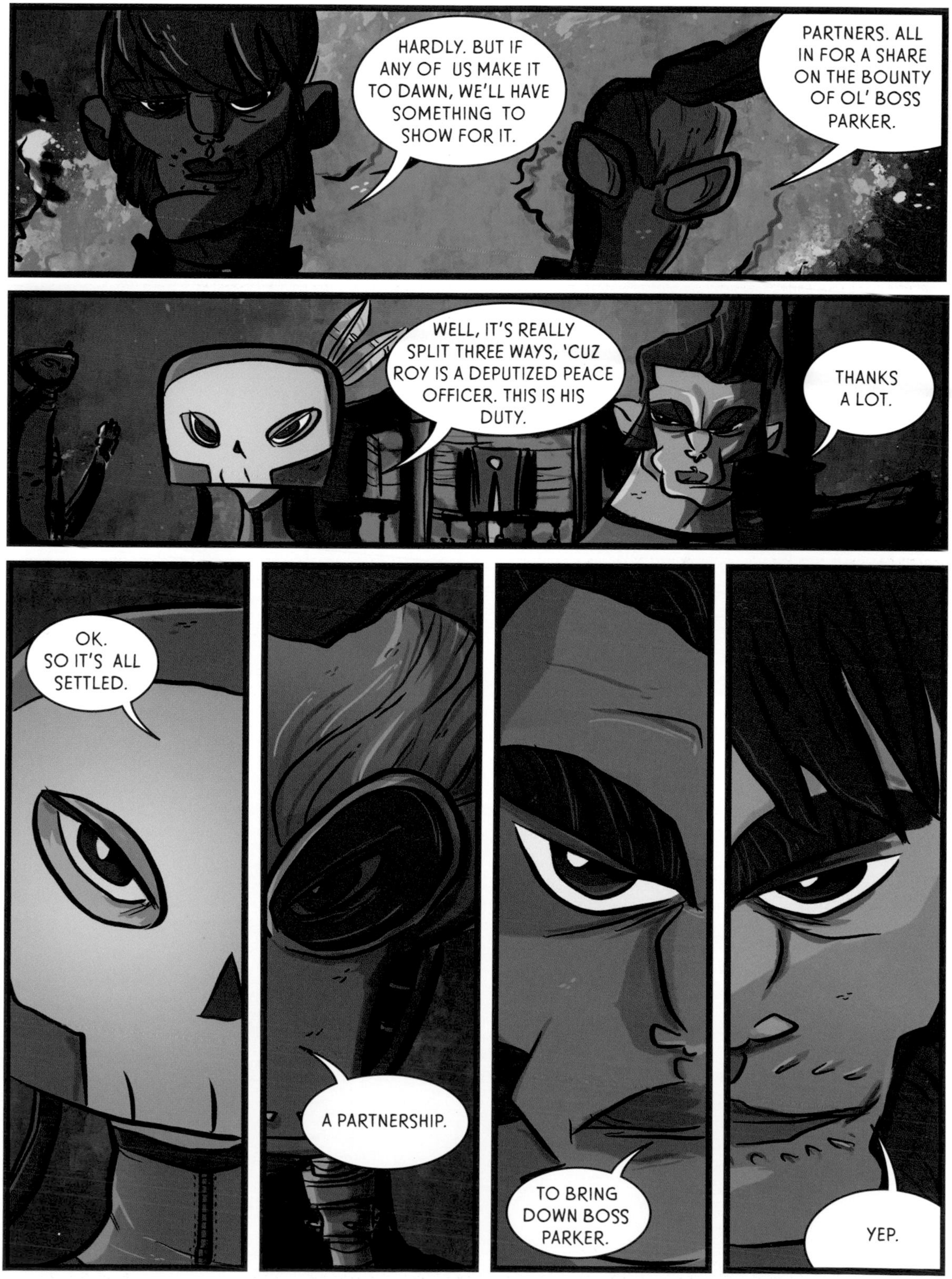
HARDLY. BUT IF ANY OF US MAKE IT TO DAWN, WE'LL HAVE SOMETHING TO SHOW FOR IT.
PARTNERS. ALL IN FOR A SHARE ON THE BOUNTY OF OL' BOSS PARKER.
WELL, IT'S REALLY SPLIT THREE WAYS, 'CUZ ROY IS A DEPUTIZED PEACE OFFICER. THIS IS HIS DUTY.
THANKS A LOT.
OK. SO IT'S ALL SETTLED.
A PARTNERSHIP.
TO BRING DOWN BOSS PARKER.
YEP.

ALRIGHT.

BOYS...

GET THE BOOM-STICK.

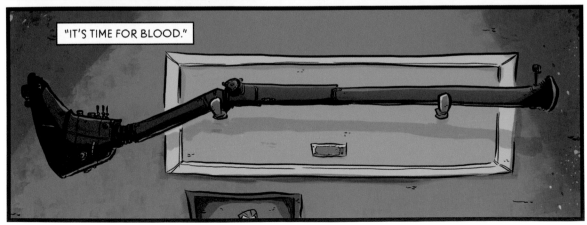

"IT'S TIME FOR BLOOD."

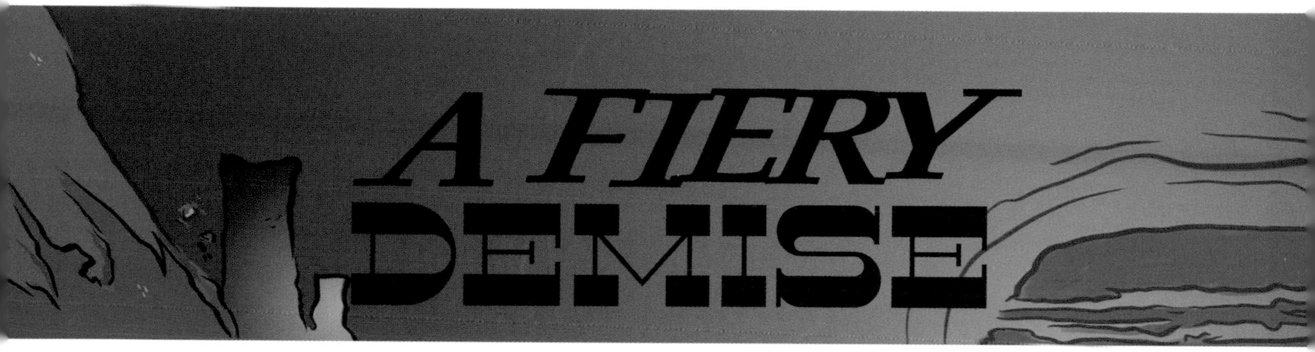
A FIERY
DEMISE

CHAPTER FIVE

MOTORCYCLE

SAMURAI

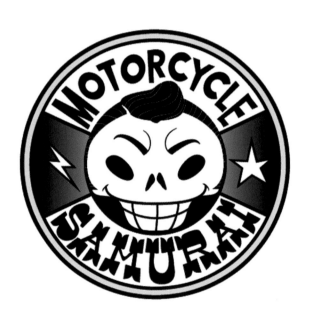

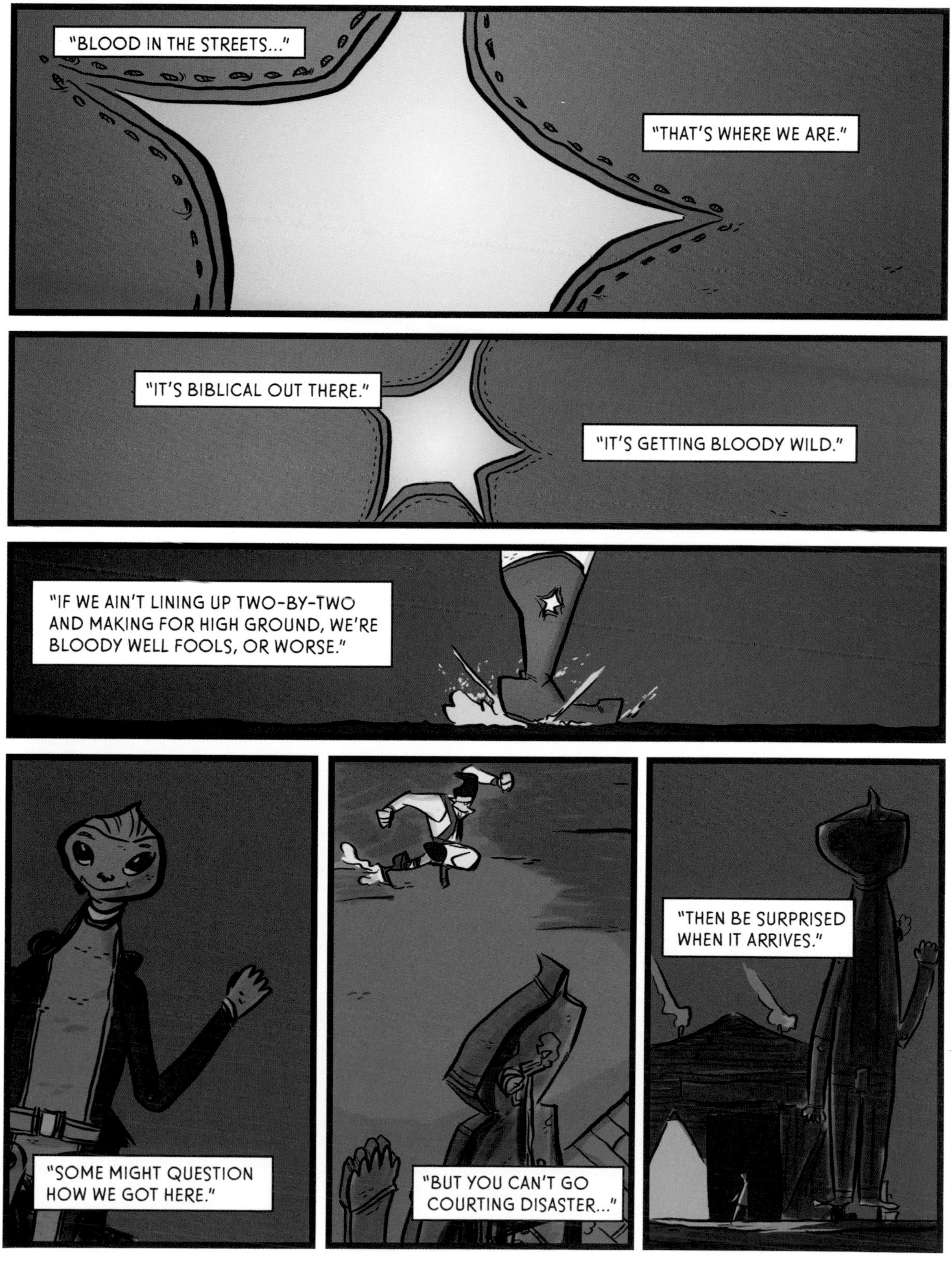
"BLOOD IN THE STREETS..."
"THAT'S WHERE WE ARE."
"IT'S BIBLICAL OUT THERE."
"IT'S GETTING BLOODY WILD."
"IF WE AIN'T LINING UP TWO-BY-TWO AND MAKING FOR HIGH GROUND, WE'RE BLOODY WELL FOOLS, OR WORSE."
"SOME MIGHT QUESTION HOW WE GOT HERE."
"BUT YOU CAN'T GO COURTING DISASTER..."
"THEN BE SURPRISED WHEN IT ARRIVES."

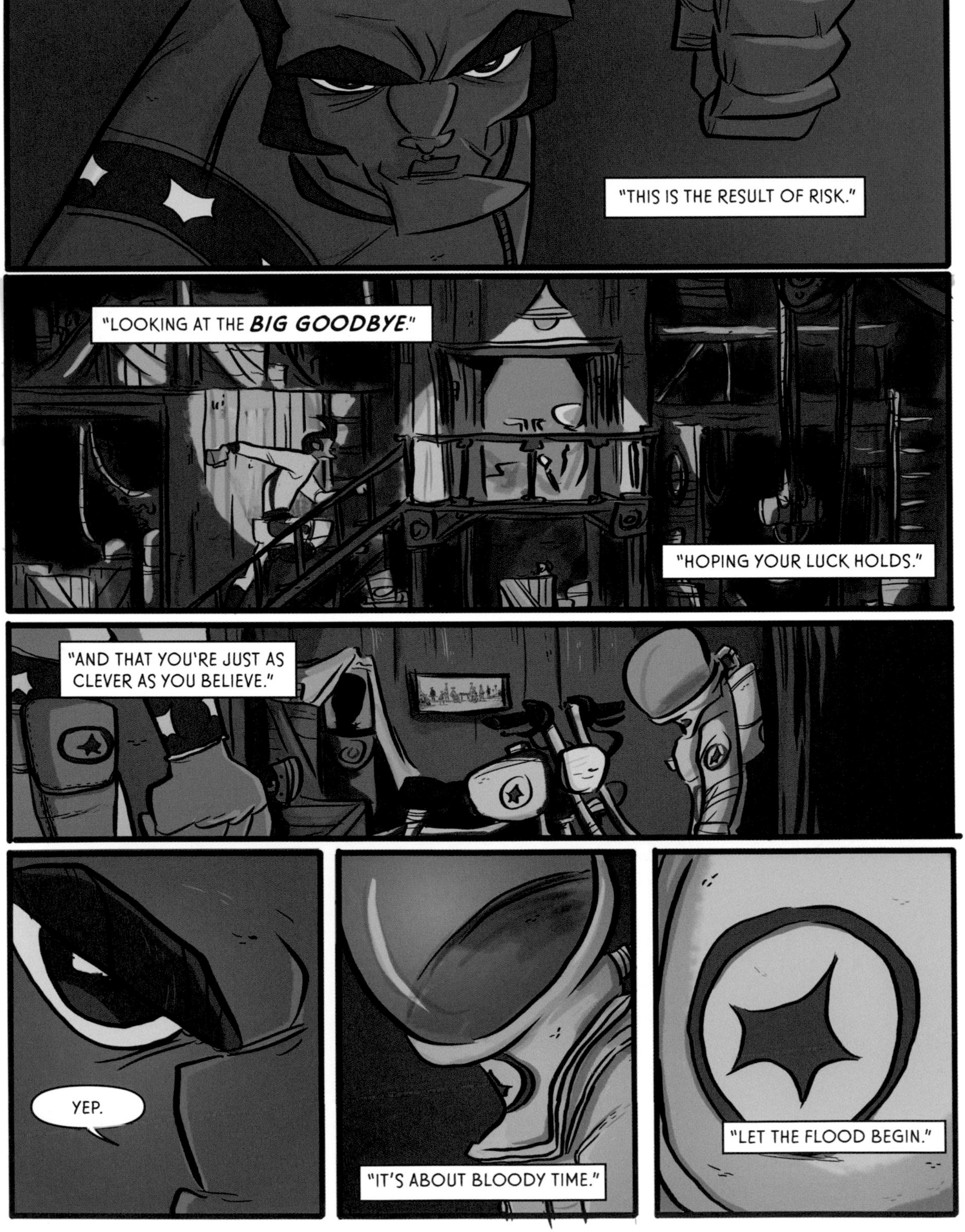
"THIS IS THE RESULT OF RISK."
"LOOKING AT THE ***BIG GOODBYE***."
"HOPING YOUR LUCK HOLDS."
"AND THAT YOU'RE JUST AS CLEVER AS YOU BELIEVE."
YEP.
"IT'S ABOUT BLOODY TIME."
"LET THE FLOOD BEGIN."

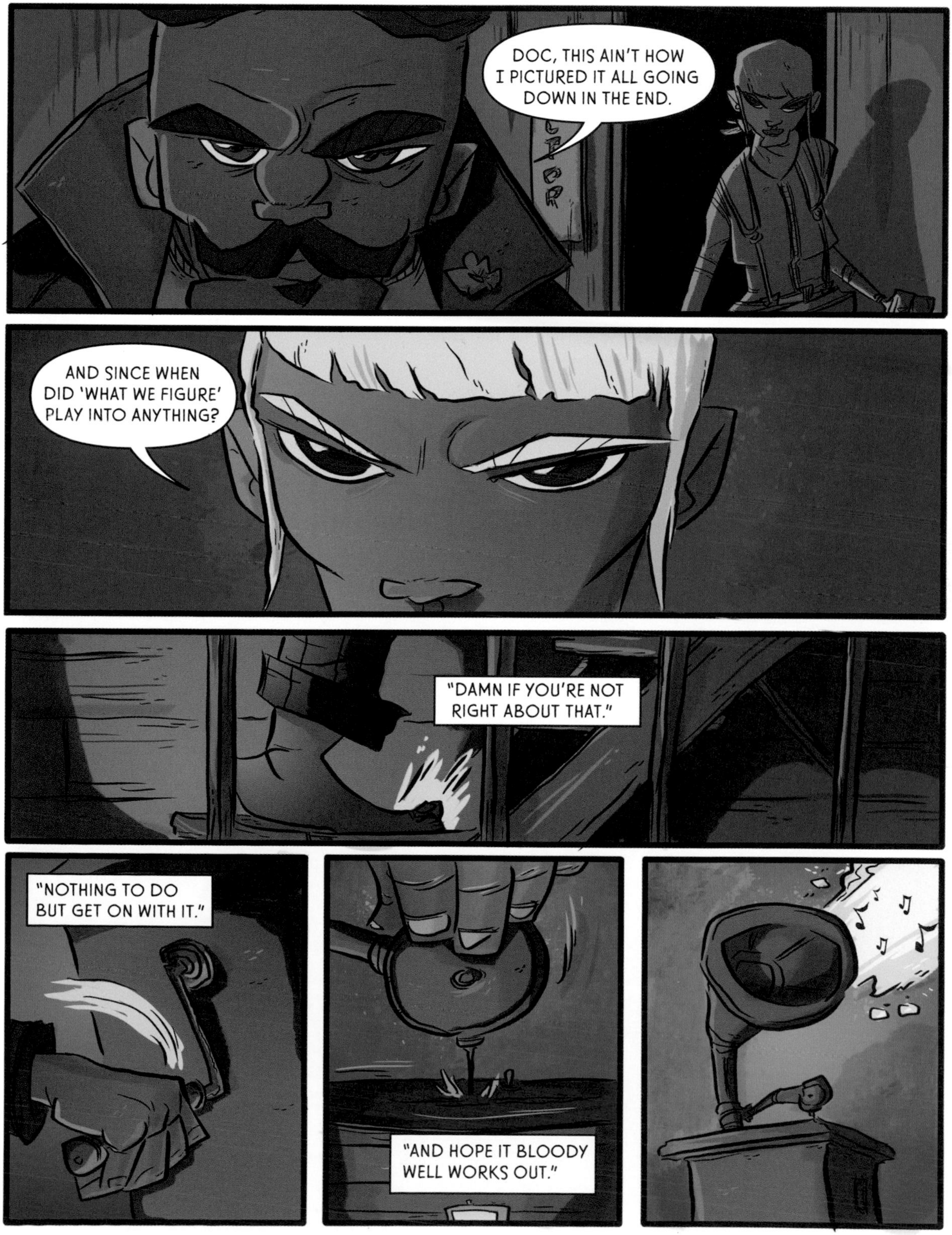
DOC, THIS AIN'T HOW I PICTURED IT ALL GOING DOWN IN THE END.
AND SINCE WHEN DID 'WHAT WE FIGURE' PLAY INTO ANYTHING?
"DAMN IF YOU'RE NOT RIGHT ABOUT THAT."
"NOTHING TO DO BUT GET ON WITH IT."
"AND HOPE IT BLOODY WELL WORKS OUT."

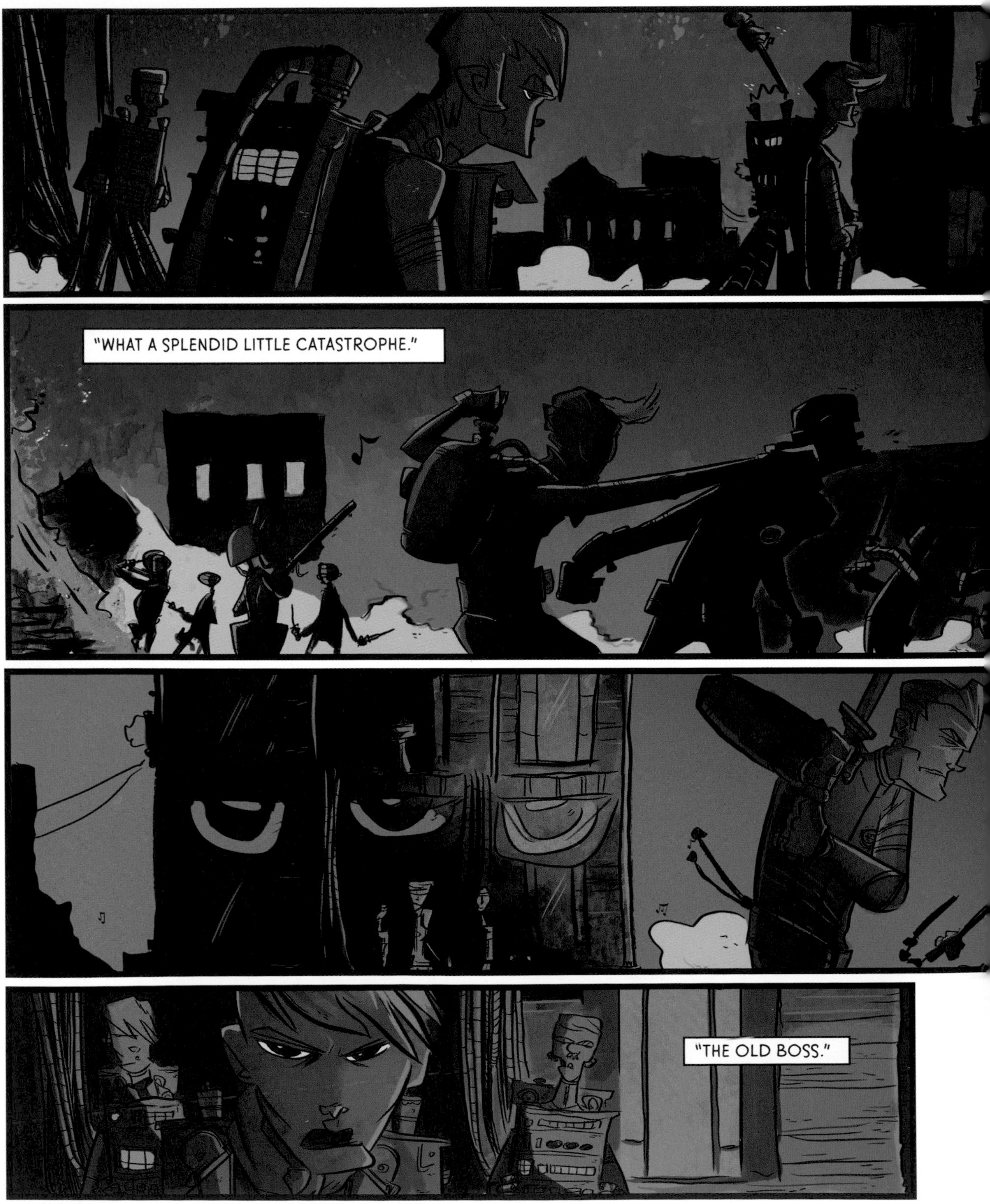
"WHAT A SPLENDID LITTLE CATASTROPHE."
"THE OLD BOSS."

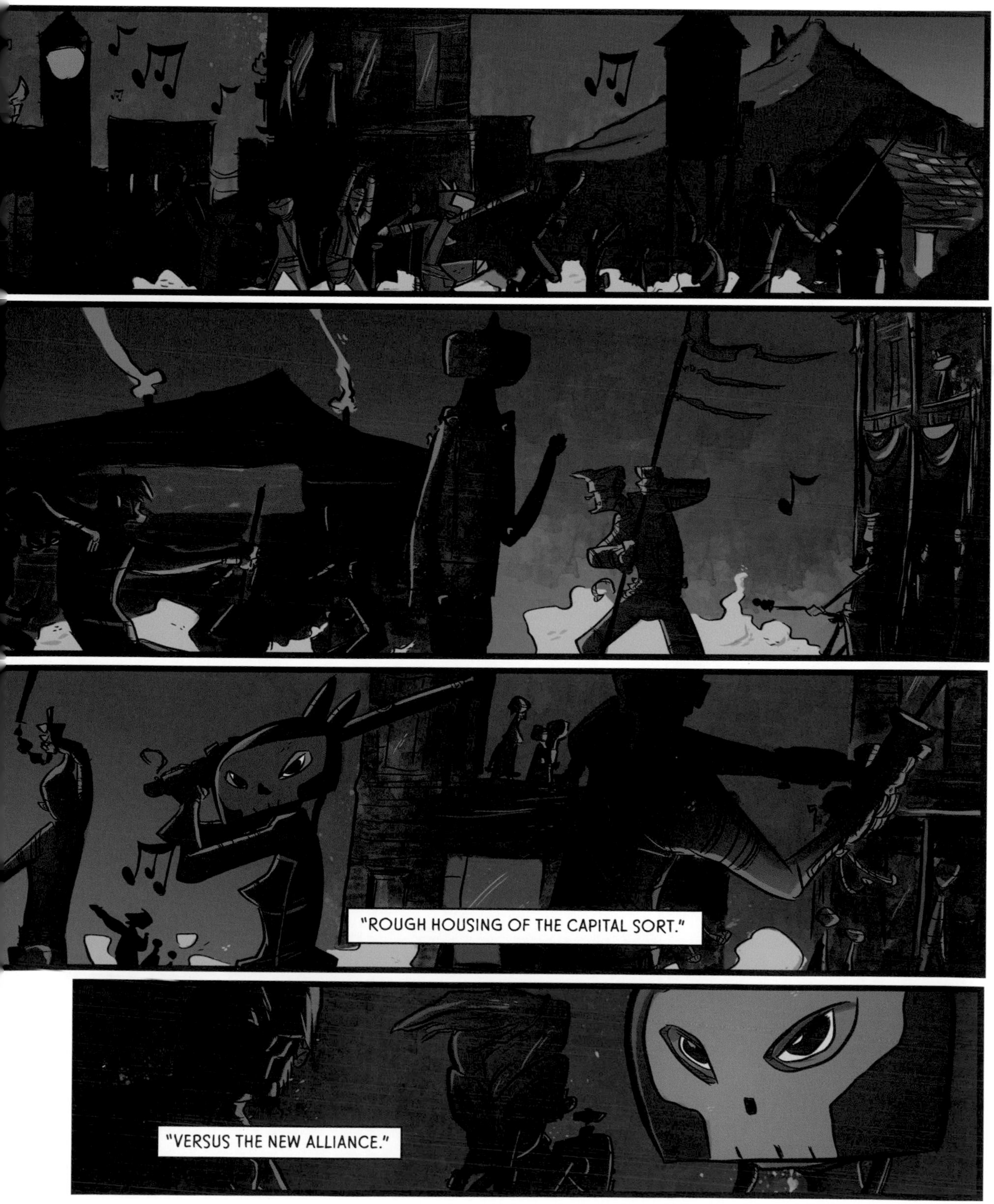
"ROUGH HOUSING OF THE CAPITAL SORT."
"VERSUS THE NEW ALLIANCE."

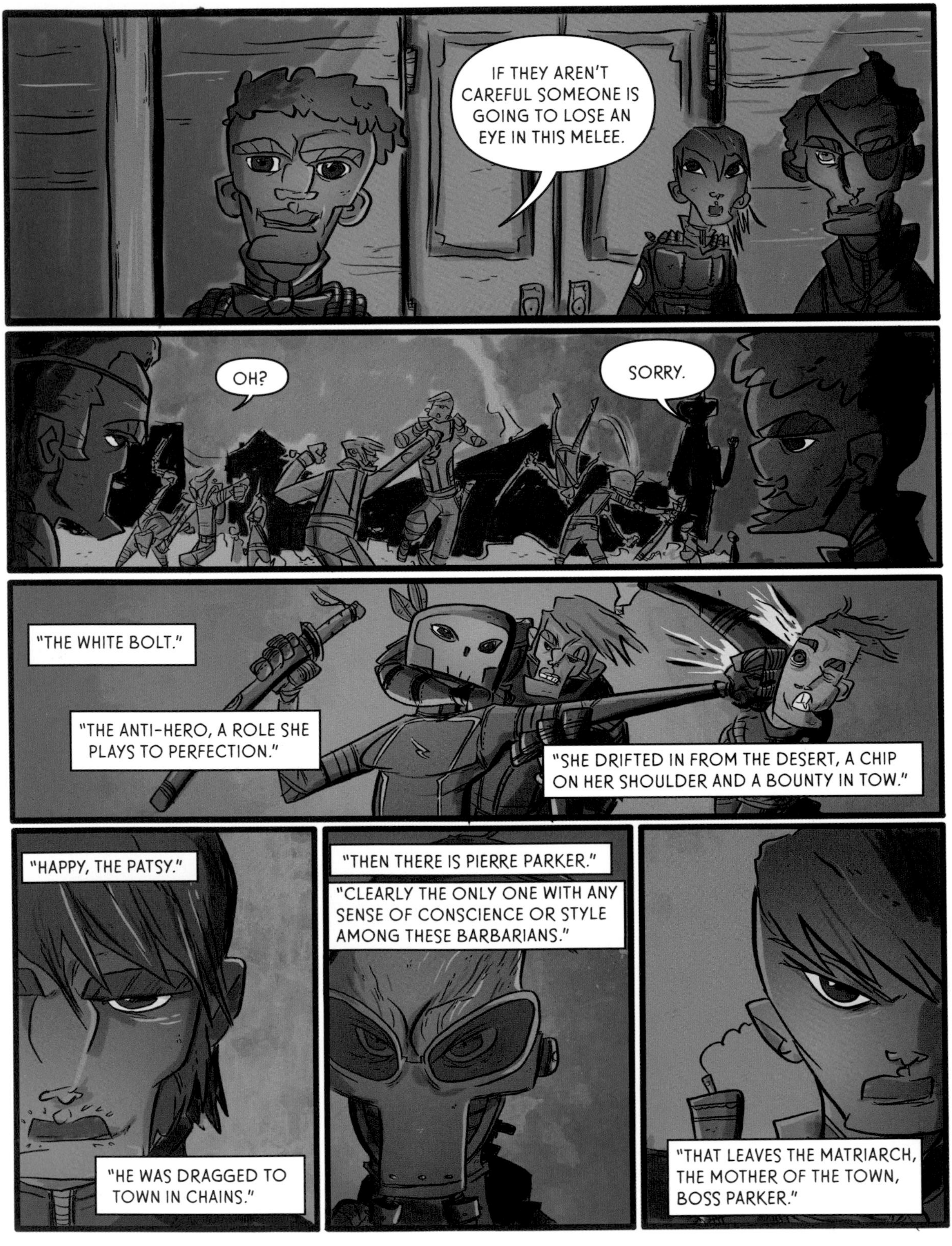
IF THEY AREN'T CAREFUL SOMEONE IS GOING TO LOSE AN EYE IN THIS MELEE.
OH?
SORRY.
"THE WHITE BOLT."
"THE ANTI-HERO, A ROLE SHE PLAYS TO PERFECTION."
"SHE DRIFTED IN FROM THE DESERT, A CHIP ON HER SHOULDER AND A BOUNTY IN TOW."
"HAPPY, THE PATSY."
"HE WAS DRAGGED TO TOWN IN CHAINS."
"THEN THERE IS PIERRE PARKER."
"CLEARLY THE ONLY ONE WITH ANY SENSE OF CONSCIENCE OR STYLE AMONG THESE BARBARIANS."
"THAT LEAVES THE MATRIARCH, THE MOTHER OF THE TOWN, BOSS PARKER."

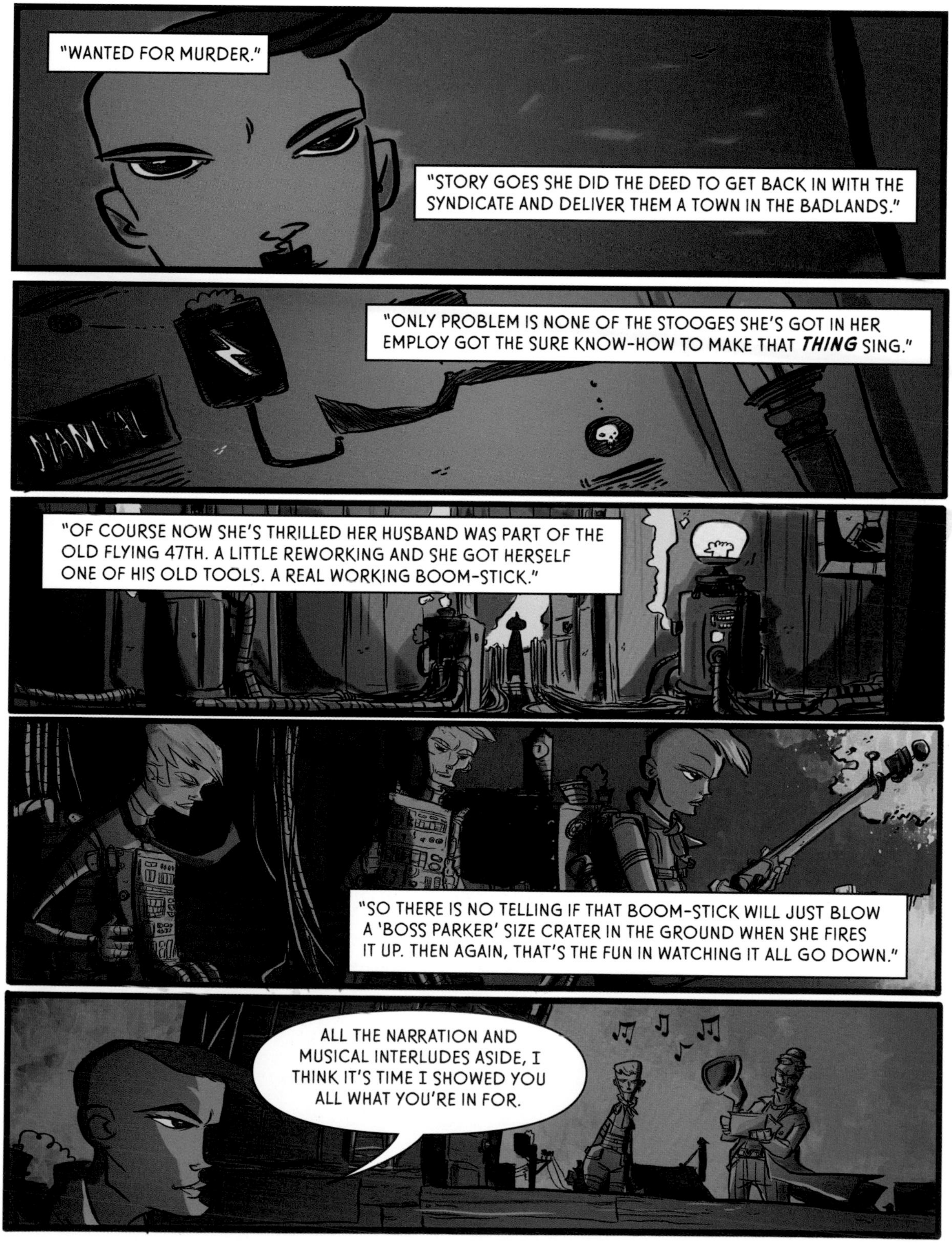
"WANTED FOR MURDER."
"STORY GOES SHE DID THE DEED TO GET BACK IN WITH THE SYNDICATE AND DELIVER THEM A TOWN IN THE BADLANDS."
"ONLY PROBLEM IS NONE OF THE STOOGES SHE'S GOT IN HER EMPLOY GOT THE SURE KNOW-HOW TO MAKE THAT ***THING*** SING."
"OF COURSE NOW SHE'S THRILLED HER HUSBAND WAS PART OF THE OLD FLYING 47TH. A LITTLE REWORKING AND SHE GOT HERSELF ONE OF HIS OLD TOOLS. A REAL WORKING BOOM-STICK."
"SO THERE IS NO TELLING IF THAT BOOM-STICK WILL JUST BLOW A 'BOSS PARKER' SIZE CRATER IN THE GROUND WHEN SHE FIRES IT UP. THEN AGAIN, THAT'S THE FUN IN WATCHING IT ALL GO DOWN."
ALL THE NARRATION AND MUSICAL INTERLUDES ASIDE, I THINK IT'S TIME I SHOWED YOU ALL WHAT YOU'RE IN FOR.

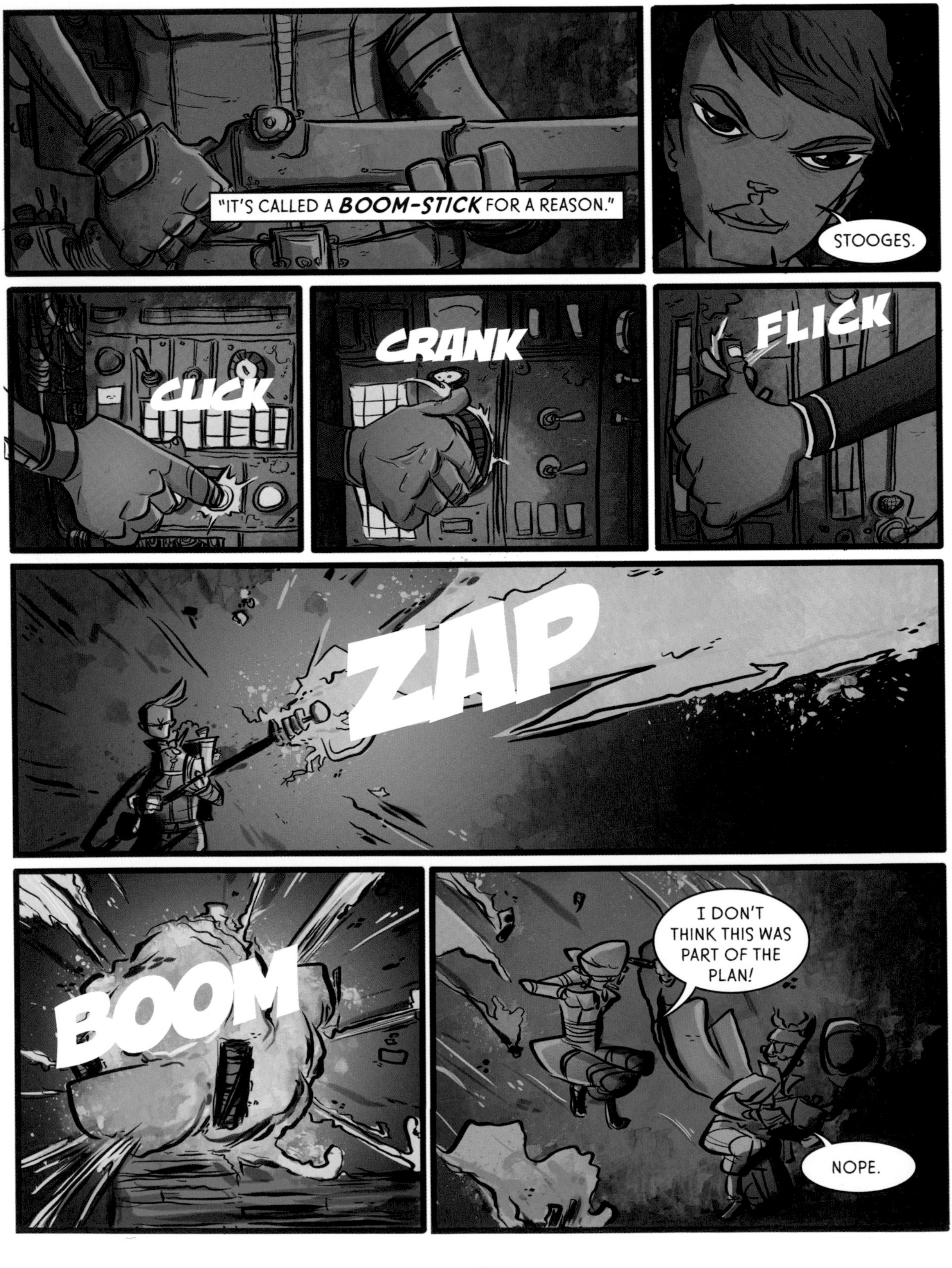
"IT'S CALLED A BOOM-STICK FOR A REASON."
STOOGES.
CLICK
CRANK
FLICK
ZAP
BOOM
I DON'T THINK THIS WAS PART OF THE PLAN!
NOPE.

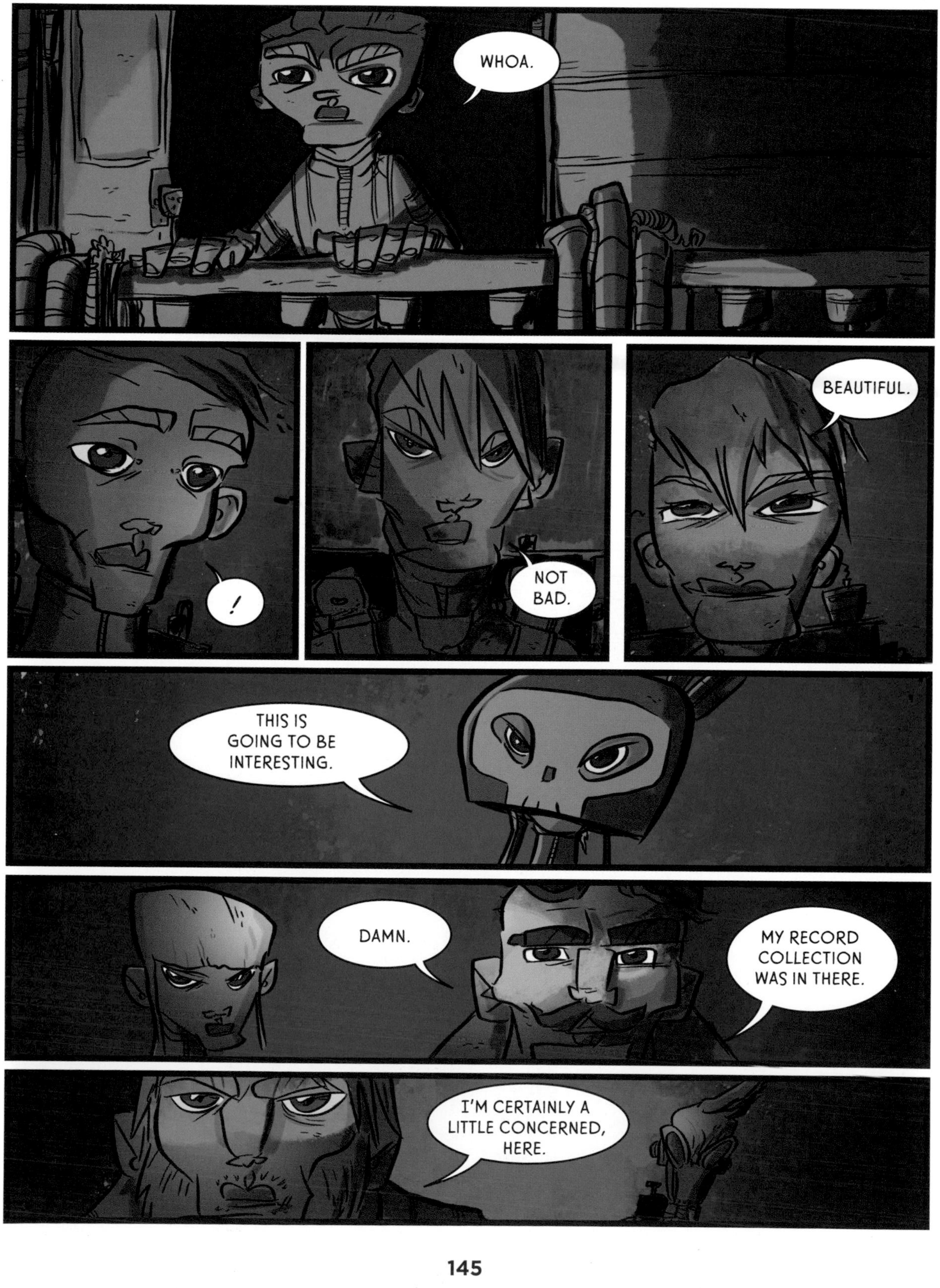
WHOA.
!
NOT BAD.
BEAUTIFUL.
THIS IS GOING TO BE INTERESTING.
DAMN.
MY RECORD COLLECTION WAS IN THERE.
I'M CERTAINLY A LITTLE CONCERNED, HERE.

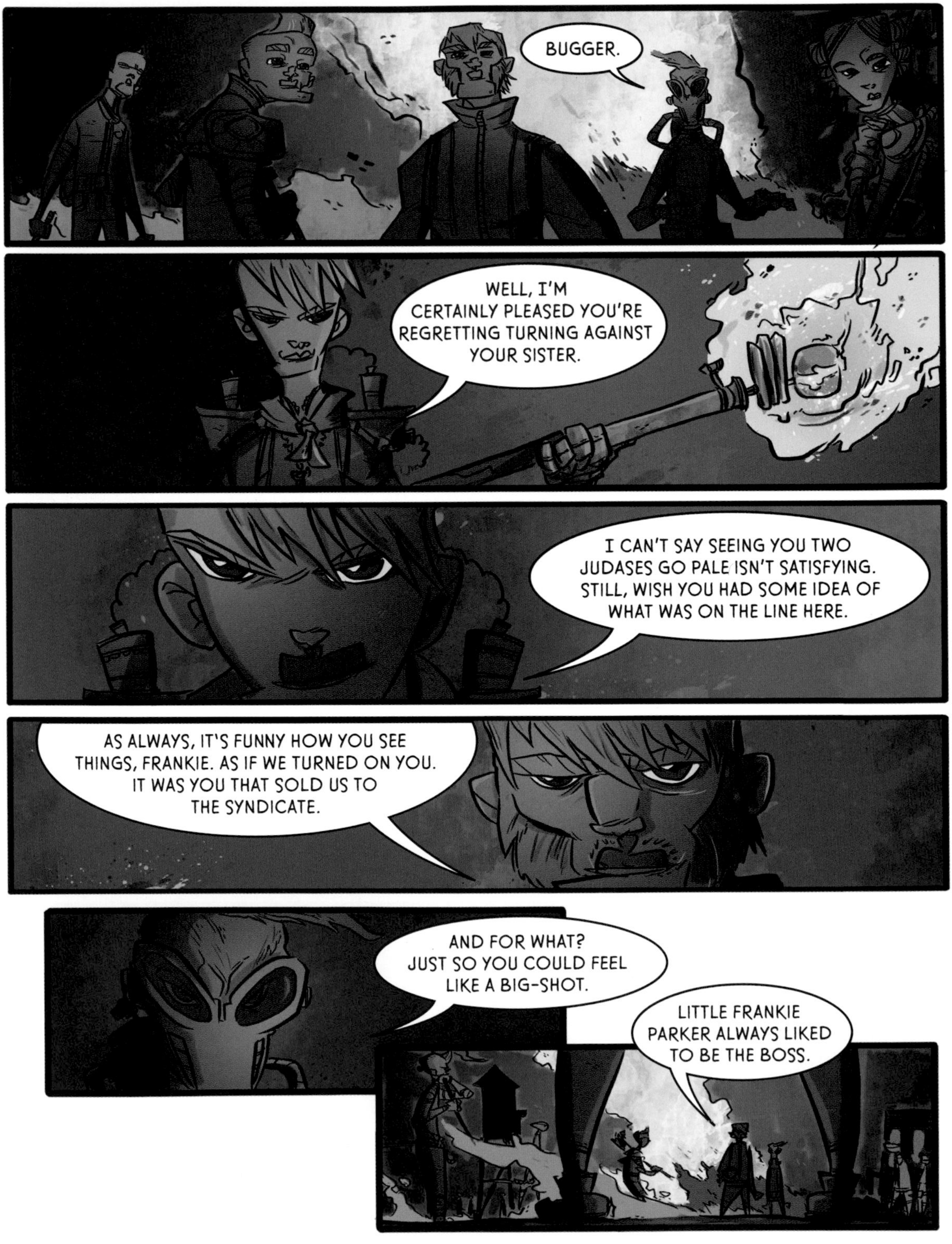
BUGGER.
WELL, I'M CERTAINLY PLEASED YOU'RE REGRETTING TURNING AGAINST YOUR SISTER.
I CAN'T SAY SEEING YOU TWO JUDASES GO PALE ISN'T SATISFYING. STILL, WISH YOU HAD SOME IDEA OF WHAT WAS ON THE LINE HERE.
AS ALWAYS, IT'S FUNNY HOW YOU SEE THINGS, FRANKIE. AS IF WE TURNED ON YOU. IT WAS YOU THAT SOLD US TO THE SYNDICATE.
AND FOR WHAT? JUST SO YOU COULD FEEL LIKE A BIG-SHOT.
LITTLE FRANKIE PARKER ALWAYS LIKED TO BE THE BOSS.

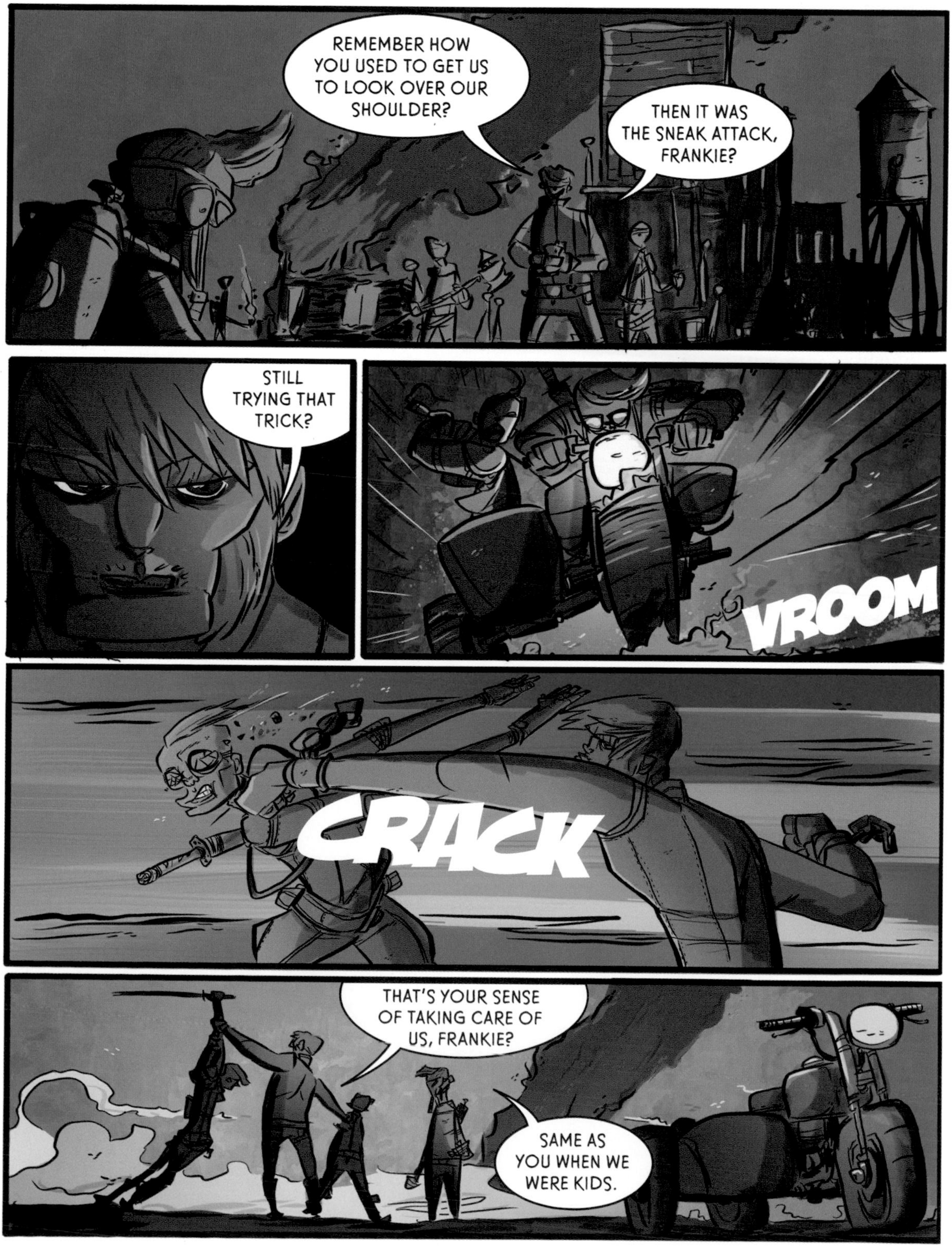

REMEMBER HOW YOU USED TO GET US TO LOOK OVER OUR SHOULDER?
THEN IT WAS THE SNEAK ATTACK, FRANKIE?
STILL TRYING THAT TRICK?
VROOM
CRACK
THAT'S YOUR SENSE OF TAKING CARE OF US, FRANKIE?
SAME AS YOU WHEN WE WERE KIDS.

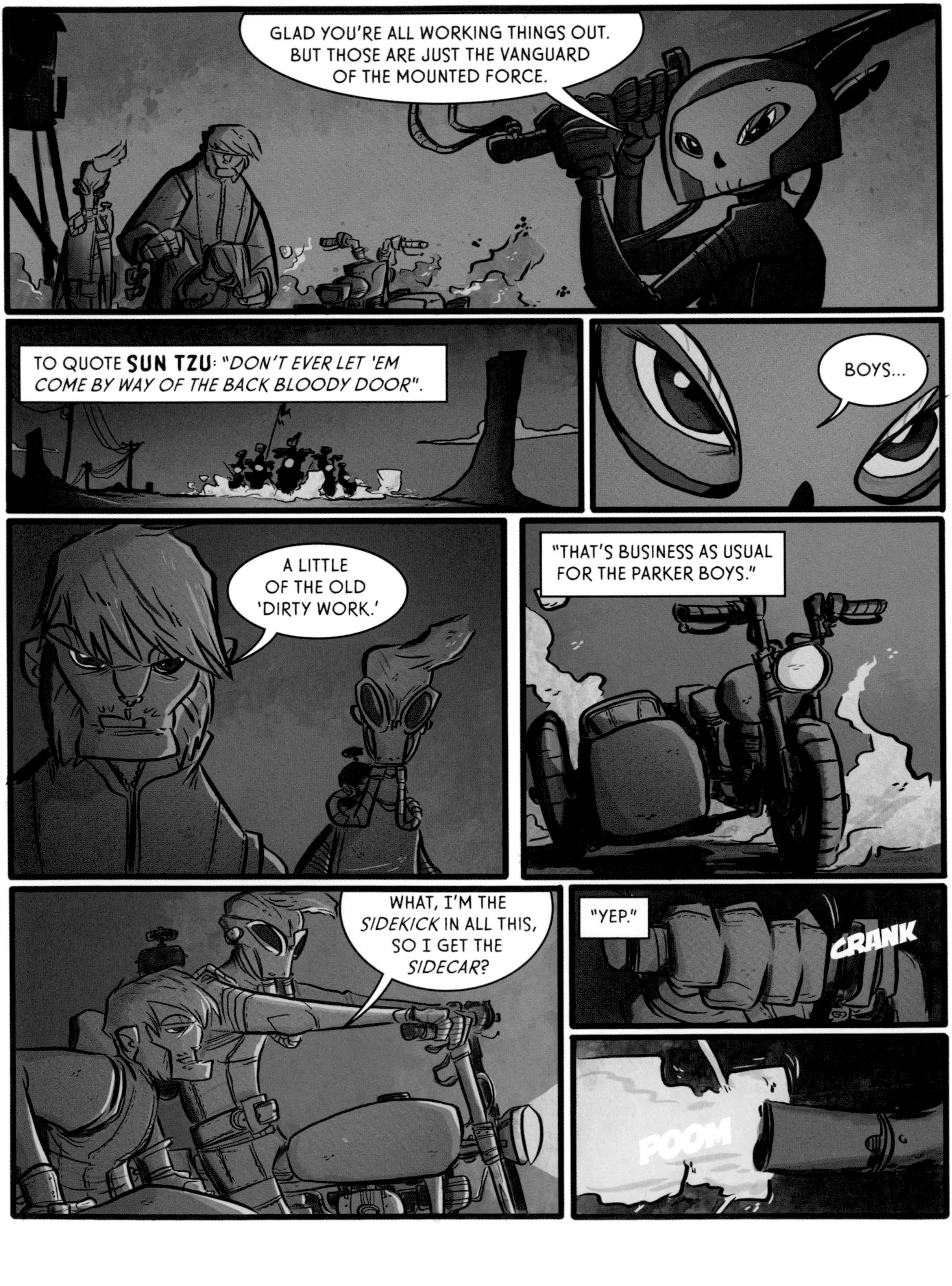
GLAD YOU'RE ALL WORKING THINGS OUT. BUT THOSE ARE JUST THE VANGUARD OF THE MOUNTED FORCE.
TO QUOTE **SUN TZU**: *"DON'T EVER LET 'EM COME BY WAY OF THE BACK BLOODY DOOR"*.
BOYS...
A LITTLE OF THE OLD 'DIRTY WORK.'
"THAT'S BUSINESS AS USUAL FOR THE PARKER BOYS."
WHAT, I'M THE *SIDEKICK* IN ALL THIS, SO I GET THE *SIDECAR*?
"YEP."
CRANK
POOM

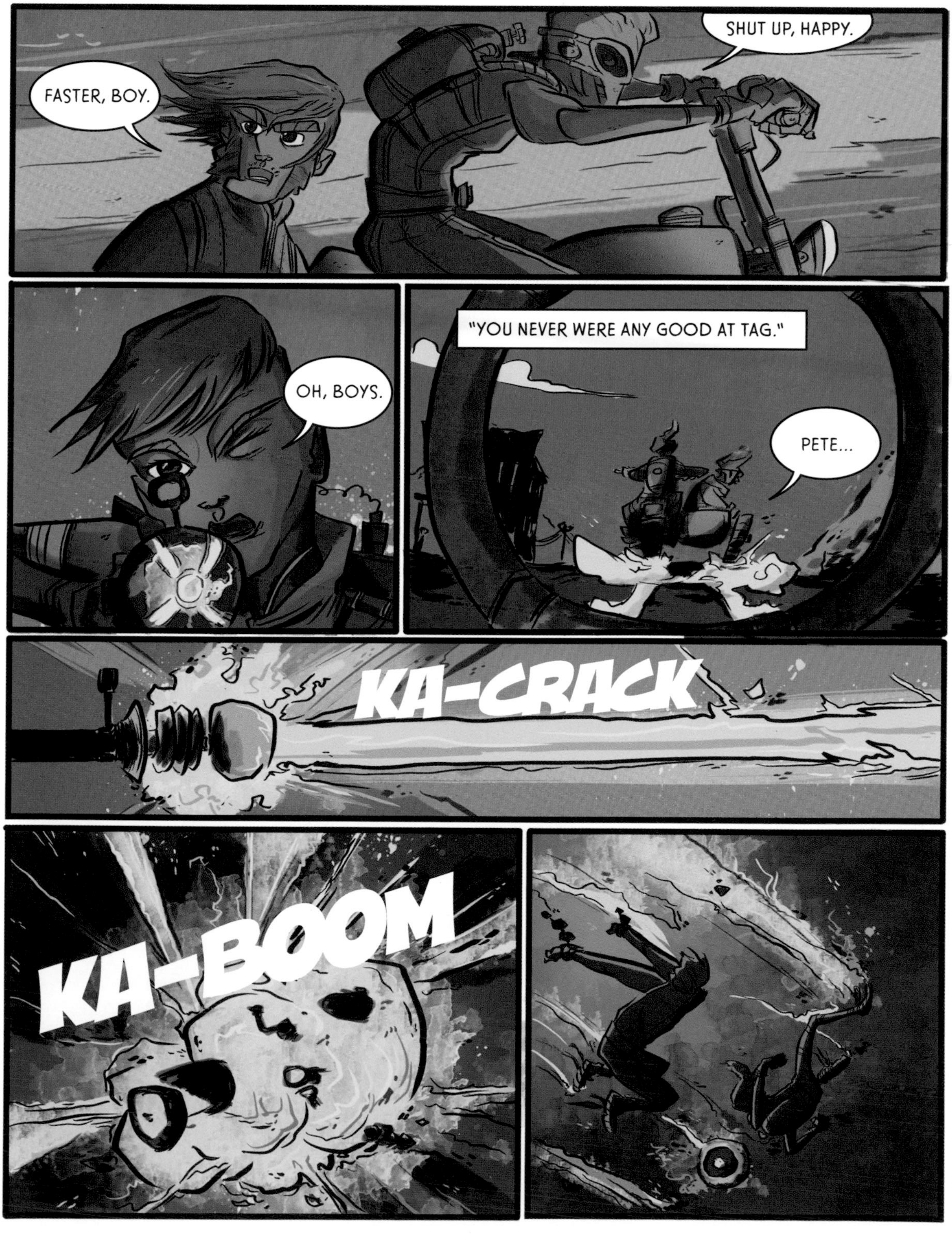
FASTER, BOY.
SHUT UP, HAPPY.
OH, BOYS.
"YOU NEVER WERE ANY GOOD AT TAG."
PETE...
KA-CRACK
KA-BOOM

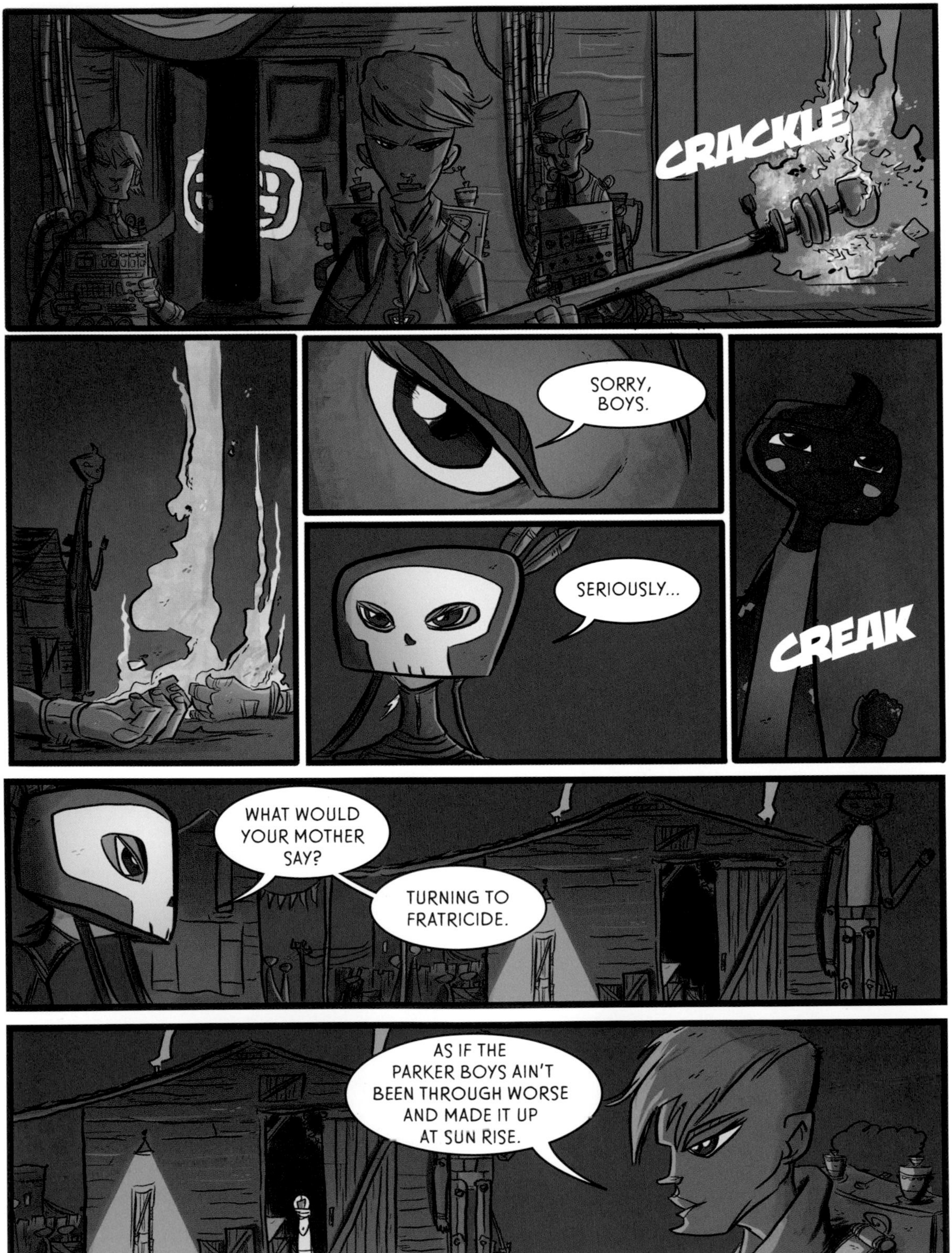
CRACKLE
SORRY, BOYS.
SERIOUSLY...
CREAK
WHAT WOULD YOUR MOTHER SAY?
TURNING TO FRATRICIDE.
AS IF THE PARKER BOYS AIN'T BEEN THROUGH WORSE AND MADE IT UP AT SUN RISE.

YOU GOT A HELL OF A WAY TO EXPRESS LOVE.

FAMILY ADVICE FROM A LITTLE GREEN MAN IN A SHINY SPACE SUIT?

FUNNY. YOU THINK YOU KNOW A THING ABOUT WHAT IS GOING ON AROUND HERE?

"JUST 'CUZ YOU APPOINTED YOURSELF SHERIFF, DON'T MEAN YOU KNOW BULL."

"YOU'RE TOO BUSY COMBING YOUR HAIR..."

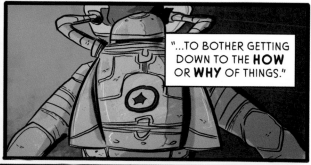

"AND GETTING DONE UP IN THAT STUPID SHINY SILVER SUIT OF YOURS..."

"...TO BOTHER GETTING DOWN TO THE **HOW** OR **WHY** OF THINGS."

"YOU GOT NO IDEA HOW YOUR FRIEND MET HIS END, OR WHAT I HAD TO DO TO KEEP THOSE PARKER BOYS SAFE."

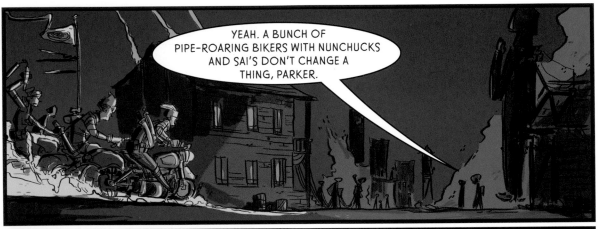

YEAH. A BUNCH OF PIPE-ROARING BIKERS WITH NUNCHUCKS AND SAI'S DON'T CHANGE A THING, PARKER.

SO UNLESS YOU WANT TO SURRENDER, GET READY FOR SOME PAIN.

I'LL TAKE MY CHANCES AGAINST YOU TWO. ALL THOSE BIG WORDS MAKE ME THINK YOU'RE GONNA FALTER.

THAT'S JUST MY SOUTHERN HOSPITALITY GETTING IN THE WAY OF SOME GOOD OLD-FASHIONED SCORE SETTLING.

THEN I'LL PAY IT NO BLOODY MIND AT ALL.

"I KNOW MY CREDO."

"I'VE LEARNED WHAT HONOR THERE IS IN THE DESERT."

"AND WHAT IT TAKES TO SURVIVE."

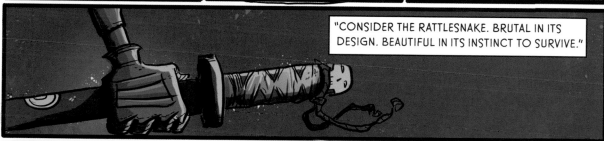

"CONSIDER THE RATTLESNAKE. BRUTAL IN ITS DESIGN. BEAUTIFUL IN ITS INSTINCT TO SURVIVE."

"PERFECTLY SUITED TO PROSPER IN A PARCHED LAND UNDER AN ACID SUN."

"TOOLS TO KILL. TOOLS TO LIVE."

YOU THRIVE ON YOUR INSTINCT TO SURVIVE.

NOT INSTINCT. BLOODY DOGGED WILL.

WELL THEN, LET'S GET ON WITH THIS PHILOSOPHY LESSON.

IT'S A LESSON COMING FOR YOU, ROY, SURE ENOUGH.

DID YOU KNOW YOU'RE WEARING A DEAD MAN'S SUIT?

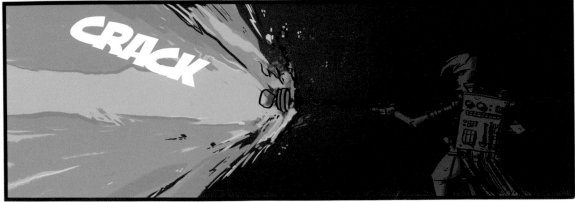

CRACK

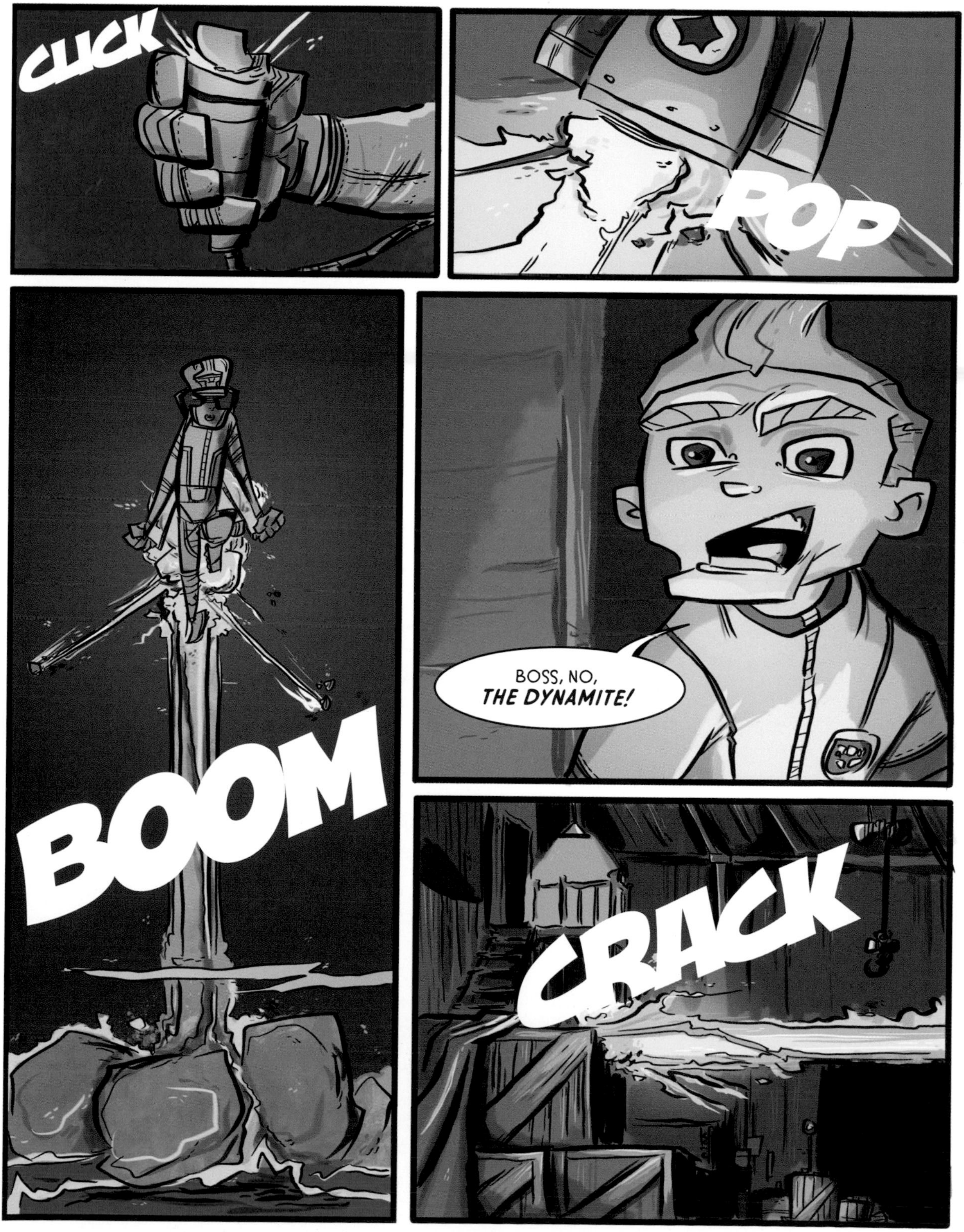
CLICK
POP
BOOM
BOSS, NO, *THE DYNAMITE!*
CRACK

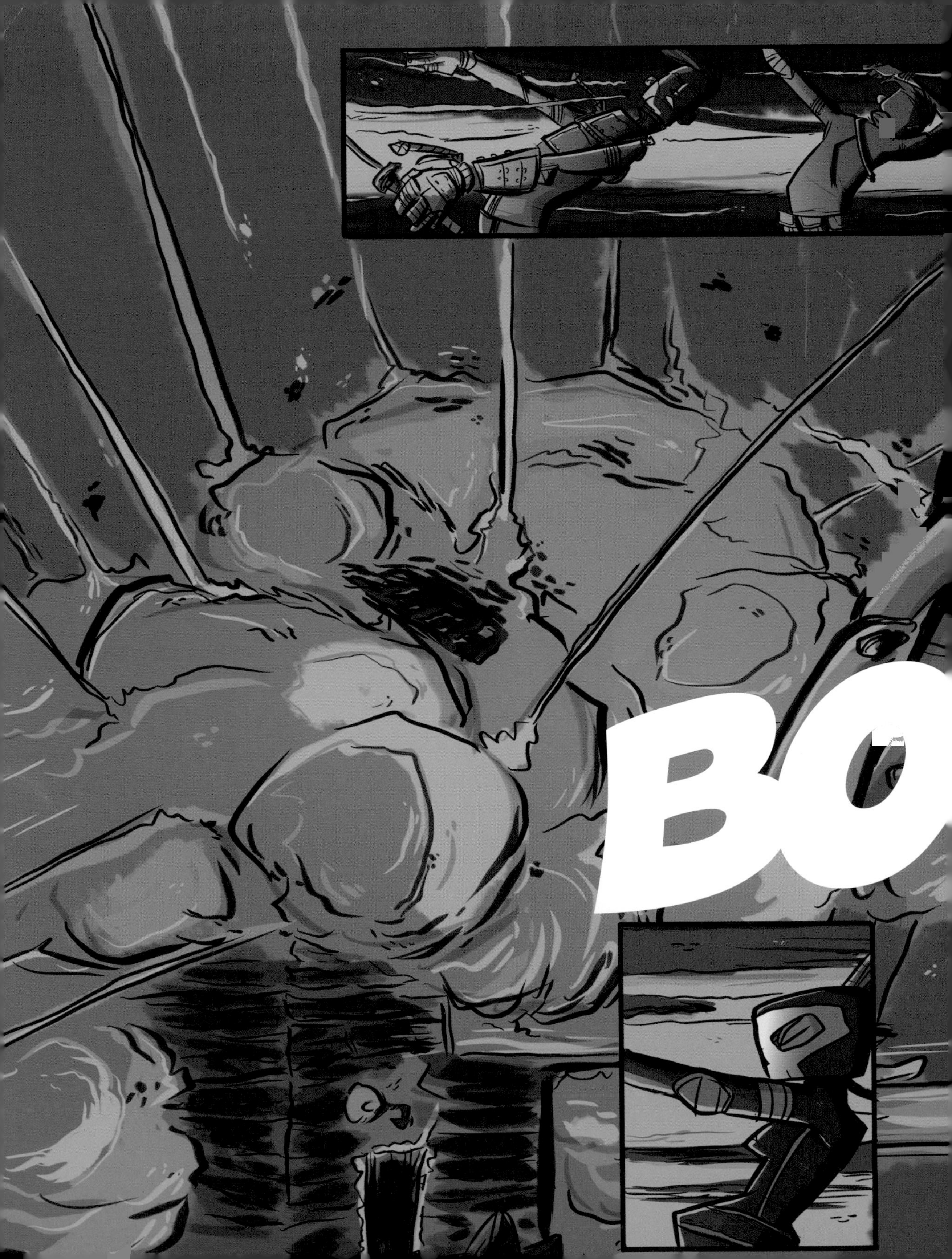
BO

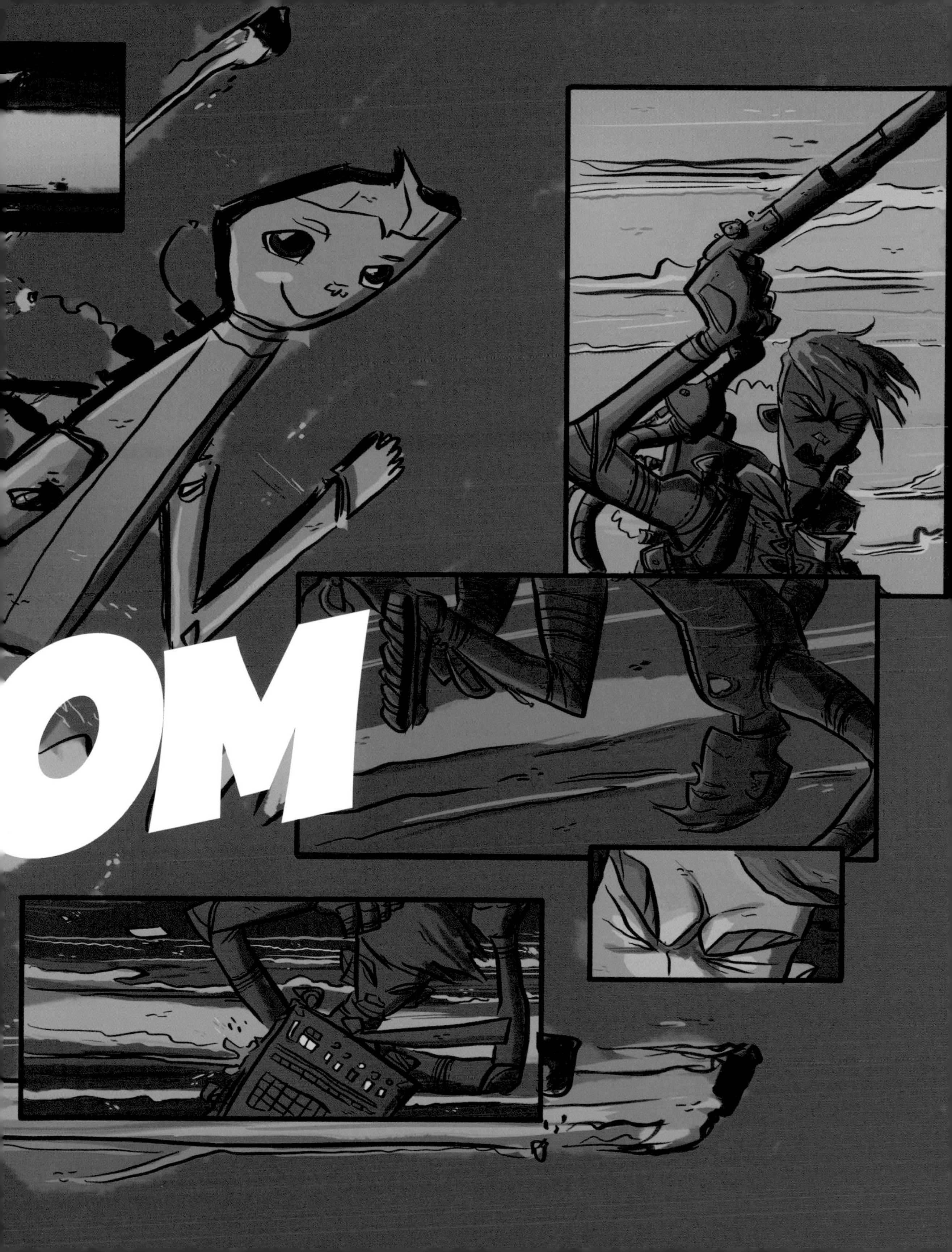
OM

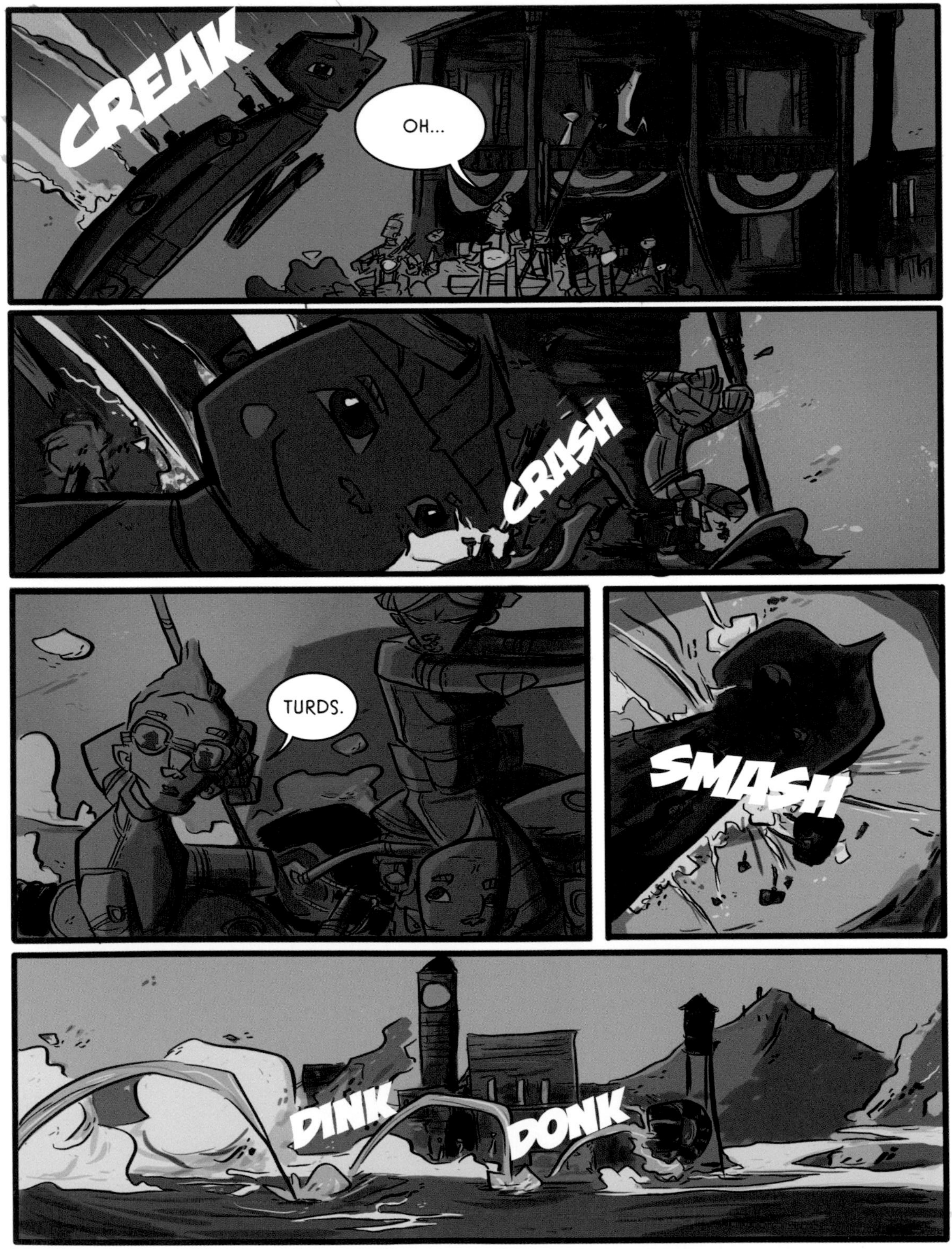
CREAK
OH...
CRASH
TURDS.
SMASH
DINK
DONK

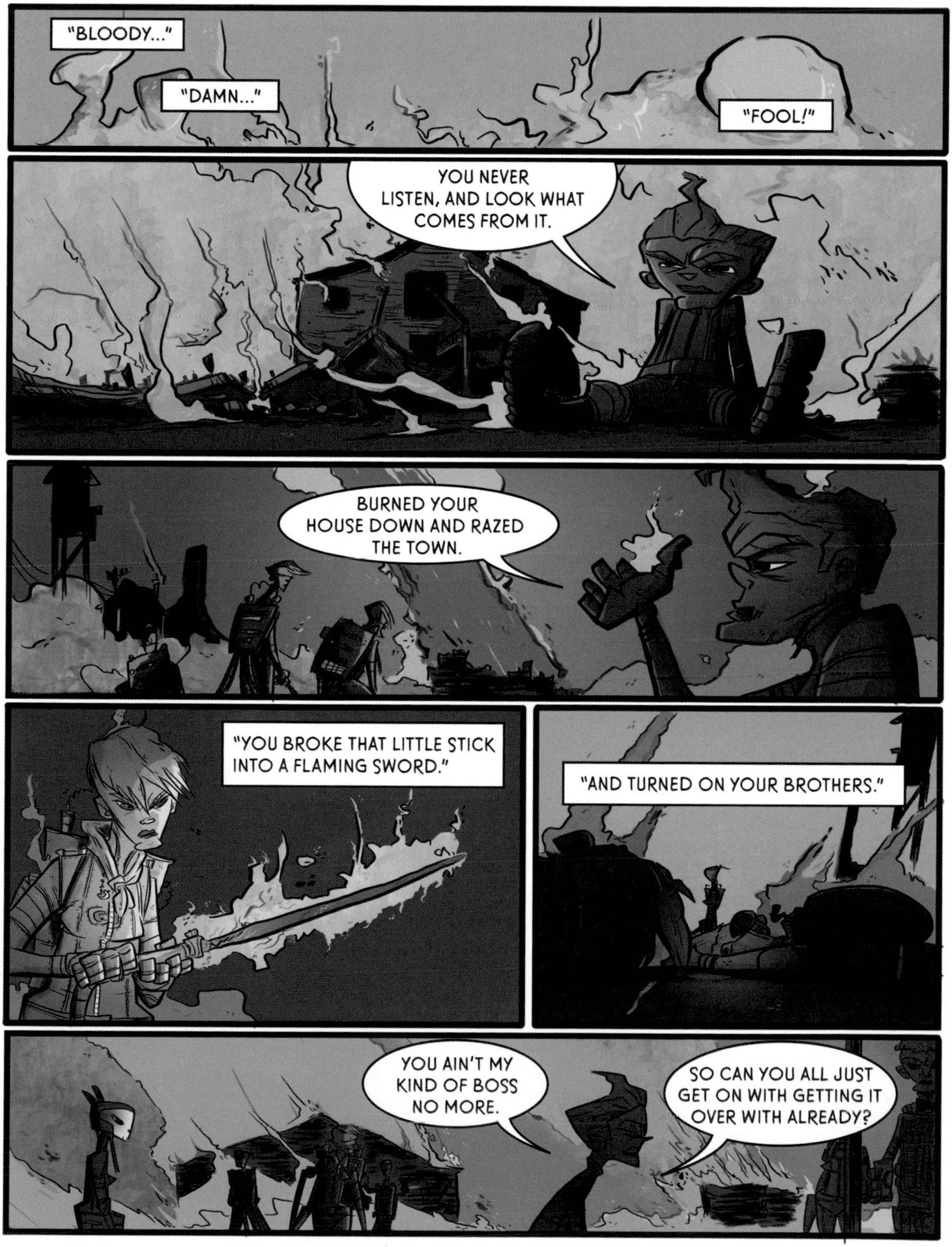
"BLOODY..."
"DAMN..."
"FOOL!"
YOU NEVER LISTEN, AND LOOK WHAT COMES FROM IT.
BURNED YOUR HOUSE DOWN AND RAZED THE TOWN.
"YOU BROKE THAT LITTLE STICK INTO A FLAMING SWORD."
"AND TURNED ON YOUR BROTHERS."
YOU AIN'T MY KIND OF BOSS NO MORE.
SO CAN YOU ALL JUST GET ON WITH GETTING IT OVER WITH ALREADY?

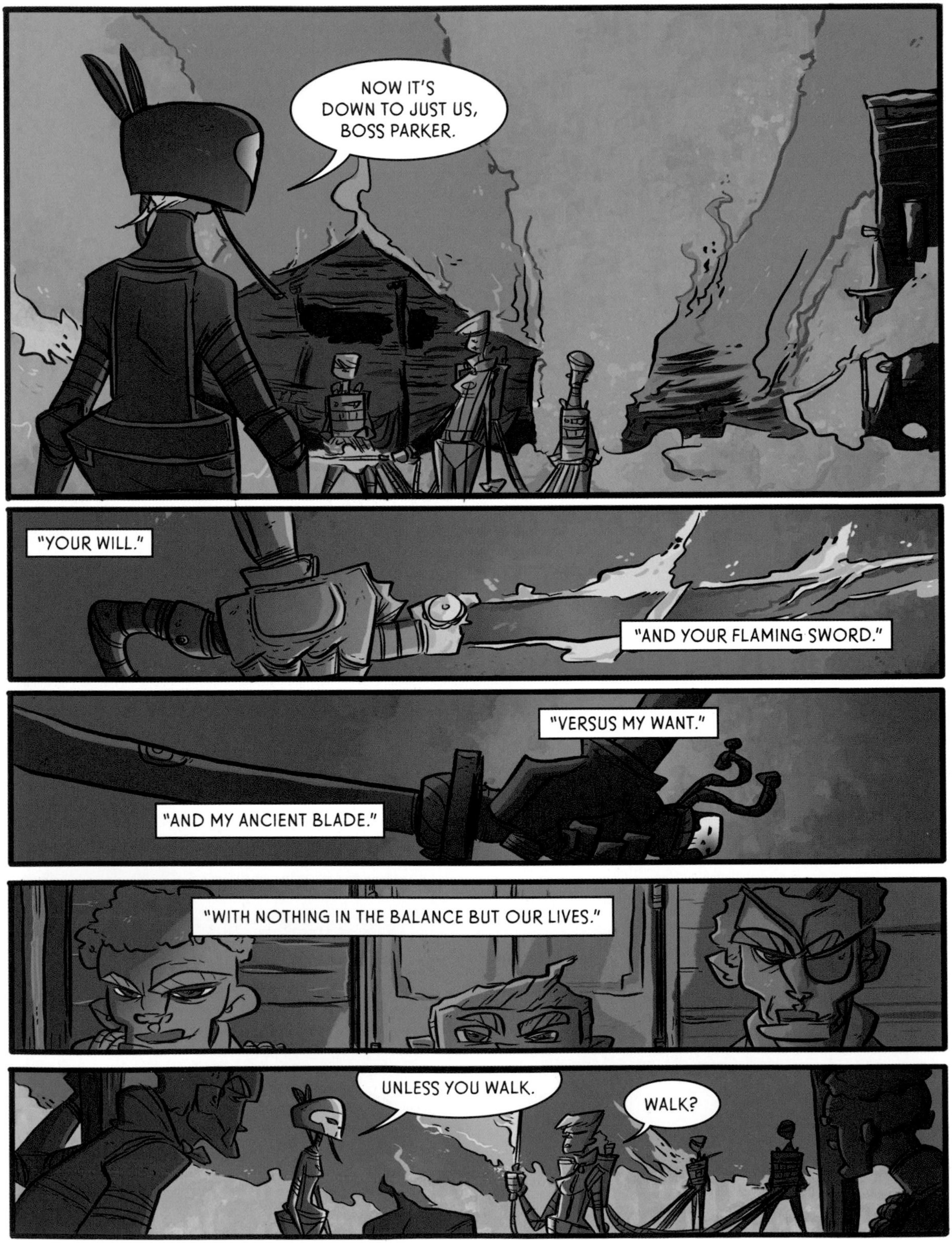
NOW IT'S DOWN TO JUST US, BOSS PARKER.
"YOUR WILL."
"AND YOUR FLAMING SWORD."
"VERSUS MY WANT."
"AND MY ANCIENT BLADE."
"WITH NOTHING IN THE BALANCE BUT OUR LIVES."
UNLESS YOU WALK.
WALK?

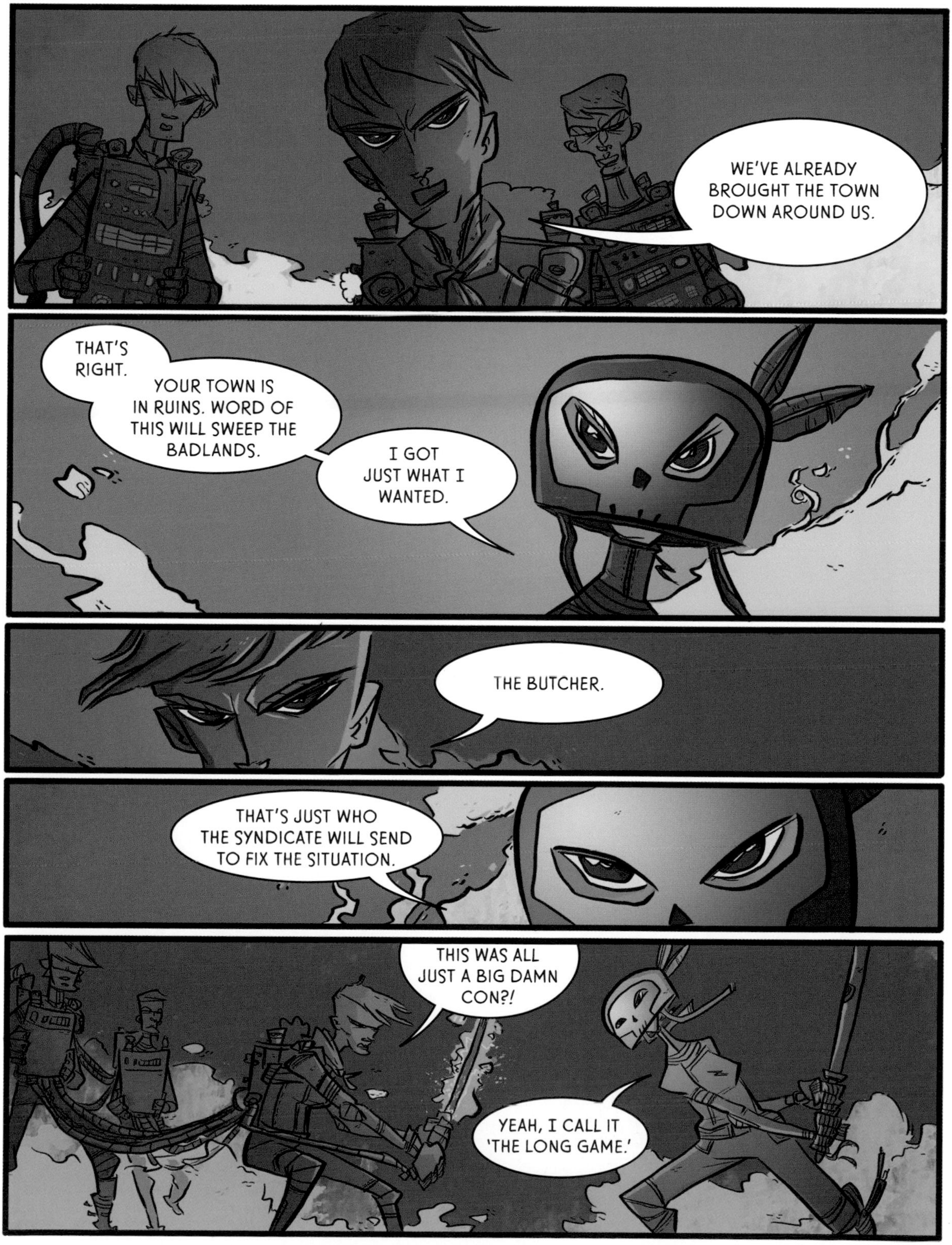

WE'VE ALREADY BROUGHT THE TOWN DOWN AROUND US.
THAT'S RIGHT.
YOUR TOWN IS IN RUINS. WORD OF THIS WILL SWEEP THE BADLANDS.
I GOT JUST WHAT I WANTED.
THE BUTCHER.
THAT'S JUST WHO THE SYNDICATE WILL SEND TO FIX THE SITUATION.
THIS WAS ALL JUST A BIG DAMN CON?!
YEAH, I CALL IT 'THE LONG GAME.'

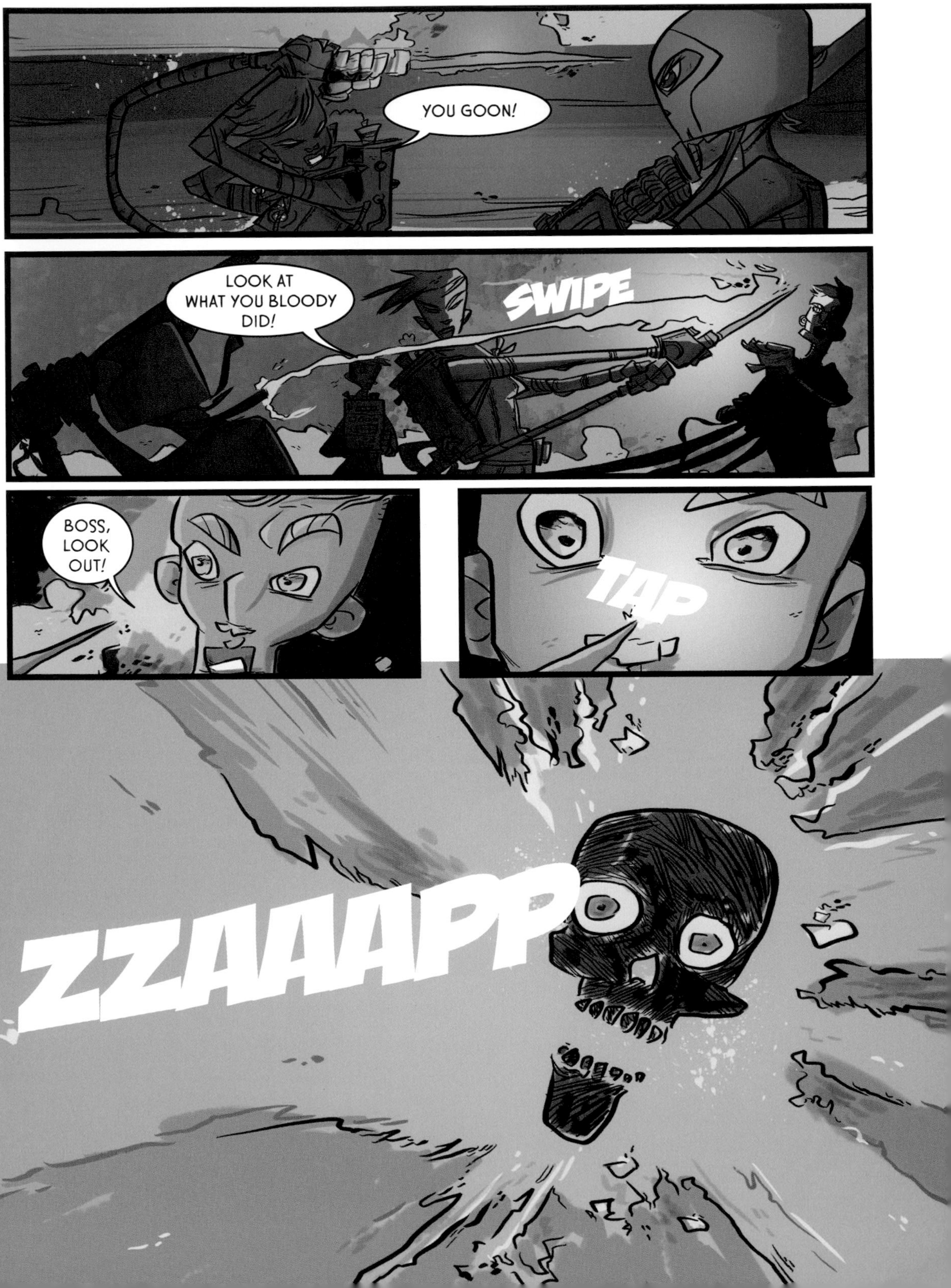
YOU GOON!
LOOK AT WHAT YOU BLOODY DID!
SWIPE
BOSS, LOOK OUT!
TAP
ZZAAAPP

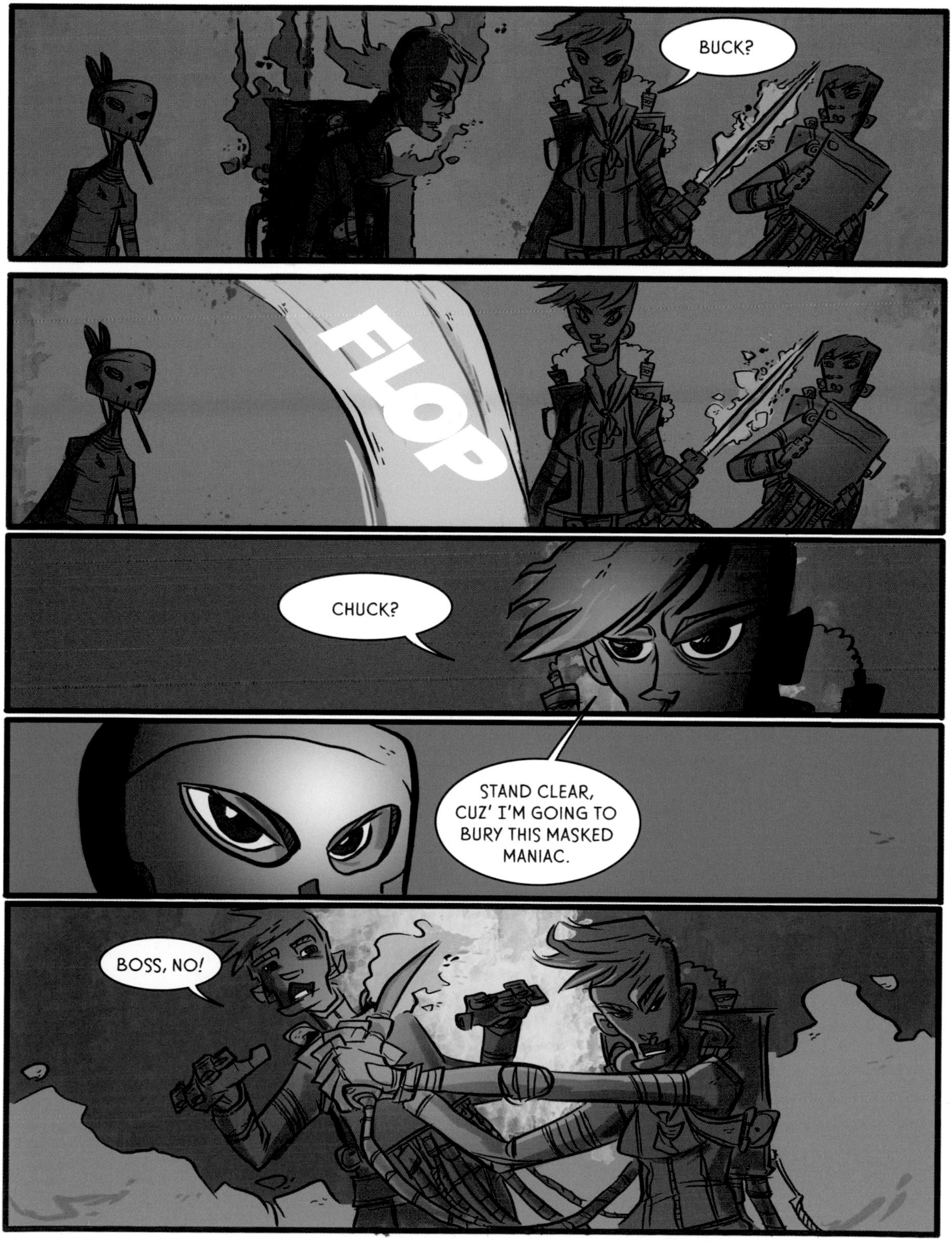
BUCK?
FLOP
CHUCK?
STAND CLEAR, CUZ' I'M GOING TO BURY THIS MASKED MANIAC.
BOSS, NO!

TINK
BOOM
SNAP
LISTEN...
FLOP
I'M GOING TO SIT FOR A MOMENT AND LET YOU CATCH YOUR BREATH.

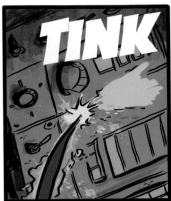

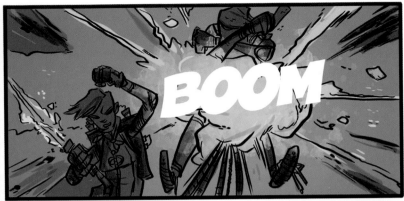

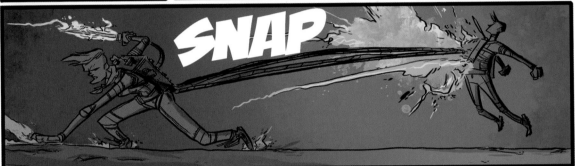

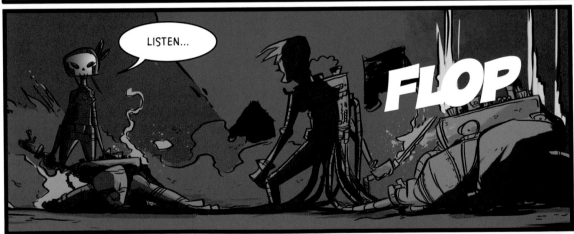

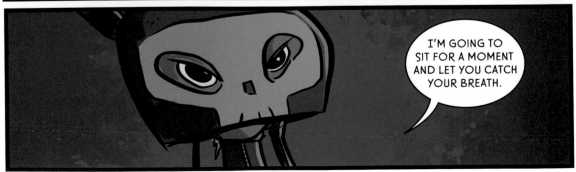

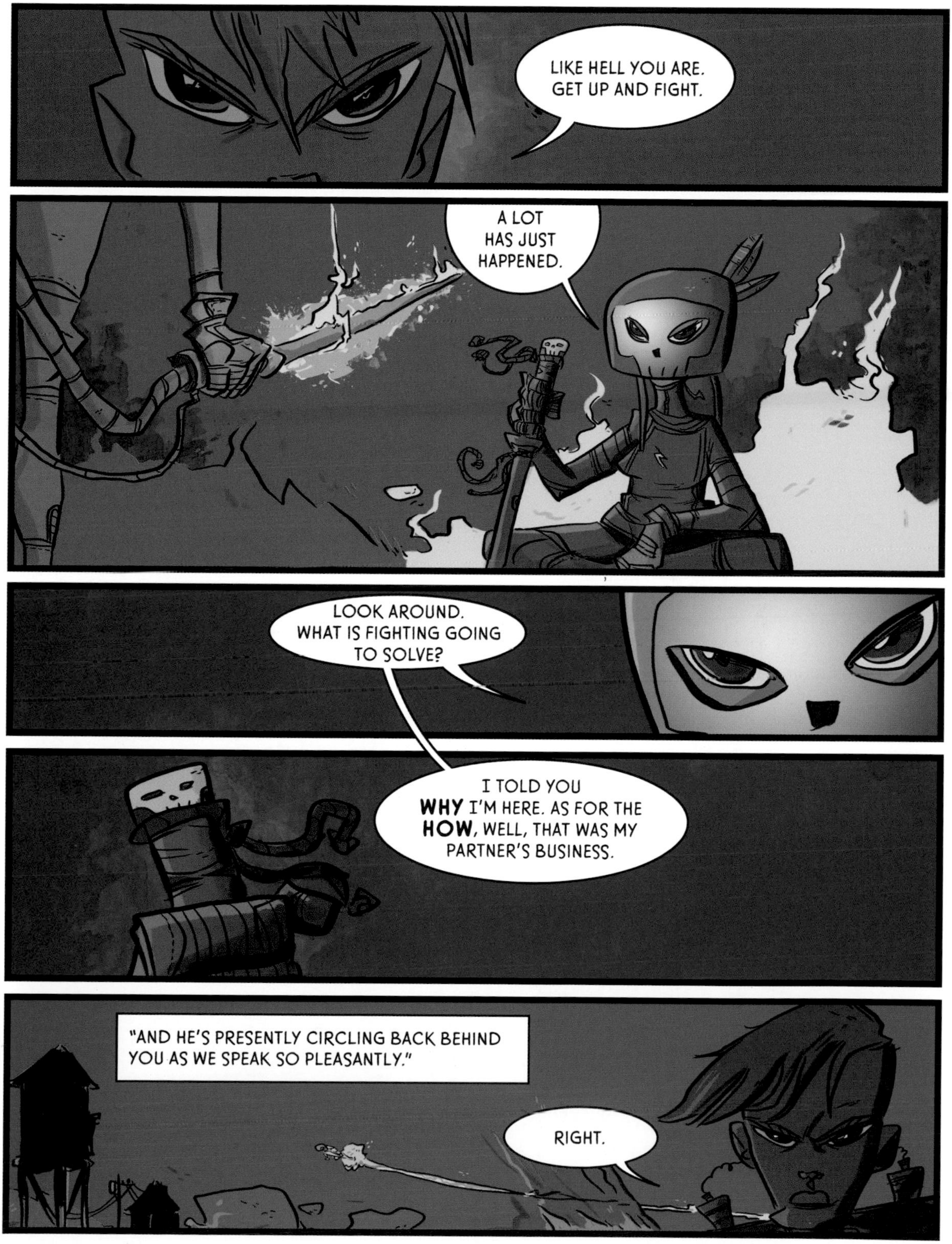
LIKE HELL YOU ARE. GET UP AND FIGHT.
A LOT HAS JUST HAPPENED.
LOOK AROUND. WHAT IS FIGHTING GOING TO SOLVE?
I TOLD YOU **WHY** I'M HERE. AS FOR THE **HOW**, WELL, THAT WAS MY PARTNER'S BUSINESS.
"AND HE'S PRESENTLY CIRCLING BACK BEHIND YOU AS WE SPEAK SO PLEASANTLY."
RIGHT.

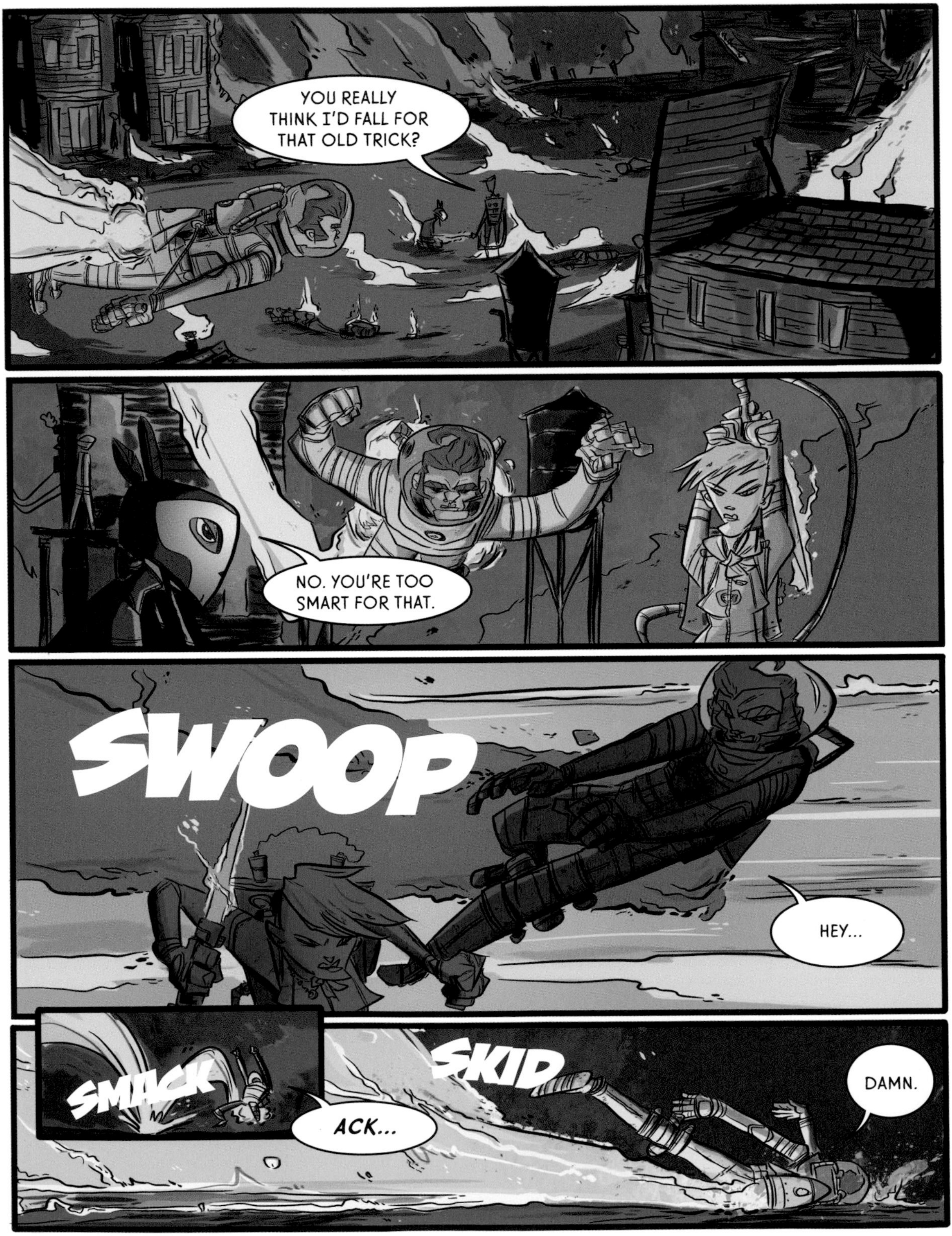
YOU REALLY THINK I'D FALL FOR THAT OLD TRICK?
NO. YOU'RE TOO SMART FOR THAT.
SWOOP
HEY...
SMACK
ACK...
SKID
DAMN.

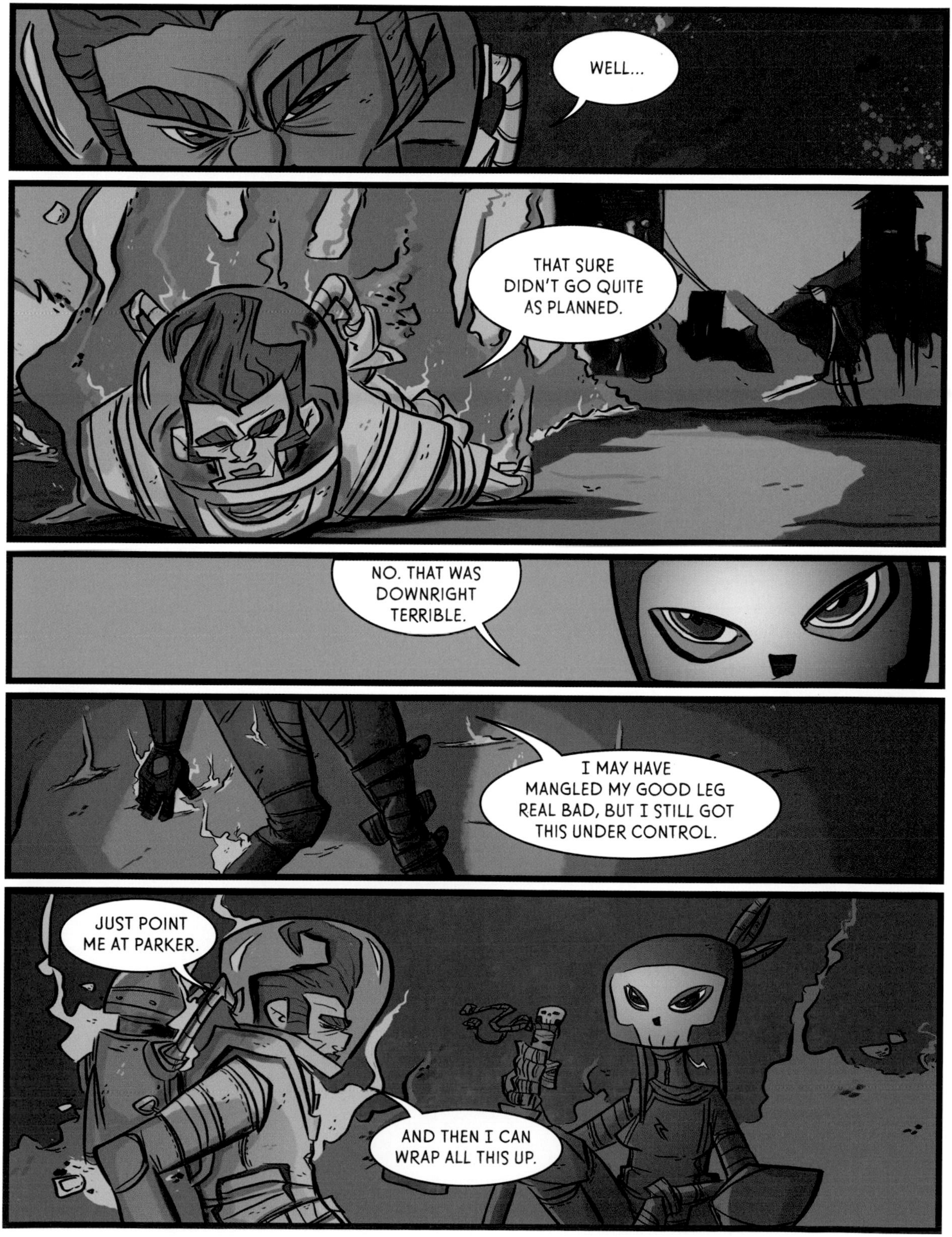
WELL...
THAT SURE DIDN'T GO QUITE AS PLANNED.
NO. THAT WAS DOWNRIGHT TERRIBLE.
I MAY HAVE MANGLED MY GOOD LEG REAL BAD, BUT I STILL GOT THIS UNDER CONTROL.
JUST POINT ME AT PARKER.
AND THEN I CAN WRAP ALL THIS UP.

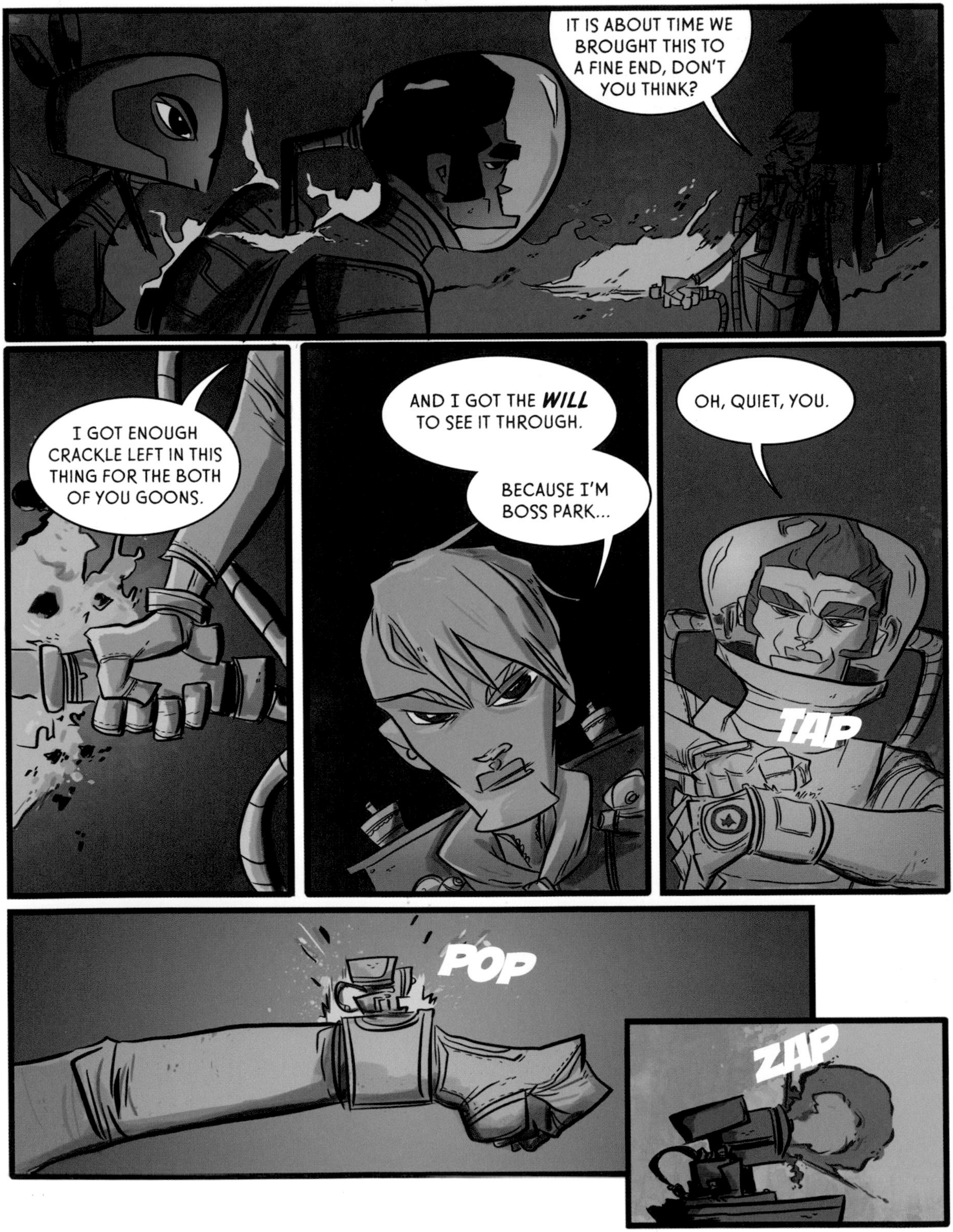
IT IS ABOUT TIME WE BROUGHT THIS TO A FINE END, DON'T YOU THINK?
I GOT ENOUGH CRACKLE LEFT IN THIS THING FOR THE BOTH OF YOU GOONS.
AND I GOT THE *WILL* TO SEE IT THROUGH.
BECAUSE I'M BOSS PARK...
OH, QUIET, YOU.
TAP
POP
ZAP

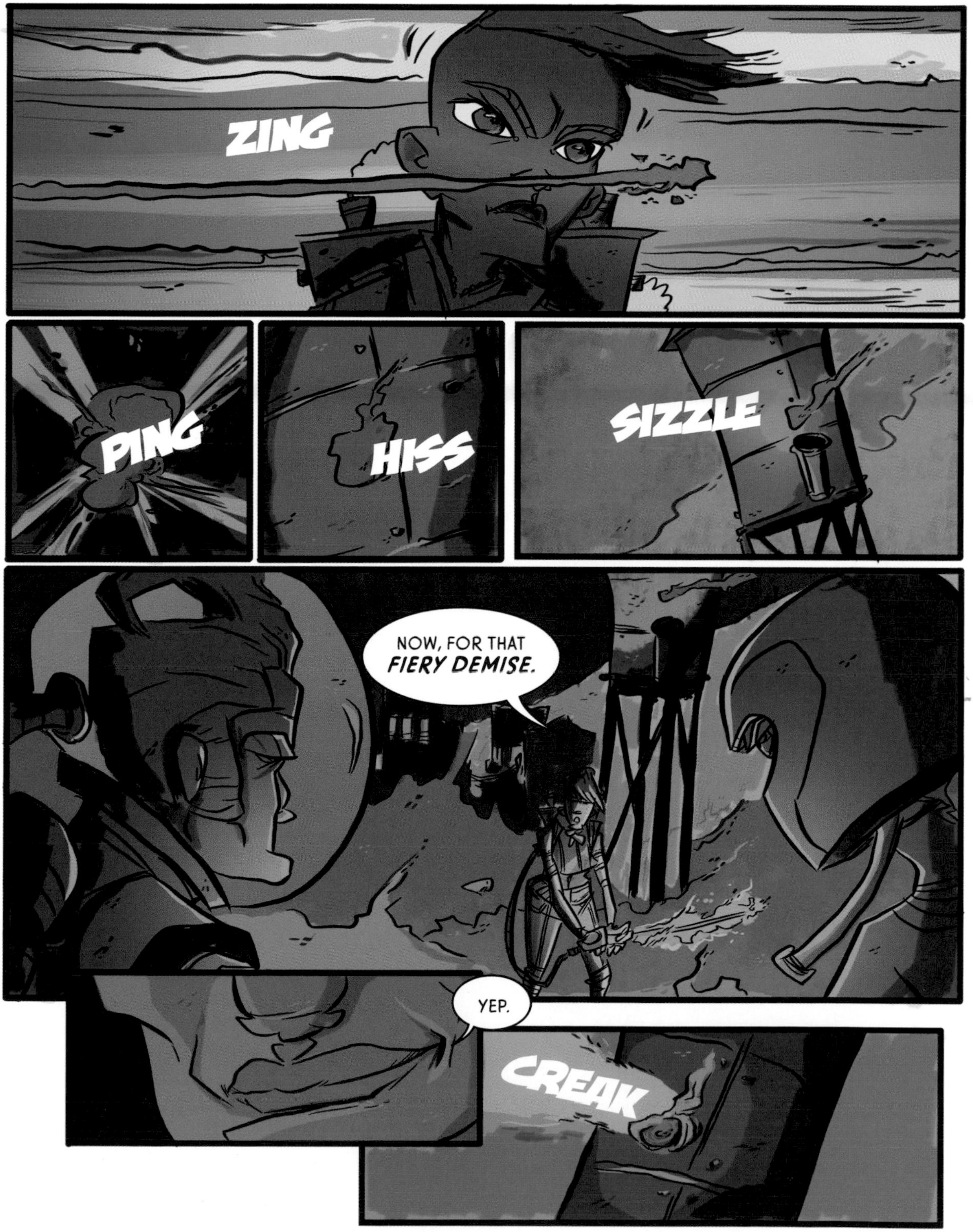
ZING
PING
HISS
SIZZLE
NOW, FOR THAT *FIERY DEMISE.*
YEP.
CREAK

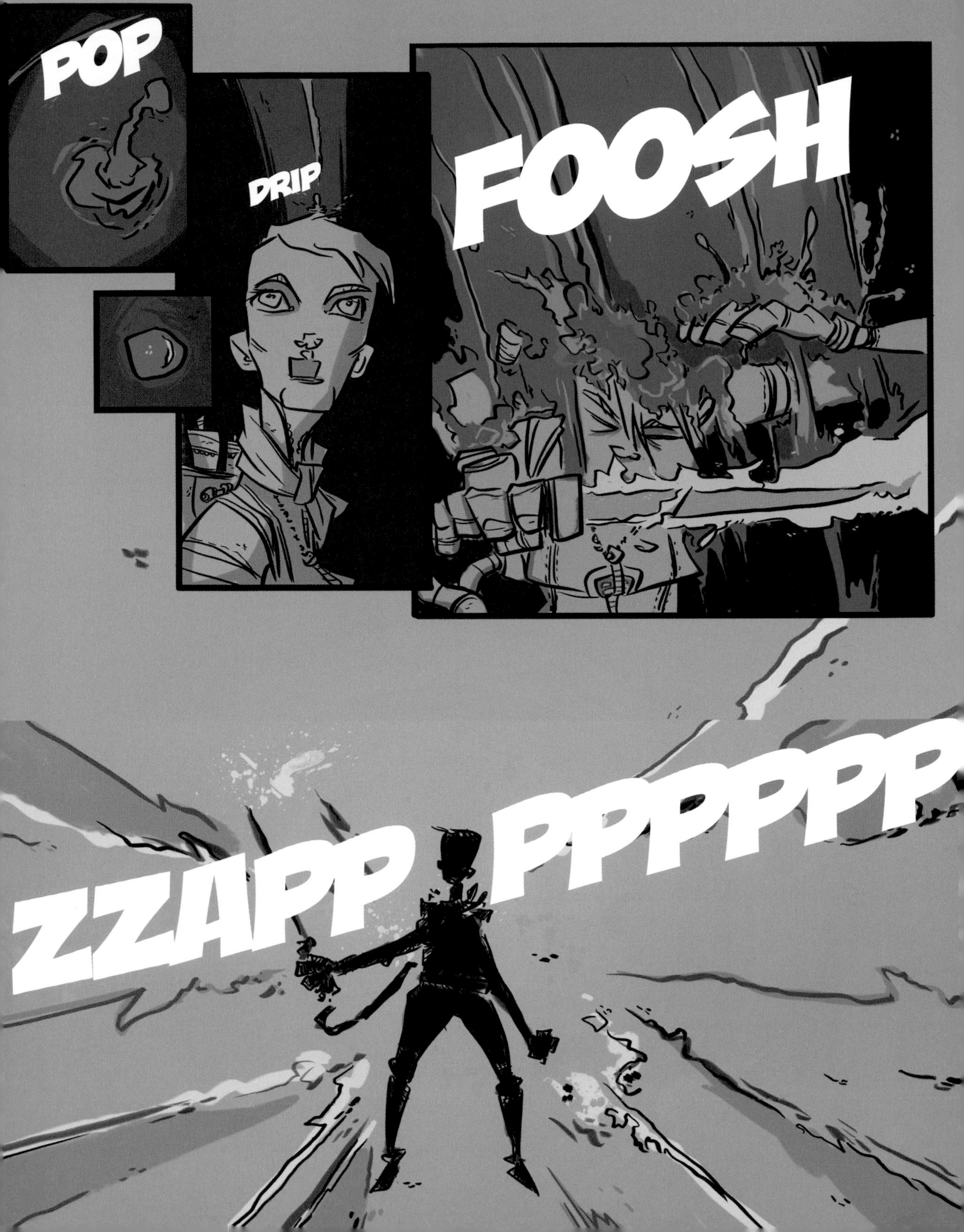
POP
DRIP
FOOSH
ZZAPP PPPPPP

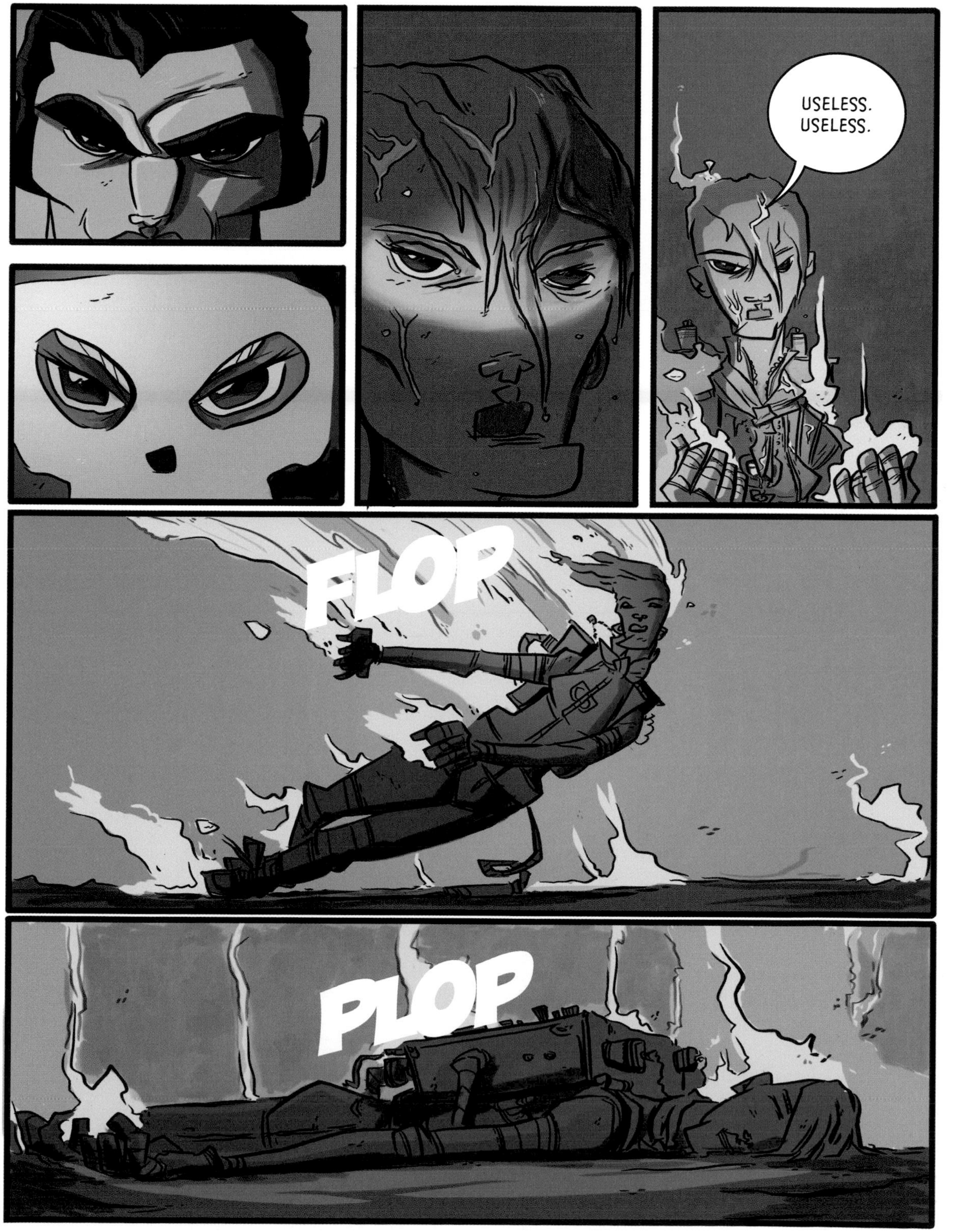
USELESS.
USELESS.
FLOP
PLOP

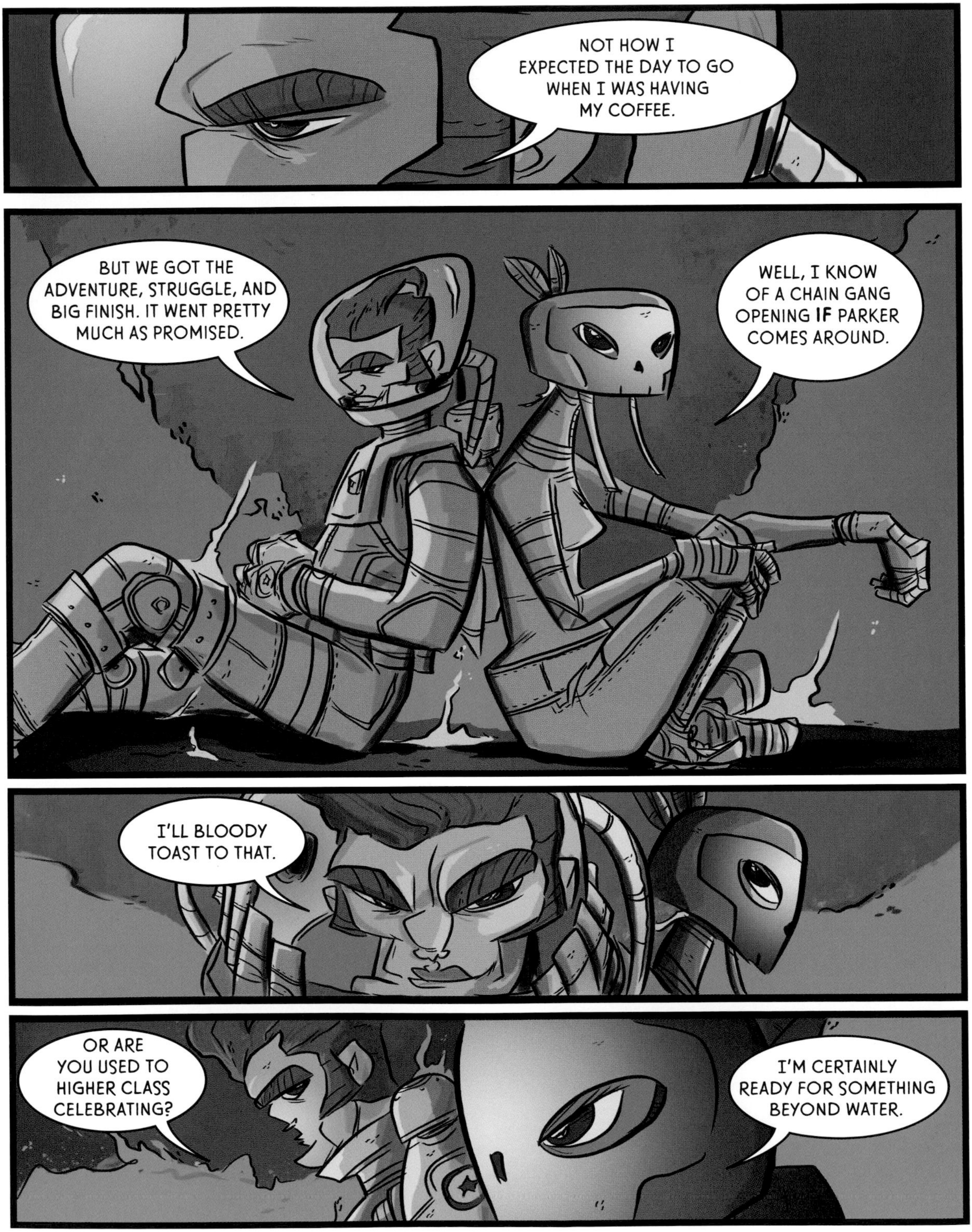
NOT HOW I EXPECTED THE DAY TO GO WHEN I WAS HAVING MY COFFEE.
BUT WE GOT THE ADVENTURE, STRUGGLE, AND BIG FINISH. IT WENT PRETTY MUCH AS PROMISED.
WELL, I KNOW OF A CHAIN GANG OPENING **IF** PARKER COMES AROUND.
I'LL BLOODY TOAST TO THAT.
OR ARE YOU USED TO HIGHER CLASS CELEBRATING?
I'M CERTAINLY READY FOR SOMETHING BEYOND WATER.

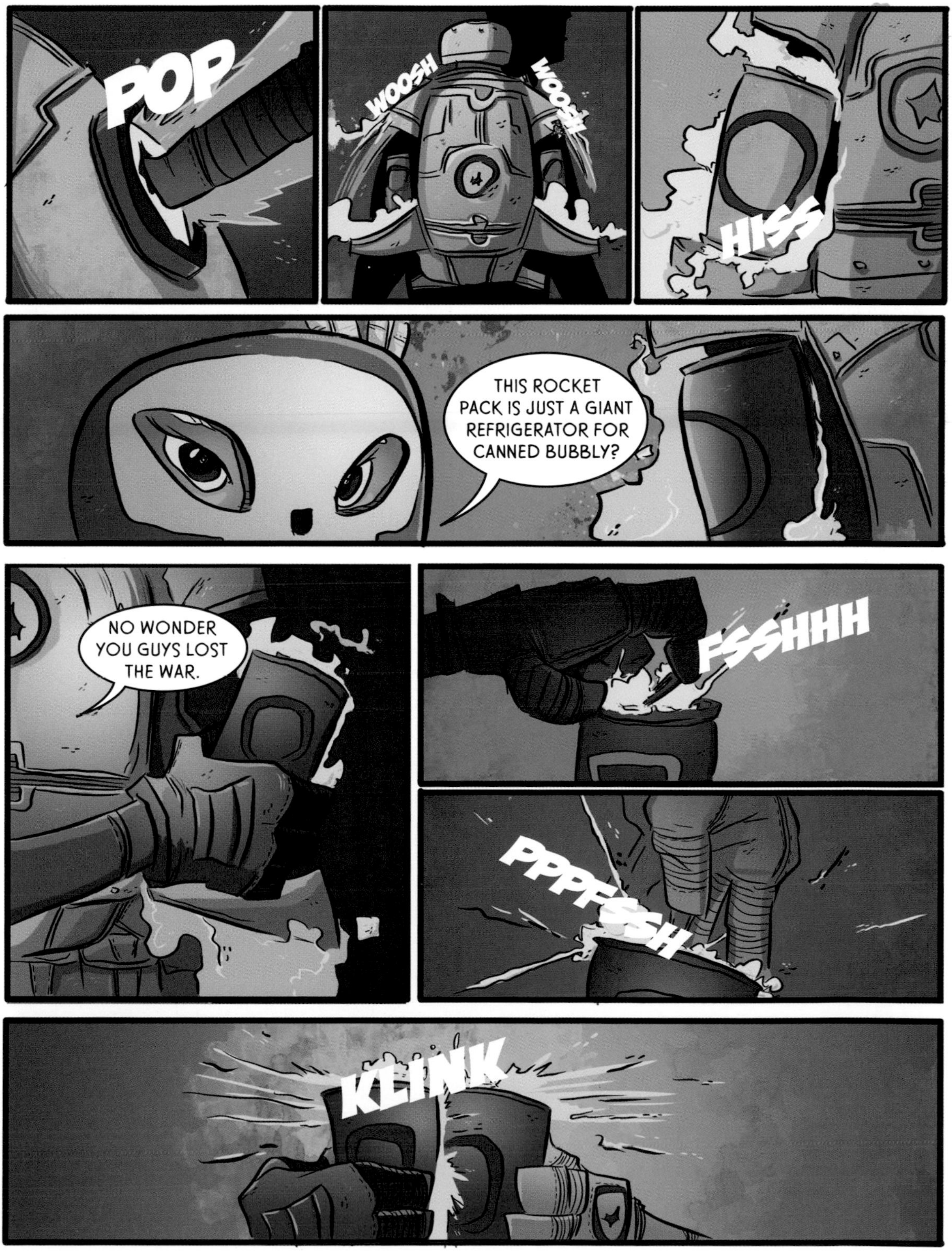
POP
WOOSH
WOOSH
HISS
THIS ROCKET PACK IS JUST A GIANT REFRIGERATOR FOR CANNED BUBBLY?
NO WONDER YOU GUYS LOST THE WAR.
FSSHHH
PPPFSSSH
KLINK

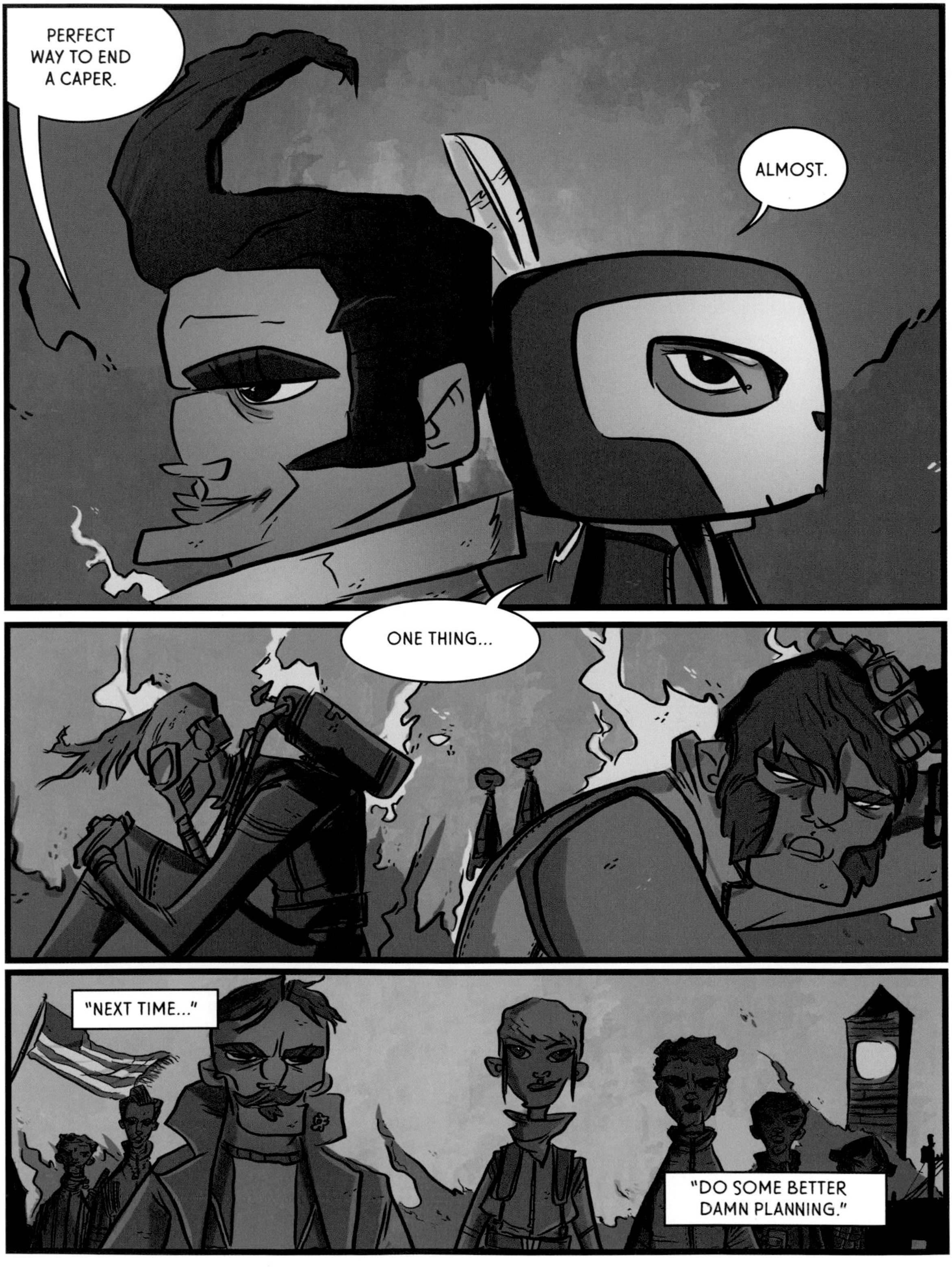
PERFECT WAY TO END A CAPER.
ALMOST.
ONE THING...
"NEXT TIME..."
"DO SOME BETTER DAMN PLANNING."

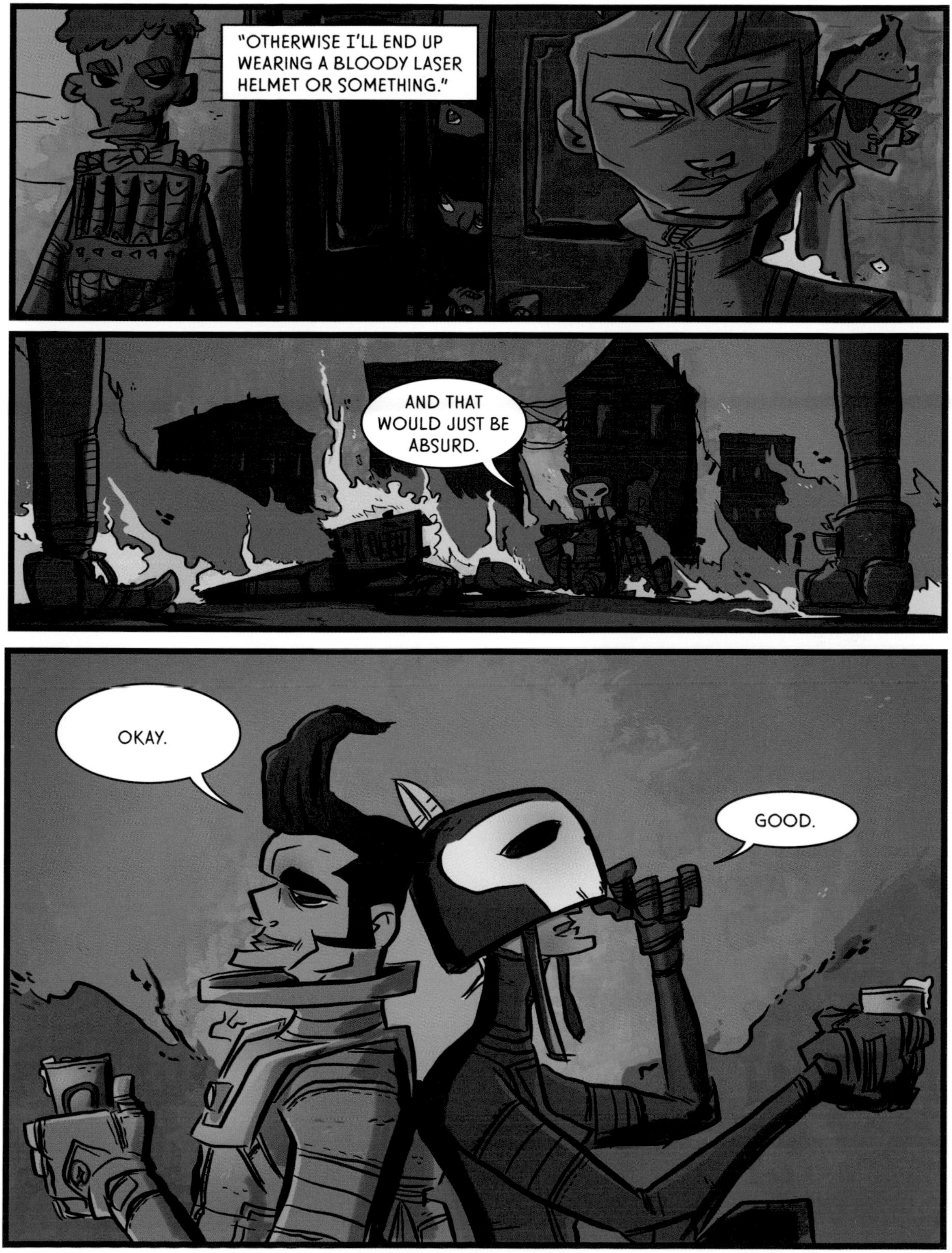
"OTHERWISE I'LL END UP WEARING A BLOODY LASER HELMET OR SOMETHING."
AND THAT WOULD JUST BE ABSURD.
OKAY.
GOOD.

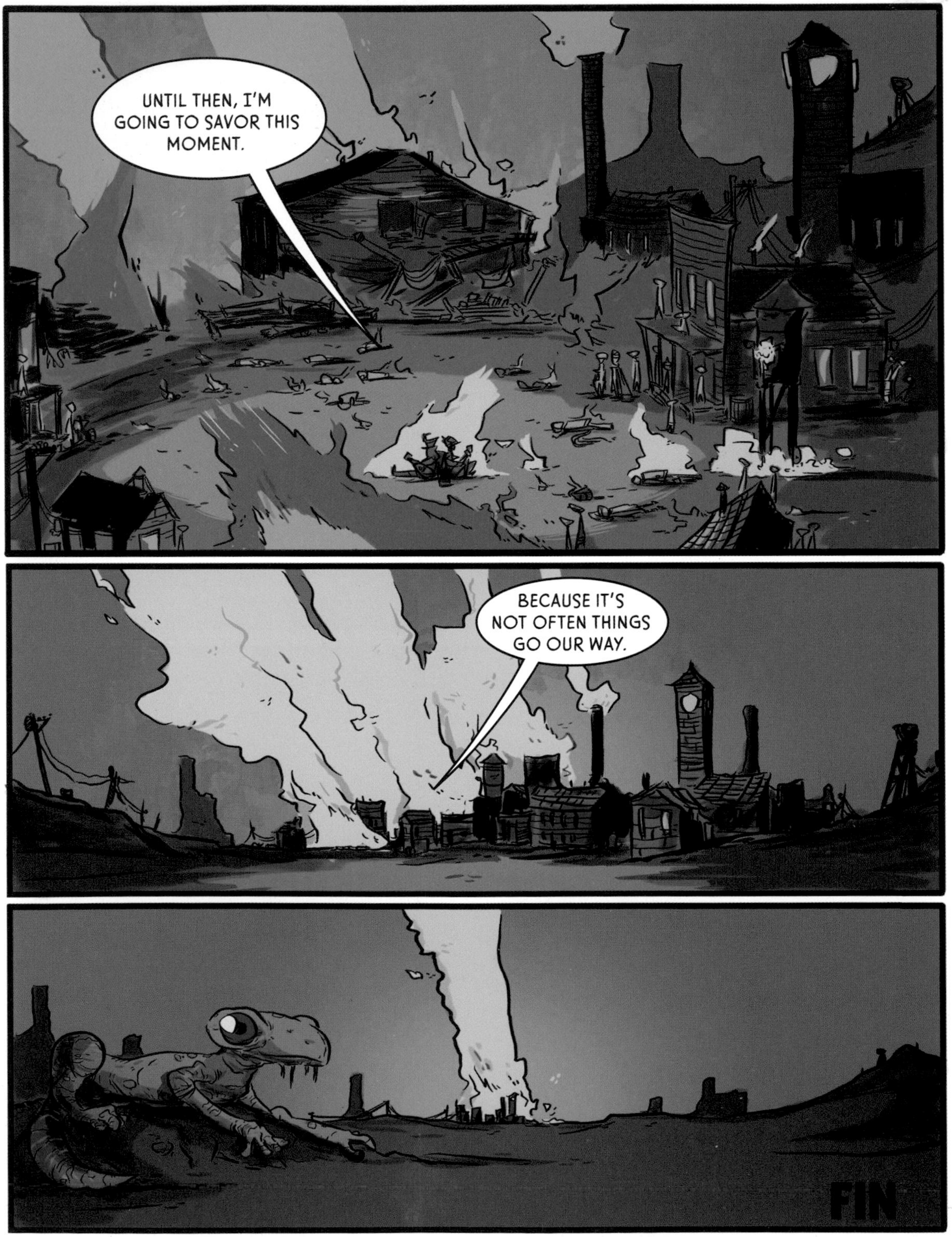
UNTIL THEN, I'M GOING TO SAVOR THIS MOMENT.
BECAUSE IT'S NOT OFTEN THINGS GO OUR WAY.
FIN